AMERICANS have always been intrigued by the question: What is a gentleman? Historically, the question was of great importance to the Federalists. Dr. Cady shows how the ideal of the gentleman was separated from the "gentry" class in America and how it was reconciled to the idea of democracy.

A native of New Jersey, Dr. Cady did his academic work in the Middle West, receiving his doctorate from the University of Wisconsin. He has taught at Ohio State and Wisconsin. He is now Associate Professor of English at Syracuse University, in charge of courses in American literature.

He is currently working on a biography of William Dean Howells.

# THE GENTLEMAN IN AMERICA

# THE GENTLEMAN IN AMERICA

*A Literary Study in American Culture*

*by*

EDWIN HARRISON CADY

*Associate Professor of English
Syracuse University*

SYRACUSE UNIVERSITY PRESS

COPYRIGHT 1949, SYRACUSE UNIVERSITY PRESS

*To*

**FRANCIS ALVA WOODARD**

—*for his faith.*

# INTRODUCTION

As a study of the gentleman in America, this is an attempt to survey a portion of American culture which seems never to have been directly investigated before. In so doing, it impinges upon but does not attempt to duplicate the work done in a number of valuable books. It is not a repetition of Dixon Wecter's fascinating and ironic *Saga of American Society*. Nor does it attempt to extend the cultural history of American patricianism laid out in Merle Curti's *Growth of American Thought*. Its purpose is distinct from that of Arthur M. Schlesinger's clever survey of American books of etiquette.

What is attempted here is a study of the fate in America of the cluster of concepts, values, attitudes, and cultural forms implied by the word "gentleman" as it is reflected in American literature. With that goes the effort to show how accurate criticism of certain interesting American authors depends upon a full reading of books which cannot be understood without a clear grasp of the gentlemanly configuration. Finally, it is hoped that something is here contributed toward a better understanding of the working relations among ideas, culture, and literature in America. To any student of American literature it will be obvious that many more authors and books could be brought into the discussion than are present. When the essential points had been made—the nature and importance of the gentlemanly configuration established; the value of its use as a critical tool illustrated—it seemed superfluous to multiply instances. Perhaps other and better critics may find it useful to refine the tool and apply it to other materials. The writer must, of course, hazard the contention that no broadly significant variations from the patterns laid down here will be found among men or groups not covered.

The list of all those who helped, wittingly or not, in the production of this book would be too long to print. But my gratitude must be extended to Nelson Blake, Howard O. Brogan, William Charvat, Sanford B. Meech, Ernest Campbell Mossner, and Roy Harvey Pearce who have read parts of the manuscript and commented helpfully. Professor Meech kindly read proof as did Douglas T. Bockes, who also helped with checking. Dr. William Miller has harried me benevolently about quotations and footnotes. For inspiration from the beginning I am indebted to Benjamin Townley Spencer. And from the time the project was an obscure enthusiasm Harry Hayden Clark has sustained it with a fertility of suggestion, information, and fatherly sympathy which no words could repay. Norma Woodard Cady has made the book possible in all the uncountable ways known only to the wives of scholars.

It is also a pleasure to acknowledge my debts to Syracuse University, which through the Faculty Research Committee and Vice-Chancellor Finla G. Crawford has provided me with time and assistance which have measurably speeded my work. For permissions to quote extensively from copyrighted material I am grateful to the Houghton Mifflin Co., which controls the *Journals* of Ralph Waldo Emerson; and to Mildred Howells for permission to quote from various writings of William Dean Howells.

# CONTENTS

|     |                                                                      | PAGE |
| --- | -------------------------------------------------------------------- | ---- |
| I   | The Gentleman: Traditions and Meanings                               | 1    |
| II  | The New England Gentleman: Theocracy and After                       | 33   |
| III | "Fine" Gentleman vs. Christian Gentleman                             | 52   |
| IV  | John Adams: How to Tame the Tiger?                                   | 68   |
| V   | Jefferson and the Democratic *Aristoi*                               | 85   |
| VI  | The Death of the Agrarian Dream: Fenimore Cooper                     | 103  |
| VII | The Gentleman as the Substance of Art: Cooper's novels               | 127  |
| VIII| Dr. Holmes and the Best Society Virus                                | 146  |
| IX  | God's Democratic Gentleman: Ralph Waldo Emerson                      | 160  |
| X   | The Gentleman as Socialist: William Dean Howells                     | 184  |
| XI  | Are There Any Gentlemen Now?                                         | 206  |
|     | Notes                                                                | 212  |
|     | Index                                                                | 229  |

CHAPTER ONE

THE GENTLEMAN: TRADITIONS AND MEANINGS

THE IDEAL of the gentleman is as old as the root-traditions of our civilization. And it is a living part of our daily experience. It figures in the *Instructions* of Ptah-Hotep, the Egyptian volume supposed to be the oldest surviving book. The millions of Americans who go to movies and read "comics," to say nothing of the hundreds of thousands who read books, are subject daily to artful expressions of the ideal. Europeans received gentlemanliness along with the other patterns of culture they absorbed from classical antiquity. Much altered and intensified, in time the constituent ideas of the concept of the gentleman were carried alive to America, there again to be shaped to fresh uses.

I

The Englishmen whose culture was dominant in young America could command a gentlemanly tradition as intellectually respectable as it was long. They could, and occasionally some did, cite such classical writers as Plato, Aristotle, and Isocrates; Quintilian, Cicero, Horace, Juvenal, Theophrastus, Plutarch, and Ovid. Medieval life, legend, and art had given them the unstably compounded notions of the courtly lover and the Christian hero (together with the inevitable reshapings of classical ideas which would as yet be several times reworked before there were Americans to use them). And the close of the Middle Ages had given them the name of gentleman and the class of gentry.

Sir George Sitwell once asserted that there was no one who "ever described himself, or was described by others as a gentleman before the year 1413"; and there was no "class of gentlemen before the third decade of the fifteenth century." Though Sitwell may not be accurate in terms of date, he suggests vividly one of the basic distinctions—between gentleman-ideal and class of gentry—upon which understanding of "the gentleman" depends. As Sitwell says, since a numerous class of professional soldiers, younger sons, and other semi-noble but unlanded men had sprung up during the wars of the fourteenth century, it became legally necessary to label them by some title below noble. The word "gentleman" was coined, and it came swiftly into use from the frequent contact of this restless and reckless group with the law. "The premier gentleman of England," then, says Sitwell, "is 'Robert Erdeswyke of Stafford, gentleman' . . . He was charged at the Staffordshire assizes with house-breaking, wounding with intent to kill, and procuring the murder of one Thomas Page, who was cut to pieces while on his knees begging for his life . . . If any earlier claimant to 'the grand old name of gentleman' be discovered, I venture to predict that it will be within the same year and in connection with some disreputable proceeding—assault, murder, robbery, or housebreaking—of a kind which would not now be accepted as an introduction to polite society."[1]

The case of Robert Erdeswyke makes it clear that the *class of gentry,* representing an overt culture-pattern which had developed in response to social needs, must be distinguished

## THE GENTLEMAN: TRADITIONS, MEANINGS

carefully from the *concept of the gentleman,* a primarily covert culture-pattern extant as a system of ideal values long before the class came into being. Even Chaucer's Wyf of Bath had been aware that "he is gentil that doeth gentil dedis." And the discrepancy between Robert Erdeswyke and the tradition of gentle magnanimity in the admirable man is a fact of fundamental significance. The tradition, the ideal, was then what it always had been: an item among what a cultural anthropologist would call the covert culture-patterns of the period. It was an idea with positive value associations, held subjectively and requiring overt, objective expression before it could be judged. To take familiar examples: the notion of courtesy is a dynamic, covert culture-pattern; but the usages of finger-bowls, dinner-jackets, or calling-cards are minor overt culture-patterns through which the covert aspects are in this case directly expressed. It seems clear, in these terms, that the class of gentry, to which Erdeswyke belonged, came into being as an overt culture-pattern which was not an expression of the old concept of the gentleman. The class was the product of overt social and political conditions completely irrelevant to the concept. Later efforts to fuse the two, to make the class a true expression of the concept, had only partial success. And failure to distinguish clearly between objective class and ideal concept has often bewildered theorists of the gentleman.

When under Tudor stability England turned from the agony of the Wars of the Roses, she found a new world about her. The ways of the Middle Ages were ceasing to be, and the ways of the Renaissance brought much that was different. The privileged classes were forced to change with the times. The still new class of gentlemen was comparatively democratized by new political conditions, by new commercial wealth, and perhaps because it had never had time to work out fixed standards of admission.

Also with the Renaissance, the model of manly excellence ceased to be the knight and became that new thing: the gentleman. Knighthood was dead, and Cervantes was laughing its remembrance out of the world. Most Renaissance writers on courtesy, moralists as they were, condemned the main holdovers from chivalric tradition, the duel and the romance. Their puritanic followers were even harsher. And the concept of the gentleman left the chivalric influence buried in its past until, glamorized and sentimentalized, it was resurrected by the literary medievalists of the nineteenth century, Scott, Tennyson, and Lanier.

In Tudor times the new class of gentlemen grew swiftly in numbers and importance, increasingly free of dependence upon noble ancestry. In 1583 Sir Thomas Smith wrote in his *De Republica Anglorum,* "whosoever studieth the lawes of the realme, who studieth in the universities, who professeth liberall sciences, and to be shorte, who can live idly and without manuall labour, and will beare the port, charge and countenaunce of a gentleman, he shall be called master, for that is the title which men give to esquires and other gentlemen, and shall be taken for a gentleman." The holders of offices in the royal service and even such civil officers as the four chief personal representatives of the Lord Mayor of London—the Sword Bearer, the Water Bailiff, the Common Crier, and the Common Hunt—were admitted automatically to the class of gentlemen. The playwright John Heywood and his younger brother Richard, a lawyer, became gentlemen while their elder brother William remained a yeoman and tenant farmer. The rise of the great mercantile group breached the wall of exclusion still wider. Wealth made it easy to bear the "charge and countenaunce" of gentlemen and to buy landed estates with all the gentleman's "port." Often merchants were associated with the great nobles and courtiers in industrial monopolies, gaining thus as a group access to the highest circles in the nation.

This fluidity of the class of English gentlemen was not a bad thing. It helped avoid the disastrous class cleavage which resulted in France from the economic immunities of gentry. The English gentleman's privileges were those of dignity and status, not of immunity. He might perpetrate such injustices as the enclosure movement, but he had in the end to meet his bills or go under like anyone else. On the average and in the long run, he could not survive as a parasite on the nation, and the man who replaced him if he tried to do so was as likely as not to be the shrewd and energetic son of a commoner.

Fast though the class of gentlemen grew, the ideal of the gentleman, with its long start, kept ahead of it. Virtue and learning and wealth—wealth for leisure and the display of liberality—were the three main elements of Elizabethan gentility. They made the gentleman in concept and ideal, and they were urged upon every candidate by the dozens of books turned off the new presses. The advent of publishing had given the concept of the gentleman an effective weapon: courtesy books could open its mysteries to any reader.

Though "courtesy books" defy precise definition, they were a sort of improvement literature which, in the Renaissance way, generally spent much of their space summarizing all the author knew and the rest in giving advice to the parent on the education of his son in the way of the gentleman, defining polite conduct, and describing the responsibilities of the gentleman and the best ways for him to meet them. The matter in Polonius's famed advice to Laertes in *Hamlet* has the rare distinction of having been twice clichéd: once by the Elizabethans, for the point of the speech is that the senile statesman is mouthing capsuled truisms from the courtesy writers; and again by American schoolchildren and elocutionists. Courtesy literature seems to have formed a large part of the Elizabethan reader's fare, and it brought the concept of the gentleman so far forward that he was made by theory the chief cornerstone of the public good. The courtesy writers gained a command of the thought of the day which made their concept of the gentleman, however it might be altered in usage or detail, a permanent part of the culture that went with English literature and institutions.

The fundamental ideal in the courtesy books was Virtue. Typically of the age, this was a mixture of pagan classicism and Christianity. It never quite reconciled stoic pride of self with self-rejecting humility. But by common consent justice, prudence, temperance, fortitude, courtesy, and liberality were the elements of Virtue. The first four of these were especially necessary for the performance of the governing functions of the gentleman, though they had further bearings. They were all capable of multiple constructions. Liberality could mean the open-handed generosity of *largesse*, conspicuous consumption, or support of the liberal arts. Fortitude could mean ordinary physical courage. But it included magnanimity, that great-heartedness far above courage which gave Hakluyt's worthies, for example, their power to hazard tremendous dangers with an air of relaxed enjoyment. Courtesy as such was the consideration which fared worst from the undeclared civil war between pagan and Christian attitudes. By comparison with later generations, the Elizabethans neglected delicacy, noting simply that every gentleman should be aware of the grades and distinctions of social rank and be able to give everyone precisely his due deference. Also, from Sir Thomas Elyot to Peacham and Brathwaite and Milton, courtesy writers took up the burden of educating the gentleman until they had laid most of the foundations for modern educational thought.

Although wealth might bring one to high station within the class of gentlemen, it was not a sure means to gentlemanliness itself. Yet only with it could the gentleman exercise the virtue of liberality or practice and patronize the liberal arts. The general decision seems to have been that one had to have wealth to live as a gentleman but that he need never expect to have it bring him to ideal gentility. As Thomas Gainsford put it in *The Rich Cabinet* (1616), "Generositie doth not account him a gentleman which is only descended of noble bloud, in power great, in jewels rich, in furniture fine, in attendants brave . . . But to be a perfect Gentleman, is to be measured in his words, liberall in giving, sober in diet, honest in living, tender in pardoning, and valiant in fighting." Virtue and character counted most.

Still Elizabethans found it hard to give up the conviction, scouted by later theorists, that the gentleman must ordinarily

## THE GENTLEMAN: TRADITIONS, MEANINGS 7

be born the son of a gentleman. Accustomed to breeding hounds and horses, and passionately attached to the ideal of monarchy, they felt that blood counted. Their political necessities made them recall the medieval fables and philosophies justifying social stratification, all the way from the legend of Eve's unlike children to the recurrent ideas of plenitude and the Great Chain of Being. Yet there was old and good authority, and even stronger contemporary fact, to back the other idea of birth: that the natural gentleman, highly capable of all the virtues and functions of the gentleman, might appear from anywhere. Since everyone could point out men who had risen from the lowest ranks to gentility and even nobility, the writers began to win out who were saying that only proved merit, virtue, and natural leadership should gain for any man the privileges and respect of the gentleman. The future lay with them.

Because so much of what we ordinarily think we know about the gentleman in this his primal period is gathered from materials incidental to the drama, movie, or historical novel where he figures principally for the romantic interest of his person, it is easy to forget that his own time thought of him as valuable first for the functions he performed in society. In that day the gentleman was most important because he was the unit of social structure. He joined to the theoretical prestige of the "common man" in our day an ability to further his own interests which the common man has never possessed, yet much was required of him. Within the pyramided hierarchies of the Elizabethan organic state, the class of gentlemen formed the critical link from the king to the people, for whose welfare the whole structure was supposed to exist. Upon them depended the good of the nation. As kings and princes were the hands of God, gentlemen were the fingers of the king.

The actual functions of the Elizabethan gentleman varied with his own personal importance. Great aristocrats performed many of the present functions of diplomatic corps and civil service without salary. They were paid, if ever, at the caprice of the sovereign. The lesser gentry at home were justices of the peace, and assumed almost the whole responsibility for local administration and justice, again without salary. Some of the courtesy books were written to help the gentleman in his performance of such functions. Being in a sense responsible for keeping the arts and ceremonies of the countryside alive, the gentleman served as an example of excellence in living to all who saw him. In dress, in manners, in interests, and in religion he must be a living model to those less fortunate. Above all else came the life-long pressure of the cares and decisions, rewards and punishments and charities, proper attention to which, in an organic society of mutual dependency, rested primarily on the class of gentlemen.

Through the Stuart reigns and the commonwealth interregnum, current concepts of the gentleman changed slowly. Sentiment continued to shift against the hereditary and in favor of the natural gentleman. Not at all surprisingly, a strong emphasis on piety as part of a gentleman's virtue began to appear. Many a militant Puritan lived in a country mansion in the days of Charles I, and good Anglicans were just as pious as Puritans. Hence no such cleavage exists between Royalist and Puritan courtesy writers over the pietistic trend as might be expected from the traditional notions of Cavalier and Roundhead. Though in essence the notion of function did not change, it was considerably strengthened by the return to the ancient idea of God's vocation or "calling" of his people to certain tasks in the world. As in Richard Allstree's *The Gentleman's Calling,* the gentleman's function became an awful responsibilty to render a good stewardship to God himself.

Except for Peacham's *Compleat Gentleman,* an encyclopedic work, seventeenth-century courtesy books do not match those of the preceding century in literary prestige. One, however, translated from a Jesuit manual by Francis Hawkins and called *Youth's Behavior, or Decency in Conversation Amongst Men* (ca. 1640), has a significance all out of proportion to its worth because it became George Washington's manual. As a school boy in 1745, Washington transcribed a number of Hawkins' maxims,

## THE GENTLEMAN: TRADITIONS, MEANINGS 9

condensing some and omitting others, onto the pages entitled "Rules of Civility" in the commonplace book he named *True Happiness*. Presumably he knew Hawkins because the second edition of the book had been dedicated to his collateral ancestresses Eleanor Partiger and Mrs. Elizabeth Washington.[2] By such a chain of chances were century-old English interpretations of still older French notions of gentlemanliness carried to shape the majesty of demeanor—and perhaps some of the stiffness—of one of the premier gentlemen of America.

With the Glorious Revolution, the class of gentry came into their own. Their success gave the gentleman a preeminence in English life so nearly absolute that he has only now lost control. By the eighteenth century proper gentlemanliness was not only a theory of excellence, and a set of responsibilities, but a full-blown way of life with its *beau monde,* for the first time significantly independent of the Court, in which to express itself. The old courtesy literature with its stuffy encyclopedism began to disappear. In its place, to edify and instruct the gentleman, came the familiar periodic essay, the didactic poem, the satire, and the moralizing novel. *The Spectator,* said Dr. Johnson, had rivalled Castiglione. Each in his own fashion, almost every significant writer of the age sought to rival Addison and Steele.

In the famous dictionary, Dr. Johnson defined the gentleman as, "*homo gentilis,* a man of ancestry. All other derivations seem to be whimsical." Gentle folk, furthermore, he defined as "persons distinguished by their birth from the vulgar." With his immense common sense and grasp of fact, Johnson was correct in so interpreting the class of gentry, but the tide of contemporary writings set strongly against him. Courtesy writers had ceased to puzzle over the origin and transmission of nobility and turned equalitarian. Hobbes had popularized the idea that men were essentially equal, and Pufendorf and Locke had hammered it home. Evangelical faith that all men are equal in the sight of God further weakened the prestige of noble birth. The age insisted on judging gentility principally by merit. Addison and Steele, Defoe, Fielding, and Chesterfield all exalted merit above birth. Yet what we know of the actualities of the age would make us believe that Johnson was closer to them than the idealists were. Theorists on the concept of the gentleman had discarded the old ideas of birth and blood and had opened the way for the natural gentleman. Gentlemen as a class remained reactionary. They held to the notion of birth out of caution and pride, conveniently blinking the fact that able upstarts yearly invaded the ranks, just as their own grandfathers had done.

The rejection of heredity did not imply any real weakening of the philosophic position of the gentleman; it merely brought his position more clearly in accord with the healthy fact that his class continued to absorb the strong products of the lower classes without inspiring revolt. With the intellectual harvest of the Renaissance in, the stock of supporting ideas must have seemed inexhaustible. The ideas of plenitude and gradation, which formed part of the concept of the Great Chain of Being which Mr. A. O. Lovejoy has so brilliantly shown to have been tremendously influential, sanctioned the gentleman in his place and function. Various strains of pessimistic or cynical antirationalism also justified the shepherding of the passion-blinded people.

Of course, thinking so philosophic as that had little immediate power to change people's behavior. But there were two fashions of thinking which did have real cultural effects. They split the concept permanently in two. The first of these was the pattern of ideas which Mr. Lovejoy, once again, has called uniformitarianism. Some of the corollaries to this doctrine, which informed a significant portion of the culture of the age, are helpful in understanding the eighteenth century gentleman. They are what Lovejoy calls intellectual equalitarianism; the antipathy to enthusiasm and originality; and cosmopolitanism. Intellectual equalitarianism, meaning that every man possesses reason, effectively ruled out special heredity: it made men depend more strongly than ever upon education and training for the originality affected the manner of the gentleman, inclining him towards coolness and formality. The same doctrine buttressed the position of his class, for it thrust against levelling innovations the whole force of what the age took to be Nature: had there not been special privilege of some sort in all times everywhere? Cosmopolitanism made gentlemen receptive to new modes from abroad, particularly from France. As Mr. Lovejoy implies in the title to his basic analysis of the pattern of uniformitarianism,[3] it represented in a sense a reversal of the seventeenth century trend toward Christian piety. These gentlemen turned back toward the coldly brilliant, this-worldly, calculating, self-centered and self-exalting classical paganism of the Renaissance. They could hardly go unopposed.

Those who fought the uniformitarian attitude were part of a culturally much stronger movement—the revival of Christian piety within Anglicanism, which produced the Society for the Reformation of Manners and such kindred groups as the Society for Promoting Christian Knowledge and the Society for the Propagation of the Gospel in Foreign Parts. Seeking to win the gentry of England to evangelical Christianity, these groups exploited the advantages of the virtue tradition in courtesy literature. Gradually they fastened on their deistic opponents the reputation of Rake-Hellism and lurid wickedness in general. Sir Richard Steele, whose *Christian Hero* was a major step toward the definition of the Christian gentleman, very early expressed, in the tone of good-humour which was the policy of the Spectator, the sense of antithesis which became bitter when lines were more tightly drawn. In *Spectator 109* he sketched the two gentleman-ancestors of Sir Roger de Coverley. One grandfather was elegant, but wasteful and idle; the other was religious, honest, and charitable. The virtuous Sir Charles Grandison and wicked, deluded Lovelace of Richardson's novels set the pattern permanently. Grandisons and Lovelaces continue to appear in popular literature and drama to this day.

Those who held to the uniformitarian pattern found themselves, like Horace Walpole, in sympathy with the ways of Castiglione and the gentlemen of France. More than English tradition had been accustomed to do, they put a stronger faith in the "accomplishments" of the gentleman than in his virtues or his duties. Creating the model of the scholar-gentleman as well as the blue-stocking salon, they established a tradition of intellectual achievement for the gentleman which was ingloriously undermined by their evangelical opponents. But they made themselves too vulnerable by their creation of *le beau monde*. It took a kind of greatness to be Chesterfield, but he was fatally easy to vulgarize. Any young fop or prig could understand shining in fashionable society, climbing in the polite world. Men of parts were revolted by the moral voids which yawned so readily beneath the peacock attractions of Society. They cooperated with the evangelical enemy to produce the caricatures of Sir Fopling which haunt contemporary comedy and satire. Eventually this creature was identified with Lord Chesterfield and firmly labelled "the fine gentleman."

The letters of Chesterfield to Philip Stanhope, published in 1774, had little to do with the formation of the fine gentleman. He was full-blown before the letters appeared. Chesterfield himself varied significantly from the pattern. But the tone and approach, and much of the content, of the letters so masterfully express everything that school has always been understood to be, that distinctions of this sort make no difference. Historically the fine gentleman was the Chesterfieldian gentleman.

No one needs to sum up Chesterfield again. But it is useful to see the fine gentleman in his relation to the other concept. Defining virtue as moderation and giving full license to temperate amounts of under-cover vice, Chesterfield enraged contemporary moralists. His definition of manners as "engaging, insinuating, shining manners; distinguished politeness, an almost irresistible address, a superior gracefulness in all you say and do," was as brilliant as the manners he described. His definition of courtesy as sacrificing "one's self-love to other people" seemed in the great tradition. But his pessimistic view of human nature and cynical technique of winning friends and influencing people gained him the warm enmity of the advocates of the Christian gentleman. His preaching of balance, dignity, and absolute self-mastery, "a real reserve toward almost everybody and a seeming reserve toward almost nobody," and his teaching of flattering hypocrisy earned him their scalding contempt.

The most noise was raised against Chesterfield's advice about women. Anxious to have Philip profit by the brilliant ladies brought to the fore by the salons, his father condemned liaisons with vulgar women but heartily recommended intrigues with those of high rank and breeding. Intrinsic values aside, such experiences would help Philip in court affairs, would aid his social standing (largely determined by women), and would improve his manners. While this was all right in terms of the ancient tradition of misogynist satire in which Chesterfield dealt, it was his historical misfortune that the devotees of the Christian gentleman were restoring the chivalric worship of womanhood and of chastity. They made his name infamous. Dozens of the great and the small caricatured him. Dr. Johnson growled that the letters "teach the morals of a whore, and the manners of a dancing master." He hoped that someone would write a play to show that a son trained according to Chesterfield would turn out a consummate rogue. "It should be contrived so that the father should be the only sufferer by the son's villainy, and thus there would be poetic justice." Cowper called Chesterfield "the gray-beard corrupter of our list'ning youth." Even Dickens attacked viciously with the caricature of Sir John Chester in *Barnaby Rudge*.

The mighty opposite of Chesterfield, the world's champion defender of the Christian gentleman, was the pioneer novelist Samuel Richardson. Obsessed with technical chastity, Richardson opposed to Chesterfieldian cynicism, piety, scrupulous candor, and the bug-eyed devotion of the commoner to gentlemanliness. His difficulty was that he never understood that he was dealing with a pattern of ideas that could be coherent, though at the suggestion of Dr. Johnson he stitched together from his novels a patch-work courtesy book: *A Collection of the Moral and Instructive Sentiments, Maxims, Cautions, and Reflections* . . .

in ... *Pamela, Clarissa,* and *Sir Charles Grandison.* Staunchly upholding rank and blood, he could yet assert that "gentleman" is a "title of distinction a prince may not deserve" if he is not a Christian. He had the snob's love of the gentleman's dignified condescension as well as the snob's fear of a mean pride—without really distinguishing between them. In his confusions, of course, Richardson mirrored the attitudes of most people in his time much more clearly than preciser theorists. His preoccupations came out clearly in such apothegms as:

> *True politeness is but another word for Virtue and Honor.*
>
> *A man who deserves the name of a gentleman, will be careful in his conversation not to offend a chaste ear.*
>
> *A man who offers freedoms to his female servant, deserves not, however rich and powerful, to be called a gentleman.*

The evangelical rejection of the pride of intellect in favor of the heart's piety also distinguished the Richardsonian from the Chesterfieldian gentleman. Richardson's ideal hero, Sir Charles Grandison, was also the ideal "man of feeling." With him the virtue of tenderheartedness which had been growing with the Anglican reformation from the start came fully into its own as the cult of sensibility, of out-gushing emotionalism which seized on any pretext to show its virtue—and its virtuosity. A new criterion of gentlemanliness had been formed. Now gentlemen must show the effects of tentacles of sensibility so fine-spun that only the teariest cultists could imagine them. In its comparatively brief span of vitality as an element in the concept of the gentleman, sensibility went far toward making a confusing situation bewildering.

In spite of the great fissure through the theory of the gentleman, it must not, of course, be supposed that everyone felt himself to belong definitely on one side or the other. The tradition of the Christian gentleman won out over-whelmingly in popular literature and in general lip-service. But many a gentleman had no intention of being nearly so saintly—and there were the silly-season aspects of sensibility to avoid. One could choose intelligently from the venerable and conveniently complex tradition: balancing head and heart, manners and morals, deed and ideal as, for instance, Thomas Jefferson did.

A conspicuously sane example of just such balance could be found in the writings of the great Mr. Locke, philosophic giant of the age. A warm supporter of the class of gentry as his *Fundamental Constitutions of Carolina* show, Locke was also an influential courtesy-writer in *Some Thoughts Concerning Education*. In the mainstream of classical and English tradition, he showed a typically common-sense concern for the ideal. Typically again, he clarified tradition by pointing out that good manners and a fine manner, to avoid offense, must come from "good breeding." And good breeding, true courtesy, is the organic expression of a sensitive and benevolent mind, of an inward "general Good-will and Regard for all People."

British influence on American life has never ceased, strong though the tide has turned today. And through the nineteenth century both countries are affected by Dickens and Thackeray, by the pejorative fates of the words "genteel" and "gentility," by Carlyle and the British proto-Fascists of the nineteenth century. Both countries react to Matthew Arnold, George Du Maurier, Cardinal Newman, and Oscar Wilde. But long before the squabbles over the fine gentleman and the Christian gentleman had ceased, American experience and thinking were having particular and home-grown effects on the concept of the gentleman, effects which in their turn became causes of thought upon which British innovations had no important influence.

Knowing that weighty segments of the American heritage were Continental rather than British, one might expect influential ideas of the gentleman from other European countries. But there seems to be hardly any evidence for this. Perhaps the explanation is that those few migrant Europeans who were interested were willing to assimilate into their own patterns whatever differences they found in a matter so far from the roots of their personal problems. The lack of significant direct French influence can be explained by the colonial antipathy to France, by the post-Revolutionary recoil from the frightfulness of revolution in France, and by the successful witch-hunts against French influence as represented by the Illuminati. What French contribution there was seems to have manifested itself in such things as dress, Society speech, and the theater.

## II

The fates of both concept and class of gentlemen in America naturally follow what for purposes of metaphoric convenience may be called the "stages" of American history. In the South cultural conditions were normally colonial during the "colonial period." Adventurers with ordinary English cultural backgrounds suffered their way to security on the frontier; and gradually altered their cultural heritage to meet new conditions. But they remained as intimate as they could with "home" and followed its changing styles with the usual colonial ineptitude, the usual cultural lag pulling against the usual fierce colonial loyalty and snobbery: always more royalist than the king, more Catholic than the Pope. There were always cultural tensions among the heritage, adapted "native" patterns, and the newest thing from London. The colonialism of the Middle States was much clouded by infusions of non-English culture. New England was made a special case by Puritanism.

Everywhere the frontier menaced the gentleman as it did all of the cultural heritage. Even when, as in Massachusetts, Puritan social discipline prevented such cultural disasters as those of the earliest Virginians, there was the more insidious problem of second and third generations. Wealth and leisure and opportunities even for literacy were often quickly consumed

## THE GENTLEMAN: TRADITIONS, MEANINGS 17

by the demands of survival in the wilderness or lost among its dense distances from village to village, even family to family. Two or three generations of dispersion and deprivation produced the back-woods cultural poverty early remarked by Colonel Byrd and Madame Knight and persisting through the "Pike" and the "hill-billy" to our own time. Such a cultural debacle made the gentleman impossible except in the sense immortalized by Cooper's Natty Bumppo. Until the fight against it was won (so far as it has been won in America in our time), all the force of class and concept alike had to be thrown into the counter-balance.

The immense success of the theocratic gentry of New England at doing precisely this and perpetuating themselves as the Brahmin caste was one of the fateful cultural achievements in American history. They prepared the ground for New England's great age, and they seeded in the intellectual attitudes which made Yankee and school-teacher almost synonyms in nineteenth century America. If there were such a thing as "the genteel tradition" in America, the indomitable fight of thinking Americans against loss of the heritage of European culture would be it. Obviously, no group of people is without culture, in the anthropological sense. But, as many of the vials of scorn poured upon the gentleman in America attest, what civilized persons value as civilization exists in America now in significant measure because of the traditions of the gentleman.

As Fenimore Cooper pointed out, after the pioneer stage came a tight, competitive time of consolidation. And in the period 1690-1790, give or take a few years either way, most of colonial America underwent such a time. Boundaries physical, political, and psychological—the Alleghenies, the French, British fur interests, the Indian Nations—dammed up the westward flow of population for about three generations. There was time for towns to grow, for community and provincial cultures to take on form, for social lines to be drawn more definitely, for the gentry to emerge and begin to function as a class according to English custom. This was the age to which American mythology looks back with great nostalgia, because it was a time of the gathering of forces.

When the forces were loosed in the revolutionary period which followed, there were deep cultural as well as political crises. And the question of the gentleman was as critical as any. For one thing, far too many members of the class went Tory, and the surging democrats found that a potent weapon against the old social structure. On the other hand, General Washington bewailed frequently the fact that so few of the officers were truly gentlemen. Yet when the Revolution was made, there remained the making of the new nation. Few if any of the men responsible for making it could conceive that it should cease to be organized around its gentlemen. In theory as well as practice they worked to adapt the tradition to new needs. The two main solutions they achieved still affect American life. The federalists, of whom the most profound spokesman was John Adams, proposed a limited reconstitution of the class-function, carefully checked and balanced, of the gentry. The democratic, or indeed Jeffersonian, proposal was to dissolve the class into the body public and depend upon democratic process, and upon education which was both general and selective, to bring the *natural* gentlemen forward to public service.

By the end of a generation of national experience, American conditions were changing sharply. Industrialism was rising to alter the premises upon which Adams and Jefferson, and after them Cooper, had based their thought. New democratic theory and new political customs made gentlemanliness irrelevant if not a handicap in politics. The swelling ranks of literate people able to maintain a comfortable standard of living emptied old distinctions of meaning and brought forward hundreds of thousands of men capable of aspiring to gentility. Two opposite adaptations resulted. One was a sharp movement toward special means of exclusiveness to maintain distinctions. Means as fantastic as the DAR or as natural, if fragile, as Charleston's St. Cecelia's Ball were used to approximate the discredited theory of gentlemanly birth. The top dogs in the battle for the vast new wealth used plutocratic means either to create their own Society or, more commonly, to force their way in among the Four Hundred or its home-town equivalent. From the top of Best Society to Mrs. Grundy, people competed recklessly to be or seem to be Best Society. Of this attitude the most graceful American spokesman was Dr. Holmes.

From snobbery and its results many Americans have turned angrily to reject the entire notion of gentlemanliness. Others, accepting the demise of the gentry as class, have seen further possibilities in Jefferson's ideas. Among them have been some of America's most sensitive and original critics. Emerson scrapped the class and made gentlemanliness purely a question of individual moral achievement. His unnumbered followers have everywhere popularized the faith that to be a gentleman is an inward richness naturally productive of outward beauty and kindness. William Dean Howells made the most coherent and influential effort thus far to adapt the Jefferson-Emersonian attitude to the need for economic as well as political democracy. Since Howells the ideal of the gentleman has lived vigorously, has had countless fragmentary expressions (and now has them). It can be confidently expected that strongly creative minds will be moved again, and in the not distant future, to use that ideal to speak to the condition of mid-twentieth century America.

### III

In the view of an intellectual historian, the concept of the gentleman came to America and has been used here as a constellation of six main ideas. There are the shaping, background factors of birth and wealth. There are the three inward attributes of being which mark the essential gentleman: character, courtesy, and cultivation. Sixth, there is the idea of the function of the gentleman in society. Handled ideally and abstractly—"philosophically"—these make a neat enough figure. But during the course of such a study as this it becomes clear that philosophic and intellectualist techniques are not equal to a description of the real situation. They cannot entirely cope with the web of tensions and contradictions between concept and class of gentleman, between interpretation and interpretation of single ideas, among the various ideas themselves, and among the inevitable value-judgements throughout the whole configuration.

Disparities between the traditions of the class of gentlemen and democratic tendencies have, to take a single complex example, furnished many American minds with materials peculiarly difficult to rationalize philosophically. On the question of birth, Americans have been much given to the praise of natural gentlemen and of an aristocracy of talent. Revolutionary propaganda made much of the long insanities of George III as evidence of the dangers of hereditary aristocracy, and Jefferson invested his best energies in clearing the way for his *aristoi*. Lincoln is, above all else, the classic natural gentleman. And so have been the heroes of popular fiction from Natty Bumppo to Joe Palooka. Nevertheless, cousin-matching and other genealogical pursuits, invidious "old American" associations, and questions of "good family," and "people" vs. "nobodies' are widespread. Among the writers, Cooper and Holmes, admitting the phenomenon of Nature's gentleman, invented elaborate rationalizations of "good birth"; and Howells was worried enough, probably by Holmes, to defend the democratic idea in a surprisingly long series of books.

Wealth and the gentleman have been even more perplexing. Without wealth there is neither leisure nor opportunity to cultivate the mind or the arts of living and expression. Yet materialism, vulgar display, conspicuous waste are ruinous to the gentleman. Where should the line be drawn? Paradoxes have come out of the controversy. John Adams, admitting the power of wealth in a wicked world, lived the life of a Yankee farmer, indulging only the scholar's thirst for books. Jefferson, while condemning the conspicuous waste of Virginia planters and praising frugality, hastened himself into bankruptcy by the expansive life of Monticello. Emerson, the lover of a wise inconsistency, saw riches as an evidence of the power of Nature's

Gentleman, a necessity to the success in manipulating wisely the fleeting illusions of this world of Society's Gentlemen, and a matter of indifference to God's Gentleman who led the way to mankind's better appreciation of the ways of the eternal, beneficent, "law, alive and beautiful." In William Dean Howells the paradox between plutocracy and morality became tragic. Seeing truth and salvation in the simplicities of Tolstoi's primitive Christianity with its call to forsake wealth, he found himself unable to forego his hardwon security of body and mind in the genteel stratum and confessed himself, ruefully, "a theoretical socialist, and a practical aristocrat." Fenimore Cooper loathed the money-changers and the merchants, but he thrilled to the heroism of great enterprises and idealized the lord of the manor. Holmes was frank in his "Contentment" with all the lovely luxuries of plutocratic existence; but he, with perhaps little more than the group of professional defenders of the plutocracy, stood virtually alone in not seeking to adjust wealth to the nicest possible balance between freedom and security for a free America.

Other paradoxes and compromises have come out of the many other tensions within the gentlemanly configuration. The need for class exclusiveness (or even for normal privacy) is not easy to reconcile with ideals of courtesy or function. Formal etiquette, conventions of manners or manner, clashes with the freedom of organic kindness which is the highest notion of courtesy. Thus Oscar Wilde was moved to amend Newman's definition to "the gentleman is he who never causes pain—unintentionally." Serviceable function and social responsibility in the gentleman pull hard against class traditions of conspicuousness and privilege.

If one sticks as close as he can to the facts, if he considers the record rather than theory, he sees that abstract, categorical thinking in familiar philosophic process can neither describe nor account for the phenomena. Theorists from Cotton Mather to Thorstein Veblen, and beyond, have confused themselves and the facts by insisting upon abstract entities, manipulating them more or less logically, and coming to rest upon one pole of paradox while maintaing firmly that the other was "false." But the living facts, denied and rejected, have continued to live.

A second inadequacy of philosophic process here is that it suggests no plausible account for the relation between the gentlemanly configuration and the books which are to be the primary evidence of this study. Why should the given writer have employed gentlemanliness in his book at all? What are the meanings for the book internally, for writer, and for audience in the way he handles these materials? Above all, why is the imaginative work of art much more effective (as it consistently is) in handling the gentleman than is the work of formal analysis? To answer such questions one has to consult much more than the history of ideas in the writer's age, or even in the writer's mind. His biography, his social environment, the thousand-figured texture of life in his time, all these are quite as important as his intellectual milieu. In short, the methods of the cultural historian, including in the long run those of the historian of ideas, are indispensable to the study of the gentleman in America.

Affording a wider view, a more versatile method, and more accurate terms, the approach of the cultural anthropologist is more enlightening.[4] If one recognizes that the concept of the gentleman is a complex item of covert or subjective culture, the obscurities of its relationship to the class of gentry become less puzzling. For it is evident that the class is an item of overt, objective culture which did not, historically, arise as an expression of the covert ideal. The class came as a response to political-economic pressure, and the connection between the two was always at least partly accidental and unreal. So that the persistence of the ideal (covert culture-pattern plus system of values), independent of the class and beyond a number of its own ephemeral overt expressions, is a normal cultural happening. And the modern tendency to jettison the class and cleave to the concept is healthful. The paradox, compromise, lagging, and confusions within the total gentlemanly configuration have answered to the nature of the situation. And so, finally, the wide variations of group and individual choices within the possibilities of the gentlemanly, while philosophically bewildering, are normal as examples of individual reactions at historical moments to any cultural configuration.

One major difficulty in dealing with the history of American culture is our poverty of vocabulary. Mr. Cleveland Amory has, for instance, measurably clarified things by popularizing his term "Proper Bostonian." Now it should be easier to return to the invaluable original significance of "Brahmin caste" as Holmes coined it: to describe the intellectual aristocracy, not wealthy, not Society, not properly Bostonian, but recruited from the clergy, professional men and local gentry around whom the fruitful village culture of New England's great age was organized.

It is not hard to understand why the vocabulary of our cultural history is both small and corrupted. Since a culture is a cluster of human behavior, the impressions which any observer can form of such a flux of action can be made meaningful only by imposing upon it patterns and symbols which are necessarily arbitrary and abstract, and therefore imperfectly accurate. The limitations of thought being what they are, these necessary and false abstractions are often best expressed as metaphors. To express historical process we familiarly use botanical metaphors, or those of the seasons, the ages of man, the times of the day. So long as they communicate and have direct, local, and immediate reference to some kind of experience, metaphors are as sane as they are indispensable. But it is too easily forgotten that they are only comparisons. Symbolic thinking gives way to what might be called metaphoric animism, the pathetic fallacy of metaphor, the pretence or even the faith that the symbol is an entity with a vitality of its own. Particularly in the hands of intellectual irresponsibles, in writings on American culture such terms as "Puritanism," "Victorianism," "the Gilded Age," "the genteel tradition," have been treated as though they were biologically alive. They have been among the Gremlins of cultural historiography.

Actually, of course, the complexities of any task of cultural analysis which seeks to be accurate become appalling. The relational aspects of even so limited a study as this, for example, are potentially endless. The ancient abstract ideal of the gentleman has been periodically expressed in culture patterns of behavior and thought, patterns in which writers have participated as individuals. Selecting idiosyncratically the portions of tradition and of contemporary covert and contemporary overt cultures which appealed to them, the writers have made books which, though objective artifacts in one sense, operate most importantly as works of art which affect their readers subjectively. The artistic means by which the writer works are selective and idiosyncratic on one side; and yet, insofar as they communicate to and affect a considerable audience, they are communal and representative or they could not communicate. But, again, it is certain that there will be some readers who misread the book, finding what is not there, and many who get only portions of what is there. The problem becomes fairly inexpressible when the assumed objectively real situation, in which the true absorption-into-behavior of the gentlemanly configuration occurred in the culture, and the new construct of the writer, and the spotty apprehension of his audience, and the deficiencies of the person trying to study them all are superimposed! The only answer seems to be to fall back again upon metaphor and abstract pattern, but to use them as intellectual counters with a humility and a caution which recognize their fragmentary and illusory natures.

Since 1913, when George Santayana coined the phrase, there has been much confusion, accompanied by much metaphoric animism, over 'the genteel tradition." Santayana's own use of his coinage was never entirely clear. His "genteel tradition" was a phrase obviously loaded with contempt both in its skillful build and in Santayana's subtly sarcastic handling of it.[5] For since Dickens "genteel" has connoted the fussy, pretentious, shallow, and ignorant imitation of gentility which is vulgarity seven times compounded. Santayana employed it to show his contempt for American pretenses to any culture not purely commercial and materialistic. Dealing with American philosophy he found "the genteel tradition" to be puritanic Christianity (as distinct from the 'real' Catholic tradition). Later, spiritually ensconced in fourteenth century Rome as he was physically in Fascist Rome, he levelled his scorn at all who supposed that American culture could genuinely share in what seemed to him the true, great tradition of Europe.

If it were possible, as it is not, to exorcise the contemptuousness from "the genteel tradition," an acceptable referent could be found for it in the tradition, well exampled historically, that an American gentleman was responsible to preserve the covert value-systems and advance their overt expression in American life. The ancient notion of the gentleman's function has been strongly alive in America. But "the genteel tradition," with all its pejorative slant, has been something to be "against." To identify the tradition of the gentleman's call to serve his society as "genteel tradition" is to smear unfairly and disastrously one of our too few traditions of magnanimity and social responsibility. There is a more accurate use for the phrase.

The variation in the ways it has been used is staggering. To borrow James Truslow Adams's neat term, many of the users have been "mucker poseurs." One source, and a fairly legitimate one, of "the mucker pose" is the revolt against respectability which swept in alternate gusts of ozone and hot air through the 1920's. To come down to the real roots of living, the revolters had to cut away much that was obsolete, inane, unhealthy and unreal. However frenetically, such a "Freudian" as Ludwig Lewisohn belongs with this group. But in the midst of all this revolt, it is not necessary also to discard the fundamental elements of self-realization, courtesy born of strength and kindliness, and personal responsibility for the *res publica* which form the basic modern concept of the gentleman.

A different source of muckerism was that which inspired (at the time) Marxian critics like Granville Hicks and Bernard Smith to belabor "the genteel tradition." A political conviction, like Marxianism, which sees gentlemanliness as a symbol of wicked privilege and exploitation or, even worse, a modern prop for a strong middle-class culture which impedes the working of the Marxian dialectic, must hate it. If one thinks the entire reworking of our culture prerequisite to political progress, he must scuttle its traditions. But a man concerned for the overt realization of the ideal of democracy has nothing to fear from the gentleman in America. From Jefferson forward some of the best of American thought has been employed in the assimilation of the doctrine of the "true" gentleman to that of democracy.

Perhaps the most influential popularizer of the term has been Vernon L. Parrington. Aside from a notable addiction to metaphoric animism brought on by over-indulgence in rhetoric, Parrington's handling of "the genteel tradition" is memorable for the instability of his usage. He employs the phrase, often as though it stood for a living entity, in five or six different senses, and without distinguishing among them. In three successive pages, at one point, he offers three discrete definitions.[6] Partly this is careless thinking, but it is motivated also by some of Parrington's ideoligical commitments. Sympathetic to the Turnerian tradition that democracy was an organic and nativist product of the West, and allied to turn-of-the-century Progressivism, Parrington found it convenient to bait the effete East as "genteel." His Progressivism rested also on a soft Social Darwinist faith in economic determinism: if one applied the right economics to America, all would be well since society, like an organism, is determined by environmental factors. In these terms he worked out his blistering critique of "the Gilded Age." But then there was the problem, since he assumed both the entire rightness of his own approach and the complacent stupidity of "the Age," of disposing of the many critics who lived and wrote during it. Embarrassed by their number, few of those who existed though he found, he resorted to dividing them carefully into the few, correct economic determinists and the many others, who were deluded by "the genteel tradition."

As one turns so often in Parrington from his prejudices to his sparkling insights, it should be said that one among his several uses of "the genteel tradition" seems to warrant permanent adoption. It gives scope to the pejorative connotations of the term, and it enriches our culture-study vocabulary by naming an important phenomenon which has hitherto gone unlabelled. "Intellectual New England," he says, retreated after 1870 to the Toryism of the 1790's. And so it succumbed to "the genteel tradition," which is "a timid and uncreative culture that lays its inhibitions on every generation that is content to live upon the past."[7]

In the cultural process by which covert ideas and values are expressed overtly in organized behavior, there is a significant rhythm of expression, use, and obsolescence. This has been particularly true of the gentlemanly configuration; and our literature has been sharply aware of it, especially in the individuals who, for reasons of sentiment, isolation, weakness or vested interest, cling desperately to outworn patterns. Irving's Bracebridge Hall people were such. So, variously, are Cooper's Leatherstocking, Major Thomas Melville immortalized in Holmes's "The Last Leaf," and very many of the characters who people the tales of Page, Cable, Jewett, Ellen Glasgow and other local colorists. Allan Tate's *The Fathers* is one among many modern studies of people lost between a genteel tradition and a cultural newness in a time of crisis. Since they happen in such a rhythm yet each with its historical uniqueness, these situations ought to be called "genteel traditions." There is recognizable reference in cultural history for them, none for a unitary *"the genteel tradition."*

## IV

Literature is written by persons who are uniquely individual, and we have been made acutely aware of that fact in the critical writing of the past hundred and fifty years. But that both writer and writing are affected by the culture from which they come, are necessarily much more "normal" and conventional than individual, is a fact so obvious that it is often overlooked. The accepted symbols and conventions of speech and writing, like the accepted conventions of artistic illusion and form, are "givens" out of the shared culture of artist and audience or nothing is communicated. Even in the work of the decidedly infrequent "original" artist the newness is a tiny portion of the whole. Too much of it intellectually in a Melville or technically in a James or a Joyce means that he must whistle for an audience in his own time. The writer must speak of life as his audience has experienced it and speak in the artistic terms and tones which the audience is prepared to hear—or he may not be heard. The gentlemanly configuration has long supplied both.

Because literature is a culture product in this way, and because of the kind of experiences art gives people, a culture is often better expressed in literature than in any other way. Overt culture—behavior, institutions, artifacts—can be described, enumerated, objectively reproduced. Yet experience, finally a subjective phenomenon anyway, happens to individuals as a fusion of sense and reaction, event and meaning, the overt and the covert. Experience cannot be communicated merely objectively any better than information can be communicated merely subjectively, on a psyche-to-psyche network. It is the special glory of art, and its distinctive human function, to communicate life in wholes, interior fused with exterior, by symbolically and suggestively causing the desired experience to happen within the reader or observer. Thus to know, as fully as knowledge is possible, what a culture was like, one turns to its art. And, because the quantity of culture-content is larger in literature than in the other arts, one turns, first and last, to its literature.

No part of a culture, of course, is merely passive; it will always affect everything which touches it. Literature often plays a decisive role in culture. In it are expressed and powerfully communicated the myths around which men seem prone to organize their thought and faiths. Imaginatively dominant and inventive persons, writers inject new meaning and importance into ordinary events for their readers. Kindling the reader's mind with his powers of narrative, symbolism, and interior suggestion, the writer sometimes secures more effective obedience to myth and ideal. Again, and perhaps at his most "creative," he sometimes interprets the overt cultural-situation into the new myth and the new ideal of value, and adds importantly to the pattern of covert culture. This has been a part of the greatness of Homer, the Old Testament writers, of Shakespeare, Milton, and Swift.

Some degree of that same kind of greatness is evident in the writers of America. And it will be one purpose of this book to show that the gentlemanly configuration supplies a useful tool for discovering and measuring that greatness in them as well as for understanding the cultural history of America newly. The matter of the gentleman has provided a normal point of view toward life for many American writers. It has also been a dependable ingredient of the minds of their audiences, thus affording a familiar meeting-ground for author and audience. Beyond that, it has possessed enough vitality as a system of values to call out earnest exploration of current experience by the writers and to command their intense efforts to express it freshly and with new adequacy for new situations.

One of the liveliest intellectual pursuits of the mid-twentieth century is the analysis and exploration of literature. Exciting work has been done in many fashions. New Humanists concerned for enduring values, the intellectual historians, the psychological critics, the New Critics, primarily concerned with "form," have all broadened the meaning and deepened the importance of criticism. Without depreciating any of these methods but by combining them eclectically and by adding certain things from the armory of the cultural historian, fundamental critical values can be advanced still more. For prior to "judgment," prior to analysis of method, prior even to full enjoyment of a literary work, is the necessity of the fullest possible reading of it. Studies of the author as individual, of historical events which affect his work, of the intellectual and artistic milieu with which he dealt, studies of his relations with his audience—all these have become commonplace preparation for reading his works, though they are much too seldom combined by the critic who supposes that he is attempting a definitive reading. Clearly the implications of cultural studies demand that they be combined and combined in accordance with what is evident about the natures of cultures and their relation to literature. Limited though it often is, this study of the gentleman in America will show, it is hoped, that one more dimension must be added to the problem of reading totally a number of important American books.

V

The elements of the gentlemanly configuration have played parts in the minutiae of American life from determining the planning and zoning of cities and the architecture of buildings to deflecting the quick-silver flow of fashions in millinery. Certainly the concept of the gentleman is in our literature so thoroughly that it is hard to say where it is not. Much even of our roughneck writing has been deliberately done in reaction against it. Though everyone would expect to find the gentleman or fragmentary gleams of his reflection all through Colonial, Revolutionary, and Ante-bellum literature, somehow a tradition of his superficiality, of concern only with fast horses and beautiful women (or the converse), black stocks, polished cavalry boots, swords, roses, and sherry, has become widespread. And it surprises the careful reader to discover how intellectually rigorous and morally strenuous the ideal could be, how natively it became a part of the marrow of Americanism, how richly it germinated in the minds and works of our classic writers and thinkers.

In their old age Adams and Jefferson composed their differences in terms of gentlemanliness, and they made it plain that each had made his unique contribution to American destiny from its premises. There are fragments of gentlemanly notions everywhere in Irving and his group, in Poe and Simms and Kennedy, Longfellow and Lowell and all the Cambridge crowd. But Cooper and Emerson made of their thinking about the gentleman central arches in the very different intellectual structures they spent their lives to build. Being gentlemanly in both life and letters was four-fifths of Holmes's career. The list is almost endless. Melville and Hawthorne use such ideas. Whittier surprises when his ruralism, sometimes almost proletarian, issues in "Among the Hills."

Nor does that list end when we pass beyond the "golden age." Howells conceives of socialism in terms of the gentleman. Henry James's estheticisms are possible only in a gentlemanly atmosphere. Clemens rages at privilege and at Teddy Roosevelt's idea of what constitutes a gentleman; yet for all the fury at Sir Walter Scottism, he treasures any part of a real gentleman he can find among "the damned human race." Passing by all the minor but best-selling people who shared popular taste and thought, there is clear influence on Frank Norris, Edith Wharton, Ellen Glasgow, Willa Cather, E. A. Robinson and Vachel Lindsay; Hergesheimer and Fitzgerald; the Neo-Humanists; the Agrarian group and W. A. Percy; J. P. Marquand, and any number of others. How important has been the tendency to reaction in Hemingway, Dos Passos, Faulkner, Steinbeck? Are many of Sinclair Lewis's frustrates trying to be ladies and gentlemen, and does the author think they should? No limit yet appears to the vitality of the gentleman in American literature,— or, and by the same token, in American life.

There is value in studying the configuration of the gentleman for what it has produced in history and in the literature of the past. There is value in seeing what its elements of vitality are in the life around us. But the greatest value it has to offer is the one which has always been held highest in the gentlemanly ideal. Assimilated to democratic theory, it is a useful and rich ideal of the conduct of life for individual Americans. With the churches stumbling, education struggling for light, politics bewildered by unforeseen demands from current history, the gentleman offers a way of looking at life and of ordering one's daily living which can give us self-disciplined, intelligent, balanced, generous citizens, and leaders equally capable of fair governance and the creation of a satisfying culture. The notion of the gentleman has no supernatural sanction; the saint and the gentleman are not the same. But our times could look to a rebirth of hope if there were enough men, whatever mistakes they might make in their normal frailty, who were trying to live according to the ideas behind the words graven on the tombstone of John L. Cogdell, who was buried in St. Michael's Church in Charleston in 1847:

> In all his relations he was a man to be cherished and loved; he united the kindest affections, with the deepest sensibility, the purest virtue, with the strictest honor; he sustained, with the greatest urbanity, and with spotless integrity, many public offices of trust and distinction; and he illustrated and graced them by an enlightened mind, a cultivated taste, and a devotion to the fine arts at once his ornament and reward. He crowned all his high and endearing qualities, by the humility and faith of the Christian, and fell asleep in the assurance of awaking to everlasting life thro' the merits of the Redeemer.

Sentimental, oratorical rhetoric aside, Cogdell's stone speaks out of a living tradition of the possibilities of excellence in man which is one of the hopes of our being able to continue to make America a hopeful human experience.

## CHAPTER TWO

## THE NEW ENGLAND GENTLEMAN: THEOCRACY AND AFTER

WHILE events south and west of the Connecticut borders took the more or less regular colonial course, in New England things were fatefully different. The difference and the reasons for it are easiest to understand when the interlocking Puritan settlements are seen as one of the earliest, weightiest, and in its time most successful of the innumerable Utopian experiments in America. Allowing for dilution by hangers-on of all kinds, its people were still the siftings of English Puritanism: determined, devoted, homogeneous as only come-outers to a Promised Land can be. And yet, of course, they were just colonials with a difference. As their religion was almost the same as that of Anglicans, so their patterns of living were almost the same as those of the rural England they had left. The difference was small, and its name was Theocracy. Because they were Puritans *and* Utopians, theocracy was in practice an accustomed intellectual discipline with a new twist; and it was an accustomed social discipline—with a newness which its leaders never managed to control for long.

As Governor John Winthrop once forcibly pointed out, his Patent permitted "a Government & Officers here in any forme used in England." Nothing could be more natural, then, than to set up the familiar form of simple administration of law and justice by the gentry. No one challenged Winthrop when he ridiculed "meer Democratie" and self-satisfiedly proclaimed that his government was "a mixt aristocratie." Accordingly, the fact that the leaders of the Bay Colony demanded the hereditary rights of the gentry did not mean that they were usurpers. They were much more successful in combatting the initial odds of settlement in the wilderness than, for instance, their Virginia predecessors. Used to performing the recognized function of the gentleman, they saved their colony from successive threats with great ability. Yet if this had been all, if they had merely transplanted the squirearchical system from England, it would be necessary to say little more about them.

The Puritans read little or no courtesy literature. They were too preoccupied with theology and with immediate practical questions. They were too sure of themselves to seek instruction outside the Bible. Religious and theocratic additions were the only ones they were concerned to make to the tradition of the class of gentlemen as they had learned it at home. But those made a radical difference. In his *Magnalia Christi Americana* Cotton Mather pointed up the distinction sharply by saying that, if the Judges of New England were not nobly born, they were "well born" and most certainly "new born!"

I

Mather's allusion to the Judges of the days of political purity among the Israelites, before a recalcitrant people had demanded a monarchy of God, takes us at once to the heart of the firm rationale of Puritan theocracy. Believing with Calvin that all men who have not been chosen of God for salvation are necessarily wicked and that God's Providence works in and around us at every moment, Puritan leaders and ministers argued that good could be expected only from those whom God had elected to salvation and had "called" to be rulers. Arguing from Scripture in his well-known letter to the Puritan Lord Say and Seal, the influential preacher John Cotton said, "democracy, I do not conceyve that God did ordeyne as a fitt government . . . as for monarchy and aristocracy, they are both of them clearely approved, and directed in scripture, yet so as referreth the soveraigntie to himselfe God, and setteth up Theocracy in both, as the best forme of government in the commonwealth, as well as in the church." Monarchy was obviously being taken care of for the colony in London. But the way seemed clear for them to set up the sort of theocratic "aristocratie" upon which the main lines of influence converged. It was scriptural, doctrinal, permitted by the Patent, and intimately woven into the social pattern brought from home.

John Cotton would have liked to try for a pure theocracy after the Old Testament form with God as King and the high priest (John Cotton) as his regent. But that seed fell on the stony ground of political inexpediency, since it threatened a violation of the Patent. And it was choked by the thorns of the gentlemen's disinclination to be put under the secular control of Cotton or any other priest. Accepting Cotton's three central aims for the colony—"authority in magistrates, liberty in people, purity in the church,"—they were willing to leave the last to the clergy if they could control the first two themselves. That is not to say that they did not cooperate with the church. On the contrary, the collaboration of rulers and clergy was as complete as it prudently could be.

These two concerns of the gentleman—authority in magistrates, and liberty in the people—John Winthrop clarified in that speech of his on liberty which is a Puritan classic. In gist what he said was that the only sort of liberty possible to a Christian civilization was that which obeyed the moral law and "the politic covenance and constitutions amongst men themselves," which were the ends for which all proper authority existed. The means of obtaining this liberty was to submit to the rule of God cheerfully as embodied in God's agents, the elected rulers. Once chosen, these men were the voice of God itself, and any complaint by the people against them "amounts to plain reproof of those whom God hath set over them, and putting dishonor upon them, against the tenor of the fifth commandment." The bringing of a special connotation of the fifth commandment into question became one of the most ingenious weapons of the theocratic magistrate. If it could be established that the magistrate became, once elected, a father of the community, then any rebel could be accused of a breach of the Decalogue, the Law of laws, and punished even when no specific law of the colony had been defied. Thus was Anne Hutchinson, the first New England feminist, answered when on being brought to trial she asked shrewdly what law she had broken: "the fifth commandment," for she had dishonored the fathers of the colony.

The traditional effort to validate a stratified society by appeals to the inequalities of Providence and to Biblical examples was naturally repeated by the theocrats. A point almost invariably made was that God had ordained the rule of some men by others and of the many by the few. The idea was defended eloquently in 1676 by William Hubbard who began by declaring that his topic, "The Happiness of a People," depended on "a sweet subordination of persons and things" because "whoever is for a parity in any society, will in the issue reduce things into an heap of confusion." It was he who produced perhaps the most impressive declaration in favor of the idea of divine aristocracy:

> some have with the Centurion power to command, while others are required to obey, *the poor and the rich meet together, the Lord is the maker of them both,* the Almighty hath appointed her that sits behind the mill, as well as him that ruleth on the throne. And herein hath he as well consulted the good of humane nature, as the glory of his own wisdome and power: Thoase of the superiour rank, but making a supply of what is wanting in the other: otherwise might not the foolish and ignorant be like to loose themselves in the Wilderness, if others were not as eyes to them? The fearful

# THE NEW ENGLAND GENTLEMAN 37

and the weak might be distroyed, if others more strong and valiant, did not protect and defend them. The poor and needy might starve with hunger and cold, were they not fed with the morsells, and warmed with the fleece of the wealthy. Is it not found by experience, that the greatest part of mankind, are but as tools and instruments for others to work by, rather than any proper Agents to effect anything of themselves . . . If the virtue and valour of the good did not interpose by their authority, to prevent and save, the vice of the bad would bring mischief enough . . . to ruine both.

The other major argument was that in a world governed by Providence rulers must be God's representatives. Since they had been appointed by agreement among the saints of God, for only church members could vote prior to 1647 and afterwards they still formed the bulk of the enfranchised, that became for Puritans an overwhelming argument. Even Roger Williams agreed that any point upon which John Winthrop and Edward Winslow were agreed was unquestionably God's will.

Direct responsibility to Jehovah made the function of the gentleman intense and awful. He had, in Mather's words, "to adorn the Doctrine of God our Saviour." Much more, as Jonathan Mitchell put it in a hard-hitting sermon entitled "Nehemiah on the Wall," Bible stories proved that the leader who went to his work "with courage, and constancy, and confidence in God" won prosperity for his community. A leader who spared to "search out and testifye against evil" might draw the righteous wrath of Heaven upon his whole people. Only he could secure them against mass disaster. Thus Theophilus Eaton of New Haven, as Cotton Mather paints him, was the ideal theocratic gentleman:

Mr. Eaton, being yearly and ever chosen their Governour, it was the admiration of all spectators to behold the discretion, the gravity, the equity with which he still managed all their publick affairs. He carried in his very countenance a majesty which cannot be described; and in his dispensations of justice he was a mirrour for the most imitable impartiality, but ungainsayable authority of his proceedings being awfully sensible of the obligations which the oath of a judge lay upon him. And he who would most patiently bear hard things offered his person in private cases, yet would never pass by any publick affronts, or neglects offered when he appeared under the character of a magistrate. But he still was the guide of the blind, the staff of the lame, the helper of the widow and the orphan, and all the distressed; none that had a good cause was afraid of coming before him: on the one side, In his Days did the righteous flourish, on the other side, he was the terror of evil doers.

The practical outcome of theocratic principles was personal government, and the main body of Bay freemen fought almost instinctively for that right to be governed by common law which Englishmen had been widening since Magna Carta days. His opponents, shortly before they failed in an attempt to oust Winthrop, characterized his *Arbitrary Government Described* as "pernicious and dangerous." But they did so before Winthrop had acknowledged his authorship of the paper and while they could still pretend not to know its author.

Over a period of years the opponents of theocracy limited, defeated, and finally discredited its philosophy. But they could not learn to do without theocrats, just as other societies in other times and places could not do without their gentlemen. That New England theocracy gave its society an immensely capable leadership is the fact which made its ideas, altered but recognizable, endure through generations of Yankee history. Initially, however, what the theocrats did was to provide a new and typically Puritan rationale to empower the seventeenth-century English gentleman to perform the recognized function of his class in a place and time of immense difficulty—when his success or failure was of the greatest historical importance.[1]

II

Not all the New England alterations in the gentlemanly tradition were dictated by theocratic logic. Thoroughly dependent on men of no special lineage, the Puritans awarded status among the gentry primarily to those who performed the functions of the class. Solid wealth, especially if it were the product of the notable enterprise and public service of a great

merchant, conspicuous service to the state, learning, and only
then heredity, won the respect of the community. A great gentleman, like a governor or an important magistrate or someone
whose place in England had been high, was distinguished by an
'Esquire" after his name; other gentlemen were called "Mr."
Ordinary people, of course, were designated as "Goodman" or
"Goodwife" (later shortened to "Goody"). Any holder of a
university degree or any minister was a gentleman.

A sumptuary law of 1651, for instance, limits all citizens
worth less than 200 pounds, "Magistrates . . . Officers, civil or
military, Soldiers in Time of Service; or such as have had a high
Education, or are sunk from a higher Fortune."[2] By this and
similar laws the lower classes were not, as has often been supposed, prohibited from wearing colors or legally bound to
drabness and humiliation. They were simply prevented from
vying with their superiors in the purchase and display of costly
materials. They were barred from the game, upon which the
Puritan doctrine of stewardship frowned, of conspicuous consumption, of the race to keep up with the Joneses. Puritan
gentlemen, who might be trusted not to go too far, were
rewarded by the right to finer clothing. For, preached Urian
Oakes, "One end of apparel is to distinguish and put a difference
between persons according to their Places and Conditions."

Aside from the gratifying privileges of title and sartorial
advantages for himself, his consort, and children, the Puritan
gentleman received various legal benefits, both implicit and
explicit. John Winthrop found an argument against the codifi-
cation of laws in urging that judges must take into consideration
"the qualitye of the person" on trial. A gentleman was by law
immune from sentence to such humiliating punishments as
public whipping which were almost as frequent for common
offenders in New England as in Europe. When the famous
Remonstrant Dr. Robert Child was imprisoned pending disposal
of his crime of an unwise attack upon the theocracy's refusal to
write down the laws of Massachusetts Bay, Winthrop warned
him against the further unwisdom of displays of vulgar temper,

advising him that the intention of the magistrates was to treat him with the leniency due a gentleman unless he forced them to treat him as a common criminal. Theocratic New England demanded real service of its gentlemen, but no one could complain that it did not make it worth their while.

With this respect for the class, New England was led to one of its most pregnant policies by the need to maintain its supply of gentlemen. The combination of information and cultivation which could give the naturally best men the powers to think and lead could only be provided through education. In effect, then, Harvard College was founded, not only for fear of leaving "an illiterate Ministery to the churches, when our present Ministers shall lie in the Dust," but also to provide intelligent gentleman rulers. An anonymous Latinist speaking just after Bacon's Rebellion in Virginia is reported to have said in a Harvard Commencement address:

> The ruling class would have been subjected to mechanics, cobblers, and tailors; the gentry would have been overwhelmed by lewd fellows of the baser sort, the sewage of Rome, the dregs of an illiterate plebs which judgeth much from emotion, little from truth; we should have seen . . . no flashing sparklets of honor; the Laws would not have been made by *senatus consulta,* nor would we have rights, honors, or magisterial ordinances worthy of preservation, but plebiscites, appeals to base passions, and revolutionary rumblings if these our fathers had not founded the University.[3]

It is easy to be too cynical in assigning the prestige of learning purely to political motivations or even concern for the wider function of the gentleman. For, as Samuel Eliot Morison assures us, there was in the Harvard curriculum full justification for the phrase and its special translation which have become a sort of rallying cry for Harvard historians. William Brattle said in his graduation address in 1689, *"Liberali liberaliter instituendi* —Gentlemen should be educated like gentlemen."[4]

For all that Cotton Mather's concern for learning and culture was a sort of vested interest, his delight in John Winthrop, Jr., as "a governor who was not only a christian and a gentleman, but also an eminent philosopher" is significant in the light of Mather's later book, *The Christian Philosopher*, 1721. There Mather draws the inevitable conclusion that the searcher into the mysteries of Nature will learn how to fear and adore its Creator. But he also sees the values of such pursuits to the inward gentleman. Through study the Christian gentleman will "rise into that superior way of thinking and of living, which the wisest of men will chuse to take; which the more polite part of mankind, and the honorable of the earth, will esteem it no dishonor for them to be acquainted with." In his learning, which was virtually all his polite culture, the theocratic gentleman was free to follow the humanist tradition of the balanced cultivation of the whole man. As he would have been the first to admit, it was a decidedly this-worldly concept. His ultimate salvation would be no whit surer or more glorious because of it. Yet, barred from no lawful use of the good life on this earth, he was as free to enjoy as he was to employ the entry into the life of the mind which the "Temporals" of his gentleman's education afforded him.[5]

The historical greatness of the Puritan gentleman consists in large part in the fact that he was able to maintain such intellectual standards, creating educational means to perpetuate them, in the face of frontier conditions. The necessity for the clergy to hold their scholarly eminence has been often discussed. But the physical and economic rigors of frontier life were on the gentleman even harder than on the minister. "In this Wildernesse-worke men of Estates speed no better than others," recorded Edward Johnson in *The Wonder Working Providence of Sion's Saviour*. Yet learning was fully as necessary to the gentleman as to the clergyman, and he did his fair share in selling the idea to the populace so successfully that Harvard College was supported as much from the scanty surpluses of stony New England farms as from all other sources together. In New England the concept of the gentleman won its battle with the frontier from the start, instead of having to struggle up from defeat as it did on most other frontiers. That success had permanent effect upon American life. In New England ideas about the gentleman began a native growth from the start.

And when the power of the theocracy had waned, the tradition of the learned gentleman survived in the famed Brahmin caste of New England. It is not too risky to predict that a thorough study of the great age of New England would show that a main source was the firm, intense culture of its villages. For two centuries they built soil around an aristocracy of scholars—ministers, doctors, lawyers, squires—who were accustomed to accepting responsibility for the public good. Then the towns and villages, not mercantile Proper Boston, brought forth the men of the great age. When industrialism and emigration broke up the village culture the great men ceased to appear. But they had made New England illustrious because theocracy had given rise to Brahminism.

The Puritan gentleman succeeded so well because, in part, he showed a hard-bitten variety of the gentlemanly virtue which the Elizabethans held highest of all: magnanimity. To him as a Puritan wealth was important, both for the reasons which theorists like Tawney and Weber have made clear and because it supported his position as gentleman. Nevertheless he might hold to the doctrine of stewardship to the point, as in Winthrop's case, of very nearly liquidating his estate for the good of the colony. As a Puritan he saw with a clarity denied many a modern religious group the reality of pain and tragedy in the world. But he faced it down in the faith that God had called him to bear it in single-minded humility and dependency on Himself. The concept of the calling explains a great deal also of the courage of these gentlemen in leaving lands and position in England to come to the howling North American wilderness. Faith with regard to the calling, they said,

> encourageth a man to the most homeliest, and difficultest and most dangerous things his calling can lead and expose himself to; if faith apprehend this or that to be the way of my calling, it encourages me to it, though it be never so homely, and difficult and dangerous. Take you a carnall proud heart, and if his calling lead him to some homely businesse, he can

## THE NEW ENGLAND GENTLEMAN 43

by no meanes embrace it, such homely employments a carnall heart knowes not how to submit unto; but now faith having put us into a calling, if it require some homely employment, it encourageth us to it, he considers. It is my calling, and therefore he goes about it freely, and though never so homely, he doth it as a work of his calling.

Men of such belief were unprepared for very little in the way of peril or privation which might afflict them, and they were not inclined to shrink from large responsibilities.

Though admirers occasionally recorded praise for social virtues in theocratic gentlemen, both Castiglione's emphasis upon the development of special graces, and the classical ideal of heroic individual expansiveness were neglected in New England. Theocrats envisaged the perfection of the God-favored few, but only in godliness. The native English tradition had seen the justification of the gentleman in the service which he could render to country and kind. This theocracy, with its burning faith in Providence, adopted readily; but it made service to society contingent on serving God. In sum the theocratic ideal is the ultimate extension of the virtue tradition. In New England, in fact, a man could be legally expelled from the ranks of gentlemen for even a petty crime.[6]

Theocracy failed, and with it the ideal of the theocratic gentleman. Its failure was partly due to the stubborn opposition of transplanted Englishmen to the threat of losing their common-law rights—an attitude which was yet to promote the American Revolution. A still greater reason for its failure was that, like most Puritan ideals, it was unattainably transcendent in concept. It was too much to ask of any group of men that they be at once saints, philosophers, and statesmen. There are no such men. Yet for all the many shortcomings of theocracy, there was permanent value in its ideal of the gentleman. When theocracy had ebbed in the eighteenth century, it left behind a provincial tendency toward petty snobbery. The earnest vitality and scope of the elder Puritan gentleman one misses sadly in Joseph Sewall and Samuel Mather, even in Cotton Mather. Yet it never ebbed away altogether. It left a sense of expectation in

New England of men with broad souls and tall minds which needed an Emerson for its expression.

### III

With the theoretical understructure of the New England concept of the gentleman in mind, it is well to remember that the pattern of ideas was derived from the real lives of colorfully real men. The most interesting of them all, a man who would amply repay full-scale biographical treatment, was the senior John Winthrop. An English country squire, lawyer, justice of the peace, and influential private figure in his own right before coming to New England, he was the leading defender of the ideals of the theocratic gentleman as well as a sort of combination Joseph and Moses to the colony. From Cotton Mather to Professors Parrington and Morison, commentators have delighted to admire him. "Our New England shall tell and boast of her WINTHROP," Mather exulted in his proudly Byzantine style. "A governor in whom the excellencies of Christianity made a most improving addition unto the virtues, where even without those he would have made a Parallel for the Great men of Greece, or of Rome, which the pen of a Plutarch has Eternized."

Winthrop's achievements warranted both the places of high trust he held in the colony and the paeans of the biographers. The seriousness with which he took his calling as the natural and chosen leader of the colony may be seen in brief in his economic dealings with it. Not only was he a moving spirit in the original plans for its planting; he acted, as his correspondence shows, as banker and agent for much of the early outfitting of the enterprise. He launched the first keel of New England's sailing-ship commerce by building *The Blessing of the Bay* and sliding her down the ways July 4, 1631. Though, as in Mather's words "the Joseph of his people," he had allowed the colony at one time to become his debtor for more than a third of his whole estate and knew it could repay him only in land when he was already land-poor, he wrote patiently in the magnani-

mous spirit of his stewardship and calling, primarily reminding the colony of its own need for integrity:
> I do account it my duty to spend and to be spent for the publique welfaire yet I think it (with all humility) also your duty honored gentlemen not to suffer me to loose more than needeth.

Tenderly, if humorously, concerned for the total success as a God-conducted experiment of the colony, Winthrop spent himself as well as his fortune. And his spending was not in vain. As a great gentleman who rose to the very peak of an opportunity to mould with an almost artistic completeness the historical footings of a culture, he became the first example of one of America's ideals: the pioneer-gentleman who creates the new and fires the faith that America is an experiment.[7]

John Winthrop, Jr. received considerably more of a legacy from his father than the family fortunes somewhat in need of retrenchment. His training as a Christian scholar and gentleman was unstintedly the best to be had. Nor was his training merely formal. To read the correspondence between father and son in the son's college, professional, and travelling years is to understand how completely he was made the heir of all his father's best. It contrasts fascinatingly with Chesterfield's epistolary efforts to bestow an equivalent gift upon his far less worthy child. Until Winthrop was sure that his son was among the elect and wholly firm in his sense of theocratic calling and responsibility, he wrote long letters in the tenor of this extract:
> I perceive by your letter that you were much possessed with the feare of death. You must be carefull that Satan does not delude you. It is good to be alwaies mindfull and prepared for death, but take heede of distrusting, perplexed thoughts about it, for that will encrease the sicknesse. Trust him with your life that gave you life and being, and hath only power over death and life, to whom we must be willing to submit to be at the disposing of his good will and pleasure. Whether in life or death learne to know God and to serve him, and to feare him and walke in his waies; and leave your selfe with him and cast your care on him who careth for all his servants and will not forsake those that trust in his name. In sickness use those meanes that you can have; and committ your selfe for the successe to the Lord.

When it became obvious that the end had been gained, the letters on salvation and stewardship ceased, and father and son wrote with equal respect and deference.

For all the normal intensity of concern of the Puritan gentleman for the welfare of his son's soul and the proper shaping of his mind and character, the elder Winthrop's letters were not all just moralizing. Welldoing in the son earned its ample reward, for Winthrop wrote him,

> and for your expenses, seeing I perceive you are considerate of my estate, I will not limit your allowance less than to the uttermost of mine own estate. So as, if £20 be too little (as I always accounted it), you shall have £30 and, when that shall not suffice, you shall have more. Only hold a sober and frugal course (yet without baseness), and I will shorten myself to enlarge you.

There is a world of significance in that single parenthetical phrase, "yet without baseness"; this is a gentleman writing to his son. And the son, proving worthy, had all he wished. He studied for two years at Trinity College, Dublin, finished his work at the Inner Temple, and took the Grand Tour of the Continent. When his father made his great decision for the New World, he was ready to serve as his right hand. His words are those of the rare blend of Puritan, humanist, and gentleman that he was:

> And for myself, I have seen so much of the vanity of the world, that I esteem no more of the diversities of countries, than as so many inns, whereof the traveller that hath lodged in the best, or in the worst, findeth no difference, when he cometh to his journey's end; and I shall call that my country where I may most glorify God, and enjoy the presence of my dearest friends. Therefore herein I submit myself to God's will and yours, and, with your leave, do dedicate myself (laying by all desire of other employments whatsoever) to the service of God and the Company herein, with the whole endeavors both of body and mind.[8]

The end result of this training was eminent success. The son united with learning the tolerance which was balked in his father by Dudley and Endicott. As Roger Williams wrote

## THE NEW ENGLAND GENTLEMAN 47

him, "You have always bene noted for tendernes toward mens soules, especially for conscience sake to God. . . . You have bene noted for tenderness toward the bodies & infirmities of poor mortalls. You have bene tender too toward the estates of men in your civall steerage of government, & toward the peace of the land, yea, of these wild savages." So successful as a governor and diplomat that he won for Connecticut her charter of self-government when Massachusetts was about to lose hers, he was undoubtedly the most popular man in the colonies of his day. Nathaniel Ward wrote him a begging letter signed by fifty-seven of Ipswich's leading citizens pleading that he come home and remain with them. John Davenport tried to bribe him to come to New Haven, providing a new house complete with provisions and servants. John Brewster besought him to take up permanent residence at New London, urging that the town was naked and headless without him. Yet in an age of international scholars he was a member of the great fraternity of minds to which modern civilization owes much of its start. Some of his correspondents were Robert Boyle, Tycho Brahe, Sir Thomas Browne, Comenius, Cromwell, Galileo, Milton, Newton, Sir Henry Wotton, Sir Christopher Wren.

As those names suggest, the younger Winthrop was well-advanced in the science of the day. He tried hard to exploit the natural resources of New England. The typical frontier shortages of everything, especially transportation and skilled manpower, balked his own efforts and postponed the exploitation of the opportunities he saw to future venturers. Typically also, he possessed the finest scientific library in the country and was a gifted physician for the times. His father's equal in strength of character and perhaps his superior in keenness of mind and of religious sensibility, the junior Winthrop was well fitted to consolidate and make available for use what his father had created. To his father's power to do, to lead and to sacrifice, the son added the qualities of tenderness and fine perception which made him the flower of theocratic gentlemanliness, fit for any company of the great gentlemen.

Seeing clearly that there was a difference in attitude and approach between theocratic gentlemen like the Winthrops and Samuel Sewall, the Boston Judge of the turn of the century who had married the daughter of Boston's wealthiest merchant, Vernon L. Parrington decided that that difference came from the fact that Sewall was properly neither a theocrat nor a gentleman. Sewall, he said, was not even really a Puritan. He was the "first Yankee,"—"a village capitalist," prudent, plodding, —"phlegmatic soul" with the religion of a shopkeeper.[9] Certainly it is true that Puritanism and a dominant materialism were incompatible. Under the doctrines of stewardship and the calling a Christian might possess or accumulate wealth; but he must do so by no unrighteous means, and he must be ready to "spend and to be spent," as John Winthrop put it, in God's causes. But so long as the genuine seeking after God's will came first, it was no more wrong for John Winthrop, Jr., to leave behind him a vast landed estate or for John Hull to accumulate capital to pass on to Hannah Hull Sewall than it had been for the senior Winthrop to liquidate his English fortune for the founding of the colony. To prove that Sewall was the "first Yankee" one would have to show that he was a hypocrite who violated Puritan economic theory.

As every historian of New England says, the death by dry-rot of the theocratic way of life did occur somewhere in the generation to which Sewall belonged. But Parrington, anxious to find a notable example, chose his man too hastily. Before his marriage Sewall was a young gentleman of good family, some fortune, considerable education, and fine prospects in the colony. If Hannah Hull brought wealth and powerful connections, it was the match of equals which Winthrop had made the sole stipulation concerning his son's marriage. While there is no evidence of conspicuous waste in Sewall's expenditures, his benevolences were substantial; and there seems to be no evidence of gaingetting activity by him which goes far beyond the moves necessary merely to conserve his inheritances.[10] If the positive evidence of live religious conviction be found in Sewall, there can be no real basis on which to read him out of the ranks of theocratic gentlemen.

In the light of Sewall's early conversion and intentions of becoming a minister, but even more in the daily experiences of search after God, he appears a staunch, sincere Puritan. Cotton Mather himself could have done little more toward the conversion and the training in orthodox faith and ways of his children than Sewall did for his. His action with regard to his part in the notorious Salem withcraft delusion is one of the finest exemplifications of the attitude of the theocratic gentleman in Puritan history. He placed the following announcement in the hands of his minister one Sunday and had it read to all the congregation, acknowledging it publicly at the close, and repeating the process yearly:

> Copy of the bill I put up on the fast day, giving it to Mr. Willard as he passed by, and standing up at the reading of it and bowing when finished; in the afternoon.
> Samuel Sewall, sensible of the reiterated strokes of God upon himself and family and being sensible that as to the guilt contracted upon the opening of the late Commission of Oyer and Terminer at Salem (to which the order of this day relates), he is upon many accounts, more concerned than any that he knows of, desires to take the blames and shame of it, asking pardon of men and especially desiring prayers that God who has an unlimited authority would pardon that sin and all other, his sins, personal and relative and according to his infinite benignity and sovereignty not visit the sin of him or of any other upon himself or any of his nor upon the land; but that he would powerfully defend him against all temptations to sin for the future and vouchsafe him the efficacious, saving conduct of his word and Spirit.

His attitude is explicit in his text. He had acted according to his calling as a magistrate, following what he conceived to be the evidence. But when it became clear to him that he had been mistaken, he considered God, not man. Certainly, Puritanism was alive and real there as it was in the spirit with which, the charter of Massachusetts withdrawn and the theocratic power broken forever, Sewall choked off protest and led the last general court in a ceremonial, if unofficial, relinquishment ruled by the spirit of the Puritan gentleman whose calling was his own only so long as God kept him in it and who laid it down cheerfully when he felt God no longer with him.

Such actions do not show any spirit in Sewall of soft acquiescence. A gentleman who had improved his opportunities so well that his diary became a brilliant exception in literary charm and historical value to its hundreds of contemporaries,[11] he was accustomed to the exercise of authority in the theocratic manner. When sure he was right, he fought stubbornly. He opposed the Quakers. He resigned a prized milita commission rather than serve under a flag with a "papist" St. George's Cross in it. He refused, against considerable pressume from the governor and a lucrative offer, to sell his heritage of John Cotton's land for an Anglican chapel. He resisted the proposition of the representatives of the crown itself that the church of which he was an elder be opened to Anglican services. As he recorded in his diary,

> Said came from England to avoid such and such things, therefore could not give to set them up here and the Bishops would have thought strange to have been ask'd to contribute towards setting up the New England Churches.

When Puritan values were threatened, he could be a surprisingly unpolitic politician, as the royal governor found in frequent clashes.

Yet the vital movement of the seventeenth century was dying with the date. By contrast to the positive, constructive Winthrops, Sewall was a defensive figure. Trying to champion fundamental values, he was forced into skirmishing the petty. He found himself fighting the introduction of wigs, the desertion of sober dress, the celebration of Christmas, the reintroduction of the Cross of St. George into the Restoration flag, and such vices of the soldiery as gambling and cock-fighting. The theocracy which had been at full strength in his boyhood was crumbling fast. On shattered foundations he could not build; he could only fight doggedly and futilely. Samuel Sewall rose to maturity a theocratic gentleman in the tradition of the Winthrops. He lived almost to become the representative of a genteel tradition. Theocracy as such was done, yet Sewall had an important tradition to pass on to the coming generations whose preoccupations were political rather than religious. He could leave for men like Putnam and Hancock and the Adamses a now native tradition of the function of the gentleman.

## CHAPTER THREE

## "FINE" GENTLEMAN VS. CHRISTIAN GENTLEMAN

By THE TIME of the third generation in America, a plateau period of stability and consolidation had been reached. With the Alleghenies as a natural barrier and the French as a military and psychological one, the frontier became almost fixed for decades. Yet it was far enough distant to permit tranquillity of life and enterprise in the seaboard settlements. Political peace in England gave direction and security to government, even though it also brought exploitation and infuriating restrictions. Participation in imperial wars brought wealth and a rising sense of American entity as well as loss and corruption. The result was a general shaking down and tightening up of society. Merchants and planters, the winners in the earlier race for economic position, began to reap the expected rewards. In the thriving ports and towns the professions came truly into their own; and the foundation and expansion of colleges showed that education was keeping pace. In the major ports from Boston to Charleston, on the great plantations, and in the rural towns of New England and of the

Middle States distinctive ways of life began to grow. Art and literature germinated. And the class of gentlemen came to the fore in America as it had in England.

New wealth and consciousness that American gentlemen did now actually have the position which the tradition demanded drew them into closer colonial bonds. Gentlemen's sons were often sent to Oxford or Cambridge and the Inner Temple. Like William Byrd the second, some of them hob-nobbed with the literary lions who were England's most publicized figures. Anglicanism took a stronger hold on American religion. A sizable proportion of American gentlemen became attached to England by ties, more cultural than political, which outlasted revolution, civil war, exile and expropriation. Even the able gentlemen who rebelled against the King stayed loyal to the intellectual and cultural standards of London.

I

Reading all the didactic literature of contemporary gentility, Americans were swept into the great controversy between the fine and the Christian gentlemen. With the prudery of colonials thrown to the side of Sir Charles Grandison in America, the Christian gentleman won tremendous vogue. The first American novels imitated Richardson. Harriet Beecher Stowe remembered her mother's confession that as a girl, after reading about Sir Charles, she had declared that "she never meant to marry until she found his like." Such American Richardsonians as Mrs. Rowson, Mrs. Murray, and Mrs. Sedgwick were ardently devoted to the gentleman both in class and idea. But they seemed to find the sinister lustre of Lovelace far more useful than the flat white virtue of Grandison.

Chesterfield himself could occasionally find dispassionate American treatment. In an open "Letter from Mrs. Mercy Warren to Her Son,"[1] the American blue-stocking applauded Chesterfield's style and "code of politeness which surpasses anything of the kind in the English language." But she could not approve the sacrifice of "truth to convenience, probity to pleasure, virtue to the graces, generosity, gratitude, and all the fine feelings of the soul, to a momentary gratification." She could think it, "by no means necessary, that a gentleman, in order to be initiated into the science of good breeding, should drop his humanity; that to acquire a courtly mien, and become an adept in politeness, he should renounce the moral feelings; or to be master of the graces, that his life should be a contrast to every principle of Christianity."

Popular denigrations of the Chesterfieldian and glorifications of the Richardsonian gentleman led to the development of specific terms. "Fine gentleman" came to denote the rake, the fake, the snob, the clotheshorse, and the bully. The "Happy Man; and True Gentleman" was, as a writer in the *New York Magazine and Literary Repository* put it, "a Man, a Christian."[2] The difference may clearly be seen in two anonymous magazine squibs of the time. In *Thomas's Massachusetts Spy* for July 1, 1795, appeared crudely ironic "Instructions for Fine Gentlemen." They were counselled to be boorish, selfish, foul-mouthed, drunken, lustful, pretentious, lying, snuff-taking. "Do you wish to be in love?" asks the climactic paragraph. "Visit your mistress when you have drank freely of your bottle. *Spirits* give *spirits;* and a man can never talk of his heart, unless something *puts it into his head;* then practise a dying speech; thump your breast, flourish your handkerchief; and present a pistol. If she is not moved with this, I shall give you leave to shoot yourself." In the *New York Weekly Magazine* for March, 1796, "A Lady" analyzed the "Character of a Well-Bred Man." The well-bred man and the fine gentleman are not the same. The well-bred man has all of the best of the courtesy tradition. The fine gentleman, by inference, is his opposite at every point. The well-bred man:

> is neither a slave nor an enemy to pleasure, but approves or rejects as his reason shall direct. He is above stooping to flatter a knave, though in an exalted station; nor ever overlooks merit, though he should find it in a cottage. His behaviour is affable and respectful, yet not cringing or formal; and his manners easy and unaffected. He misses no oppor-

tunity wherein he can oblige his friends, yet does it in so delicate a manner, that he seems rather to have received than conferred a favor. He does not profess a passion he never felt to impose upon the credulity of a silly woman; nor will he injure another's reputation to please her vanity. He cannot love where he does not esteem, nor ever suffers his passions to overcome his reason. In his friendship he is steady and sincere, and lives less for himself than his friends.

No one ever really pretended that every Christian man was automatically a gentleman. But it was held, most strongly at the popular level, that the true gentleman began by being Christian. The distinction in terms as well as in concept went on triumphantly through the next century. In 1863 George Calvert, writing his own courtesy volume, *The Gentleman*, held that true gentlemanhood was a "deep, moral inwardness" ultimately independent of heredity and even conventional training. It finds organic expression in the "flowers of spiritual beauty" of that courteous behavior which follows the precept of Christ which Calvert paraphrases as *"whosoever would reign, let him serve."* The core of Calvert's thought is in the firm statement: "The gentleman is a Christian product"; he is "a cultured Christian." On the other tack, Samuel McChord Crothers, gathering an essay called "The Evolution of the Gentleman" into *The Gentle Reader* (1903), distinguished carefully between the "true" and "fine" gentlemen. The fine gentleman is, he said, artificial and Machiavellian. As the gaudy butterfly of various summers, he has been "the dude, the swell, the dandy, the fop, the spark, the macaroni, the blade, the popinjay, the coxcomb." Crothers makes great capital of the contrast between the imagined meetings, one grave, pleasant and beautiful, of the true gentlemen of the ages; the other a motley hubbub of the fine gentlemen met to sneer and snicker at each other's grotesque clothing.

The two kinds of gentlemen are to be met in literature written any time in the past 150 years. They are much alive as character-conventions now. Tom Brainless in *The Progress of Dulness* is a comic fine-gentleman as parson. The distinction is implicit in Hawthorne's *House of Seven Gables* as between Judge Pyncheon and Clifford, for instance. And Hawthorne's "Feathertop" is the last word in scorn of the fine gentleman. Devil-animated by witch-craft into classic caricature of Chesterfieldianism, Feathertop was on his way to perfect worldly success when he saw his promenading self in a truth-telling mirror. Then the horrible incongruity between his seeming and his being took the heart out of him, out of even a scarecrow, and he refused to go on where many an equally false man (Hawthorne intimates) would have persisted. On the other hand, Herman Melville, who had an eye for a gentleman, made his *Pierre* a Christian gentleman to show how terribly the abysses of moral ambiguity opened beneath even the man conventionally recognized as humanly perfect.

One of the most interesting results in an earlier America of the conflict between the fine and the true gentlemen was Royal Tyler's play, *The Contrast*, 1787. Tyler asserted that his play was the representation of rugged, native American gentility in contrast to the effete and wicked Europeanism of Chesterfield. In reality his hero seems to have been made up of a large amount of Grandison with a little of Sterne and something more of George Washington thrown in. The heroine, Maria, has found her ideal of a gentleman and husband in *Clarissa, Grandison,* the *Sentimental Journey* and the poems of Shenstone. But she sees in Billy Dimple, the man fatally betrothed to her by her family, a man who has been "polished" to complete viciousness in Europe: "the wickedness of Lovelace without his wit, and the politeness of Sir Charles Grandison without his generosity." Maria's conflicting fear of the rake and extreme filial piety are both typically Richardsonian.

Dimple himself is a first-class caricature of Chesterfieldian doctrine, yet he seems to have been a type plausible to Tyler's audience. "A depraved wretch, whose only virtue is a polished exterior," he is an aggressive rake and no patriot. Vice has made him so pallid and languorous that any future wife may hope soon for the joy of widowhood. The Chesterfieldian effect upon men is mirrored in the scenes featuring Dimple's servant, Jessamy. Jessamy tells rustic Yankee Jonathan that he is a "vulgar, horrid brute" for thinking of being faithful to his fiancee a hundred miles away. There is fairly brisk satire when he tries to tutor Jonathan, á la Chesterfield, in just how, when, and how much to laugh and smile.³ The germ of the villainous scheme by which Billy Dimple ruins himself—he will "break with Maria, wed Letitia" (for her money) and make Charlotte Manly his mistress—he credits to his reading Chesterfield. At the end of the play, when all this machination is uncovered by the device borrowed from *The School for Scandal* of having all the principal characters hidden where they can watch Billy compromise himself, he leaves in pseudo-dignity with the tag-line: "You will please to observe, in the case of my deportment, the contrast between a gentleman, who has read Chesterfield and received the polish of Europe, and an unpolished, untravelled American."

The character of the hero, Colonel Manly, was formed on Grandison, with a dash of Sterne's sensibility. His flippant sister Charlotte says, "His heart is like an old maiden lady's bandbox; it contains many costly things, arranged with the most scrupulous nicety, yet the misfortune is, that they are too delicate, costly, and antiquated, for common use." He is a solemn Man of Feeling whose conversation may at any moment set Charlotte to crying and "spoil her eyes." Sententiously religious, he courts popularity like Grandison—by correcting the faults of ladies at public gatherings. Like Grandison's, too, his conversation is as stiff as "a rich old fashioned brocade, it will stand alone; every sentence is a sentiment." He condemns Dimple's first hint of trifling with a lady's affections in a fashion which would have warmed Richardson's heart, intoning "I should with reluctance suppose that these pernicious sentiments could find admittance into the heart of a gentleman."

Though Manly's condemnation of travelling is in line with the nationalistic theme of the play, he agrees with Richardson in finding it demoralizing. Similarly Richardsonian are his concurrence with Maria in her filialism and his refusal to fight a duel with Dimple. The one thing which saves Manly from fatuousness is that part of his character formed after America's premier gentleman, George Washington. Manly seeks to imitate Washington in noble self-sacrifice for his country and in the self-denying care he takes for his "family" of brave men who have fought under him in the war. This devotion to the gentleman's function and his curtain speech save him:

> I have learned that probity, virtue, honour, though they should not have received the polish of Europe, will secure to an honest American the good graces of his fair countrywoman, and, I hope, the applause of The Public.

Although both Chesterfield and Richardson had been in wholehearted agreement in opposing the institution of the duel, it is one of the significant differences in *The Contrast* that the fine gentleman challenged and that the true gentleman, a brave soldier, refused the challenge. For two centuries past the concept of the gentleman had been in unalterable opposition [4] to the "brutal bravery" of duelling by the class of gentlemen. A vestigial remnant of trial by combat, the code duello had been almost unknown in America before the importation, with French and British army officers and London-educated colonial sparks, of the mode of the fine gentleman.[5] The desperate colonial inferiority complex of the more unstable young American aspirants turned them to "the code" as a gross and easy way of proving that they were gentlemen. What better proof could there be than a man's willingness to kill or be killed? Yet all courtesy literature worthy the name, the tradition of the true, Christian gentleman, and Chesterfield himself were unequivocably against both duelling and its blockheaded notion of honor.

In that light it is interesting to examine the most famous of American duels, that between Aaron Burr and Alexander Hamilton. Although Burr and Hamilton had clashed politically, they maintained what was, on Hamilton's part at least, the pretense of friendship until the close of the New York State election of 1804. Then the Albany *Register* printed letters which referred to the "despicable" opinion of Burr which Hamilton had been sowing in a whispering campaign upstate. Burr wrote to Hamilton demanding that he at once acknowledge or deny his authorship of the slanders. Hamilton, having just wormed his way out of another challenge, tried to put Burr off. His answer equivocates as only a lawyer stalling for time can. He quibbles at length about the meaning of the word, "despicable"; it is, after all, a relative term. Since the letters published do not absolutely quote words of his, he refuses to be called to account for a technically indirect use of his opinions by his political friends. In short, he will make no answer at all. Obviously he hopes to confuse and unsettle Burr until he cools off or Hamilton has time to make new moves.

But he has mistaken his man. Burr replied at once, reminding him that politics "never absolve gentlemen from the necessity of a rigid adherence to the laws of honour, and the rules of decorum." Hamilton's equivocation only gave him "new reasons for requiring a definite reply." Hamilton again asked desperately that Burr produce actual quotations of slanders before he require an answer. He was insinuating a lie in attempting to prove himself innocent because Burr could produce no concrete evidence; for he wrote just before the duel that "I, in common with many others, have made very unfavourable criticisms on particular instances of the private conduct of this gentleman." Yet he insisted publicly that Burr had no right to call him out. Burr did call him out, however, and shot him dead on the misty Wednesday morning of July 11, 1804, on Weehawken Heights.

Hamilton's conduct in the affair was not gentlemanly. Since he could not deny what had appeared in print, there were three other courses of action open to him. He could have apologized, but that would have been political suicide. He had already broken with Adams and smashed the Federalist party. He had already publicly admitted to being a libertine; he could scarcely afford to have the name of "liar" added. He could have taken the highest ground of the Christian and gentlemanly tradition and refused Burr's challenge. Sentimentalists have made much of his statement just before the duel that his "religious and moral principles were opposed to duelling." He could have followed those principles, if genuine, in the very flower of the gentlemanly tradition. Yet he was lying again. His son Philip had died in a duel. He had stood second to Laurens in his encounter with General Greene, an encounter which Hamilton himself had sought. He had issued a challenge to Monroe which, when it was accepted, he had failed to follow up. He had called out Commodore Nicholson, then allowed friends to intervene. Finally, Hamilton could have turned his back once more upon the high tradition, accepted again the code of honor, and met Burr as Burr met him: coolly and sincerely. Instead, he spent the night before writing a long self-justification to the world and appeared on the field in such a state that opinion was divided as to whether he fought or not. Alexander Hamilton was a great financier, industrial prophet, politician. The Hamilton myth as it appears, for instance, in Gertrude Atherton's *The Conqueror* notwithstanding, he was not a great gentleman.[6]

The tremendous sensation produced by Hamilton's death at Burr's hand effectually put a stop to the institution of the duel in the Middle States as well as New England. Through most of the nation the decision of communities and individuals to treat murder as murder and duelling as a crime became one of the symbols of cultural victory for the gentlemanly ideal. The "code" was handed over to the keeping of the vanishing fine gentleman; and honor became defined as a guide to conduct "which springs from that self-respect and intellectual refinement"[7] which could never condone brutal bravery.

In parts of the South, despite the active opposition of such classic Southern gentlemen as Washington, Jefferson, and Robert E. Lee, the duel survived as a cause for international scandal. When it survived as an Ivanhoeish genteel tradition of jousting or elaborate formalities of diction to avoid "offense," it was harmless. But Mark Twain made unforgettable its frightfulness when he watched a Granger-Shepherdson feud through Huck Finn's eyes. And he made every reader feel the sickening squalor of Colonel Sherburn's shooting down drunken Old Man Boggs. As operative culture the survivals of the fine gentleman's "code," bush-whacking, attack at sight, feuding, have been a deadly, criminal genteel tradition.

## II

The cultural crisis of the Revolution brought the question of the gentleman to crossroads both theoretical and practical. The theoretic problem of reconciling the gentleman-concept to new republican or democratic thought was easily solved. The tradition held many such notions as those of the natural gentleman, the efficacy of education, and the primacy of organic courtesy, all of which could be easily converted into a theory of the democratic gentleman. Jefferson's allies and followers like Freneau, Hugh Henry Brackenridge, and even Thomas Paine took quick advantage of the possibilities. The more liberal, agrarian Federalists such as Adams and Dwight followed suit cautiously.

There was also a need to work out practical questions of social and political organization. In the past the gentry had been the piers on which social structure had rested. Now few responsible thinkers were ready to dispense with the gentry, but there became clear a bed-rock difference between Federalists and Jeffersonians as to where the gentry should stand in the new order. Broadly speaking, and both sides spoke broadly, the Federalists were afraid of anarchy and equalitarianism and so favored a system as close to the old structural one as they could come and still have a representative, republican policy. The Jeffersonians, eager for a new, libertarian world, were afraid only of oppression and restriction. Hoping to tap great new reservoirs of energy and talent, they fought for a democratic society and polity. When this was expressed in practical politics, the country seethed in the consequent heat.

At once gentlemanliness became a political issue. The Jeffersonians saw themselves as Nature's gentlemen, in love with simplicity, humility, and liberty, and battling hordes of Tories and profiteers who were eager to toady to British aristocracy and to fasten the chains of servitude and humiliation on the plain men of "the swinish multitude." From the Federalist side, the same struggle was seen as that of true, Christian gentlemen nobly bent on securing the power of the class of gentlemen in America in the interests of justice, righteousness, the rights of property, and that true liberty under which the lower classes were to be restrained from destroying themselves in a holocaust of society like the French Terror. Against themselves the Federalists saw men who were simultaneously Jacobinic rabble-rousers and sansculotte adventurers,—as well as atheistic, morally contemptible, and filthy-minded fine gentlemen.

It was a day when the partisan press of both sides practiced the gentle art of character assassination with enthusiasm. At the trial for outrageous libel of Federalist editor William Cobbett, the malodorous Peter Porcupine, the Chief Justice of the Supreme Court of Pennsylvania, remarked that at such "envenomed scurrility" every man "who has in him the sentiments of either a Christian or a gentleman cannot but be highly offended."[8] So successful was Federalist propaganda that Elbridge Gerry complained at the height of the debate over ratifying the Constitution that, "It is beginning to become fashionable to consider the opponents of the Constitution as embodying themselves with the lower classes of the people, and that one forfeits all title to the respect of a gentleman unless he is one of the privileged (Federalist) order."[9]

This Federalist appeal was especially effective in New England. Though the theocracy was dead, the traditional prestige of the theocratic gentleman had lived on. Support was given the class of gentlemen by both the liberal and conservative branches of the clergy. Tory and Anglican influences aside, the men who, like John Wise, adopted the theory of the equal rights of men under the laws of nature and the social compact had no intention of doing away with the practical "distinctions between men."[10] Their great authorities, Locke and Pufendorf, were also authors of courtesy books. Radical on one side as was

## "FINE" GENTLEMAN VS. CHRISTIAN GENTLEMAN

Jonathan Edwards's "New Light," Edwards was a strong champion of the ancient social forms. In such essays as *The Nature of True Virtue* and the posthumous *Charity and Its Fruits* Edwards threw the sanction of salvation behind "the beauty of order in society" and a rephrasing of the old doctrines of stewardship and God's calling of some men to be rulers and others to be ruled. The Christian spirit alive only in the elect was the only source of the genuine spirit of benevolence, earnestness and disinterestedness necessary to rulers.[11]

The New England tradition still exalted the gentleman, then, by differentiating him practically (in terms of his economic and political advantages), socially (both by according him prestige and by admitting theoretically his intrinsic superiority to other men), and religiously (by conceiving of his status and his ability to lead as gifts of Providence). Not every individual would have subscribed to all or even any part of this; yet it was in the tradition and a part of the fabric of daily life. And much of the earnestness with which the Federalists fought for their political faith may be accounted for by the vitality of the tradition of New England.

Earnest though the Federalists were, their failure to understand American social and political conditions and the fundamental contradictions in their thought tricked them into a curious sort of self-betrayal. It was all very well to rail at the opposition in the style of the time and to exalt one's own motives to the acme of altruism. But especially with the mercantile Federalists, that process ceased to be just good politics. The true-blue portion of them began to read the times with the eyes of their theocratic fathers, to credit their own enlistment on the side of the angels, to know passionately that the other party meant ruin, corruption and unlimited wickedness. They painted themselves into a historical corner, so to speak, and were left to sit there and wither into a genteel tradition while America followed the Jeffersonians off down the road of national destiny. Adherents of agrarian Federalism, the men like Noah Webster and Timothy Dwight who followed John Adams, seem to have had far less trouble surviving and adjusting to party defeat and changing times, bitter though they were. It was the silk-stocking Federalists, adherents of Hamilton, who gave way to reactionary despair.

Dandified little Joseph Dennie, at the peak of his career editor of the *Port Folio* in Philadelphia, was named by Jefferson, with no little malice, the Federalist "oracle." A failure at the law who believed himself a literary genius thwarted and frustrated by the vulgarity of America, Dennie yearned to be the toast of a glamorous literary metropolis. He thought of himself as a very special sort of gentleman: "The Polite Scholar" like Horace, "careless, inimitable Horace . . . the very Mansfield, Chesterfield, and Bolingbroke of Rome . . . always courteous, bland, and smiling." In this role, Dennie told his readers, "I will endeavour not to forget the duties and decorum of my title . . . I shall add all the urbanity in my power. I will not thrust an author into my reader's presence without the formality of an introduction. I will sometimes make a complimentary speech or two; and, although I have no dancing master's attitudes, yet I shall always salute the gentle and courteous with my lowest bow and kindest greeting."[12] The odd twist which appears in the thought of the chagrined and isolated representative of a genteel tradition is evident in his handling of Steele's *Christian Hero*. He gets the purpose of the book upside down, exulting that Steele has shown that Christianity could be gentlemanly and that St. Paul "was certainly the polished scholar of the Apostles . . . and a courtier with every blandishment."[13] The ultimate source of infection within Dennie, an eighteenth century "Miniver Cheevy," was bared in a letter to his parents when he said.

> Had not the *Revolution* happened; had I continued a subject to the King, had I been fortunately born in *England* or resided in the City of London for the last 7 years, my fame would have been enhanced; and as to fortune I feel a moral certainty that I should have acquired by my writings 3 or 4 thousand pounds. But, in this *Republic*, this region covered with the Jewish and canting and cheating descendants of those

men, who during the reign of a Stuart, *fled away* from the claims of the Creditor, from the tithes of the Church, from their allegiance to their Sovereign and from their duty to their God, what can men of liberality and letters expect but such polar icy treatment as I have experienced?[14]

The simple truth is that this pattern of high-flown pretense, furious struggle, and lugubrious sulking in defeat was inspired by an adventurous effort to establish the class of gentlemen in America, with the adventurers as leading members. Many an already established gentleman was engaged in the distinctively American attempt to do away with the political class of gentry and to assimilate the whole ideal to democratic theory. Others were simply riding out the times, hoping for security from the Constitution. But men like Dennie and his friend Thomas Green Fessenden had substantial stakes in high Federalism. Less ready than Dennie to admit to monarchism, Fessenden worked to convince "the American people . . . that *subordination* is the soul of freedom" and that "a government on any other basis will terminate in America as in France in a *military despotism.*" His *Democracy Unveiled* (1805) preaches the willing deference of the many to the well-trained few, even suggesting the rigid limitation of education in order to discourage climbers. A few stanzas will illustrate how far he was willing to go:

> Next, every man throughout the nation
> Must be contented in his station,
> Nor think to cut a figure greater,
> Than was designed for him by Nature.

\* \* \* \* \*

> The greatest number's greatest good,
> Should, doubtless, be pursu'd;
> But that consists, *sans* disputation,
> In order and subordination.

\* \* \* \* \*

And finally,

> There must be limits put to suffrage,
> Although the step excite enough rage,
> Lest men devoid of information
> And honesty should rule the nation.[15]

Even in a well-established scion of the New England class of gentlemen the high Federalist delusion eventually blocked positive thinking. Fisher Ames was a major prophet of that reactionary and out-distanced group which his Jeffersonian brother, Nathaniel Ames, called the "Prigarchy." His writings are packed with forecasts of doom and destruction. Though he lauded stern patricianism in all ages, Ames was unwilling to defend any system of government. If he espoused Federalism, he took it as a lesser evil. The one thing he did really well was to curse democracy:

> The truth is, and let it humble our pride, the most ferocious of all animals, when his passions are roused to fury and are uncontrolled, is man; and of all governments, the worst is that which never fails to excite, but was never found to restrain those passions, that is, democracy. It is an illuminated hell, that in the midst of remorse, horrour, and torture, rings with festivity; for experience shews, that one joy remains to this most malignant description of the damned, the power to make others wretched.[16]

It was either on this note of blaspheming, impotent rage, or on the pathetic one of Robert Treat Paine, who changed his very Christian name because it happened to be Thomas, that reactionary Federalism ended. It had become a futile genteel tradition. But that did not mean that the dynamic of Federalism was dead; it moves yet in American history and culture. Nor did it prove that all Federalists were incapable of adjusting their concept of the gentleman to the new American way.

Timothy Dwight, longtime president of Yale and an agrarian in spite of his nickname of "the Pope of Federalism," worked the New England tradition into a picture of the gentleman which is refreshingly sane after Dennie, Fessenden, and Ames. Suspicious of mere wealth and station,[17] Dwight sought an aristocracy of mind and soul like that of the theocrats. While he held that any citizen of merit should be eligible for public office, he believed that the best government was that of gentlemen fulfilling their function in life. We are almost back in the days of theocracy again as he lists the motives which ought to control the gentleman as public servant. He should seek "to lessen the public distress, to increase the public happiness, to discourage vice, to uphold religion, to stand approved to the awful tribunal of his conscience, and to gain the approbation of him, from whose judgment there is no appeal."[18]

Dwight's main business in life was education, and he has several significant things to say about the education of the gentleman. He snorted at the notion of class-restricted schooling, since only an intelligent and informed constituency could support stable government. But in the colleges, fearing to produce fine gentlemen, he proposed to suppress "the trifles" of fashionable training in favor of "an old-fashioned, rigid, academical education." Mere shallow, genteel schools were dangerous. They produced, "Not a man, nor a woman; but a well-dressed bundle of accomplishments. Not a blessing, nor an heir of immortality; but a fribble, or a doll." [19] With all this traditional moral and intellectual strenuousness, Dwight was not blind to the need of men to live in a pleasant and cultivated community. He praised the advantages of good company which "softens and polishes man," opening the way to "gentle and pleasing manners," and stimulating some of the most worthy things in human life—"thought, affection, hospitality, and pleasure." [20] And, as a good clergyman and educator, Dwight had his sermon in the wake of Hamilton's demise in which to blast the wicked, witless, and anti-social institution of the duel.[21]

Dwight's ability to be a strong Federalist and still use the gentleman to accomplish something he thought genuinely valuable to America measures by contrast with the sick futility of Ames and Dennie the difference between a living concept of the gentleman and a genteel tradition. It shows that there was vitality in the ideal even when the ancient political power of the class was stripped away. And the nature of that vitality becomes far more evident in the thought of two vastly more important Americans, Adams and Jefferson, for whom their ideas of the gentleman were simultaneously an enduring intellectual bond and a final philosophic barrier.

## CHAPTER FOUR
## JOHN ADAMS: HOW TO TAME THE TIGER?

JOHN ADAMS was spectacularly a natural gentleman. He rose from an ordinary boyhood on the farm to fortune and leadership in Boston, to key position among the Founding Fathers, to be Ambassador to the Court of St. James, to be first occupant of the White House. His rise was the result of intellectual brillance, energy, courage, and extraordinary integrity. To a degree not dreamt of in his own philosophy, he passed these qualities to his descendants to establish America's first intellectual dynasty. From the time he left the farm to take the first upward steps at Harvard, through all of Adams's life and writing, his concept of the gentleman shines out at every turning.

With the New England tradition and an unusually wide reading in courtesy literature behind him,[1] it is not surprising that the farm boy on his way up should have been very conscious of gentility. The *Journal* which forms the early volumes of his *Works* is packed with references to gentlemen and little judgments of their qualifications. Occasionally he kept score on himself, especially in the years when he was a young lawyer just out of Harvard. He resolved to check his tendencies toward censoriousness and "to take notice chiefly of the amiable qualities of other people . . . and to labor more for an inoffensive and amiable, than for a shining and invidious character."

## I

Since his genteel "advantages" had come from Harvard, he took comfort in the idea that "good sense, some say, is enough to regulate our conduct, and to dictate thought and actions which are proper upon certain occasions. This, they say, will soften and refine the motions of our limbs into an easy and agreeable air. Although the dancing master was never applied to; and this will suggest good answers, good observations, and good expressions to us better than refined breeding." Yet he never attained the air or the ways of the man of the world. He remained stiff, basically awkward, and often ill at ease. Jonathan Sewall, who had become a Tory and been forced to leave America, hit Adams where it hurt when he came to London as American Ambassador. Said Sewall:

> He is not qualified, by nature or education, to shine in courts. His abilities are, undoubtedly, quite equal to the mechanical parts of his business as ambassador; but this is not enough. He cannot dance, drink, game, flatter, promise, dress, swear with the gentlemen, and talk small talk and flirt with the ladies; in short, he has none of the essential arts or ornaments which constitute a courtier. There are thousands, who, with a tenth part of his understanding and without a spark of his honesty, would distance him infinitely in any court in Europe.[2]

In consequence, Adams become contemptuous of the *savoir faire* he could not, and in part would not, have.

Holding in the tradition of John Cotton that "the man who lives wholly to himself is of less worth than the cattle in his barn," [3] Adams took up the cause of the true against the fine gentleman with gusto. Sneering at the "foppery and affectation" of "modern fine gentlemen," [4] he retailed the typical Richardsonian fable of "a fine gentleman with laced hat and waistcoat, and a sword" who had seduced a poor farmer's daughter with empty promises and even counterfeit money.[5] Later he found it politically expedient to charge that American Tories were nothing but "fine gentlemen" whose treason took its rise in immorality. Thus he was free to disparage the Chesterfieldian notion of studied elegance and to quote Adam Smith on the superiority for "a private man" of "modesty and plainness."

So John Adams went all out for virtue. As a Boston lawyer he published essays against duelling, stacking up all the reasons he could think of to show that "private revenge" is stupid, brutal, illegal, irreligious, uncivilized, anti-social, and founded on "little, narrow, sordid notions." His whole career, during which he consistently sacrificed advantage to principle, illustrated the maxim Abigail Adams wrote their son John Quincy. It could just as well have been the father saying, "Great learning and superior abilities, should you ever possess them, will be of little value and small estimation, unless virtue, honor, truth, and integrity are added to them."

A haze of contradiction hangs over the question of John Adams's love for high etiquette and punctilio. When he was in Europe as American minister and to negotiate the treaty of peace following the American Revolution, he deplored almost continuously the folly of European diplomatic and courtly etiquette. He had adopted plainness and modesty as his watchwords. Yet there is indubitable evidence that he was tempted by his own rise to a promience second only to that of Washington in the first American government to desert republican simplicity. Granting that William Maclay was a Jeffersonian and personally annoyed by Adams, the observations in his *Journal* on Adams's conduct in presiding over the first American Senate seem to be solidly founded. Maclay recorded repeatedly and with rancor that Adams's "supreme delight seemed to be in etiquette." Maclay viewed the heirs of theocracy with jaundiced eyes; compared, he said, to the

> gentlemen of New England . . . no people in the Union dwell more on trivial distinctions and matters of mere form. They

## HOW TO TAME THE TIGER?

really seem to show a readiness to stand on punctilio and ceremony. A little learning is a dangerous thing ('tis said). May not the same be said of breeding? . . . They are an unmixed people in New England, and used only to see neighbors like themselves; and once an error of behavior has crept in among them, there is small chance of its being cured; for should they go abroad, being early used to ceremonious and reserved behavior, and believing that good manners consists entirely in punctilios, they only add a few more stiffened airs to their deportment, excluding good humor, affability of conversation, and accommodation of temper and sentiment as qualities too vulgar for a gentleman.[6]

In a sense, Adams is self-convicted of the truth of at least a part of the charges made against him by Maclay and others. He had worn a little sword as ice-President chairing the Senate. He had recognized from youth that, "Vanity . . . is my cardinal vice and cardinal folly; and I am in continual danger, when in company, of being led an *ignis fatuus* chase by it, without the strictest caution and watchfulness over myself." Furthermore, he was duped by one of the most subtly powerful of the temptations that can lure a puritan mind such as his: an appeal to vanity coupled with an appeal to principle. Without glitter and trappings and formalities to catch the eyes and to win the awe of the masses, he thought, representative government could not succeed; to love such things is human nature. As early as 1776 he had written to James Warren, "There is one thing, my dear Sir, that must be attempted and sacredly observed, or we are all undone. There must be decency and respect and veneration introduced for persons in authority, of every rank, or we are undone. In a popular government this is the only way of supporting order, and in our circumstances, as our people have been so long without any government at all, it is more necessary than in any other."

He never receded entirely from this conviction, but such shafts as those of Maclay from the Senate floor and those of the more obvious partisan press stung him enough to make him recede from his awkward attempts to establish traditions of punctilio. By 1792 he was writing meekly, "I think decent and moderate titles, as distinctions of offices, are not only harmless, but useful in society . . . There is not, however, in the United States, personally, a citizen more indifferent upon the subject, or more willing to conform to the public will or wish concerning it." He proved his basic sincerity in this at his own Inauguration, when he balked expectation by rejecting all he could of the military pomp which had rightfully surrounded Washington. John Adams did not quite know when he was acting like a man of the world and a gentleman, but he did know when he had been mistaken and perhaps ridiculous. The sure remedy for past folly was a return to good sense.

## II

Such facts about Adams's struggles with overt culture-patterns of gentlemanliness give us a clearer picture of the man, but they have little importance beyond that. Primarily he was a political theorist, and his concept of the gentleman lay at the heart of his theory. For Adams the basic political problem was not, as has been charged since his own day, how to keep the "rich, the well-born, and the able" in power. He had no doubt that they would always be in power. To him the problem was how to tame the tiger: how to keep the well-nigh boundless power of the natural gentlemen in America from re-enacting its role in European history, from taking over the government and establishing themselves as an artificial, hereditary, wicked aristocracy. Where Jefferson was anxious that the way be cleared for the true natural gentlemen to rise and provide able leadership for democracy, Adams believed grimly that nothing on earth could stop their rise and that only the firmest and canniest of governmental structures could contain both them and republican liberties.

As he wrote to Jefferson in that mellow twilight correspondence in which they so nearly agreed on everything and so clearly defined the point of faith upon which they disagreed, no one need quibble about "the word *gentleman:* it is a part of the natural history of man." Every thinker must recognize one political fact:

> The people, in all nations, are naturally divided into two sorts, the gentlemen and the simplemen, a word which is here chosen to signify the common people. By gentlemen are not meant the rich or the poor, the high-born or the low-born, the industrious or the idle; but all those who have received a liberal education, an ordinary degree of erudition in liberal arts and sciences, whether by birth they be descended from magistrates and officers of government, or from husbandmen, merchants, mechanics, or laborers; or whether they be rich or poor. We must, nevertheless, remember that generally those who are rich, and descended from families in public life, will have the best education in arts and sciences, and therefore the gentlemen will ordinarily, notwithstanding some exceptions to the rule, be the richer, and born of more noted families. By the common people we mean laborers, husbandmen, mechanics, and merchants in general, who pursue their occupations and industry without any knowledge in liberal arts or sciences, or in any thing but their own trades or pursuits; though there may be exceptions to this rule and individuals may be found in each of these classes who may really be gentlemen.

Although "the gentlemen in every country are, and ever must be, few in number, in comparison with the simplemen," their superiority is so great as to make them inevitably leaders, executives, and rulers. Indeed, Adams found it hard to conceive of successful social organization not formed around them. "The army, the navy, revenue, excise, customs, police, justice, and all foreign ministers must be gentlemen," he said. To him this was not a matter of class distinctions or snobbery; he simply believed that the power to think and to act was concentrated in gentlemen. Yet he was not, though many a good democrat accused him of it, attempting to erect a hereditary aristocracy after the English pattern in America.

Adams used the word "aristocrat" in preference to the word "gentleman" when he wished to theorize concerning the gentleman's political nature and destiny. With his hair-splitting legal and classical mind, he used "aristocrat" as more immediately expressing, by its etymology, his meaning. His "aristocrat" and "gentleman" are equivalent when he is engaged in political speculation. His "aristocrat" is the natural gentleman considered as a political entity. He brought his definition to a lawyer's long and thin-drawn point:

> Once for all, I give you notice, that whenever I use the word *aristocrat*, I mean a citizen who can command or govern two votes or more in society, whether by his virtues, his talents, his learning, his loquacity, his taciturnity, his frankness, his reserve, his face, figure, eloquence, grace, air, attitude, movements, wealth, birth, art, address, intrigue, good fellowship, drunkenness, debauchery, fraud, perjury, violence, treachery, pyrrhonism, deism, or atheism; for by every one of these instruments have votes been obtained and will be obtained. You seem to think aristocracy consists altogether in artificial titles, tinsel decorations of stars, garters, ribbons, golden eagles and golden fleeces, crosses and roses and lilies, exclusive privileges, hereditary descents, established by kings or by positive law of society. No such thing! Aristocracy was, from the beginning, now is, and ever will be, world without end, independent of all these artificial regulations, as really and as efficaciously as with them.

No matter what exceptions might be taken against them, "abilities form a DISTINCTION," and must be taken into the wise man's account as aristocracy. Anything at all which leads to "inequality of influence" produces "aristocracy with a witness." [7] Yet as soon as he argued that aristocracy meant inequality of influence within state and society, he was forced to admit that not all such inequalities arose from natural differences among men. Thus he was forced to recognize both natural and artificial aristocracy. He summed up his whole position ably as he said:

> By *natural aristocracy,* in general, may be understood those superiorities of influence in society which grow out of the constitution of human nature. By *artificial aristocracy,* those inequalities of weight and superiorities of influence which are created and established by civil laws. Terms must be defined before we can reason. By aristocracy, I understand all those men who can command, influence, or procure more than an average of votes; by an aristocrat, every man who can and will influence one man to vote besides himself. Few men will deny that there is a natural aristocracy of virtues and talents

## HOW TO TAME THE TIGER? 75

in every nation and in every party, in every city and village. Inequalities are a part of the natural history of man.[8]

In the face of such statements of the inevitability of aristocracy, what shall be said of Adams's relationship to the idea of democracy? The truth seems to be that he regarded true democracy as a beautiful ideal which could be only relatively approached in a wicked world. Speaking of himself in the third person, Adams said, "he has through life asserted the moral equality of mankind." He meant to be final when he wrote, "Democracy . . . must not be disgraced; democracy must not be despised. Democracy must be respected; democracy must be honored; democracy must be cherished; democracy must be an essential, an integral part of the sovereignty, and have a control over the whole government, or moral liberty cannot exist, or any other liberty. I have been always grieved by the gross abuses of this respectable word." [9] Defending himself against charges made in the partisan press that he was attempting to sabotage the American republic, he wrote to Jefferson in 1791: "If you suppose that I have, or ever had, a design or desire of attempting to introduce a government of King, Lords, and Commons, or in other words, an hereditary executive, or an hereditary senate, either into the government of the United States or that of any individual State, you are wholly mistaken. There is not such a thought expressed or intimated in any public writing or private letter, and I may safely challenge all mankind to produce such a passage, and quote the chapter and verse." [10] Yet Adams had definite objections to what he regarded as the starry-eyed efforts of idealists to put a pure and unarmored democracy into practical effect.

Most of his objections may be reduced to one main point: pure democracy cannot be made to work in a world where aristocracy is so potent as it is in this. In his view even "demagogues and popular orators" are aristocrats, for they wield a tremendous influence. "John Cade and Wat Tyler were aristocrats," he averred. "Callender and Paine were aristocrats. Shays and Fries were aristocrats. Mobs never follow any but aristocrats." And aristocracy might take over the people's assemblies as well as their leaders, he thought. Suppose there were an assembly of a hundred representatives met to conduct the affairs of a democracy. In the first session a majority would be formed of, let us say, twenty-six aristocrats each of whom could somehow control one vote more than his own. Falling back on his extensive legislative experience, Adams continued:

> In the second session it will become an oligarchical republic; because the seventy-four democrats and the twenty-six aristocrats will, by this time, discover that thirteen of the aristocrats can command four votes each . . . In the third session, it will be found that among these thirteen oligarchs there are seven, each of whom can command eight votes . . . In the fourth session, it will be found that there are among these seven oligarchs four who can command thirteen votes apiece . . . In the fifth session, it will be discovered that two of the four can command six-and-twenty votes each. Then two will have the command of the sovereign oligarchy. In the sixth session, there will be a sharp contention between the two which shall have the command of the fifty-two votes. Here will commence the squabble of Danton and Robespierre, of Julius and Pompey, of Anthony and Augustus, of the white rose and the red rose, of Jefferson and Adams, of Burr and Jefferson, of Clinton and Madison, or, if you will, of Napoleon and Alexander.[11]

Therefore, unintelligent democracy is "always . . . desperate and destructive to the community."[12] It leads at once to an uninhibited struggle for power. Adams's experiences in watching popular protest against the British rule in Boston had made him realize how difficult it might be to restore social stability once it had been swept away. And the gory tales from Paris during the Reign of Terror confirmed an earlier impression. Then, too, his reading of history showed that pure democracies always lead directly to monarchy and tyranny. Not only did the inevitable struggle for power already noticed eventuate in the selection of a single leader, but the "simplemen' themselves, if unrestrained, responded to a natural tendency toward the appointment of a monarch. Rather than be squeezed forever among the contending parties of gentlemen, simplemen would, if they could, place one strong man over themselves and the gentlemen, one who could be trusted to restrain the exploiters. Finally, pure democracy is too fine for the weaknesses of human nature. "No love of equality, at least since Adam's fall, ever existed in human nature," says Adams, "any otherwise than as a desire of bringing others down to our own level, which implies a desire of raising ourselves above them, or depressing them below us." [13]

His conviction of human weakness stood in Adams's way at all points. With what seemed to him realism and what must have seemed to Jeffersonians damnable iteration, he pointed again and again to the blocks of folly and cupidity over which human nature forever stumbled on its way toward perfection. He believed most strongly that only natural aristocracy should be allowed to count. Artificial aristocracy ought to be done away with; mankind needs "no church canonicals, no lawyer's robes, no distinctions in society, but such as sense and honesty make."[14] Nevertheless, mere ideal desirability would not bring the supremacy of the natural gentleman to pass. As he wrote to Jefferson in 1813:

> We are now explicitly agreed on one important point, viz., that there is a natural aristocracy among men, the grounds of which are virtue and talents. You very justly indulge a little merriment upon this solemn subject of aristocracy. I often laugh at it too, for there is nothing in this laughable world more ridiculous than the management of it by all the nations of the earth; but while we smile, mankind have reason to say to us as the frogs said to the boys, what is sport to you, are wounds and death to us. When I consider the weakness, the folly, the pride, the vanity, the selfishness, the artifice, the low craft and mean cunning, the want of principle, . . . the unfeeling cruelty of a majority of those (in all nations) who are allowed an aristocratical influence, and, on the other hand, the stupidity with which the more numerous multitude not only become their dupes, but even love to be taken in by their tricks, I feel a stronger disposition to weep at their destiny, than to laugh at their folly.

Though from any reasonable point of view "intellectual and moral qualities" ought to attract the most attention, with "the personal qualities of health, strength, and agility . . . next in importance," in reality the artificial and fortuitous "qualities of fortune, such as birth, riches, and honors, though a man has less reason to esteem himself for these than for those of his mind or body, are everywhere acknowledged to glitter with the brightest lustre in the eyes of the world."[15] Furthermore, where an aristocracy of virtue was easy to pick, men were likely to become confused about aristocracy of talents, particularly since the class of gentlemen habitually consolidate their natural gains artificially. The confusion of the human mind, as well as the weakness of its principles and morals jeopardized pure natural aristocracy. All these things taken into consideration, he could not share Jefferson's hope that a strong and lasting democracy could be founded on a well-trained, altruistic, and fluid natural aristocracy.

It is interesting to see what factors Adams thought gave the gentlemen their power. "The five pillars of aristocracy," he said, "are beauty, wealth, birth, genius, and virtue." Virtue could evidently be taken more or less for granted. Everyone had a fairly clear idea of its importance. By "genius" he means ability, and he seems willing to have it taken for granted too. Wealth, though not essential, was an intriguing factor. "I remember the time," he said, "when three gentlemen,—Thomas Hancock, Charles Apthorp, and Thomas Green, the three most opulent merchants in Boston, all honorable, virtuous, and humane men, —if united could have carried any election almost unanimously in the town of Boston."[16]

Unfortunately Adams is not always clear when talking about birth. Sometimes he means descent from a line of ancient nobility, and sometimes he means the capacities given a child at birth, without particular reference to his ancestry. In general it can be assumed that when he praises the influence of birth he has the latter idea in mind, since he repeatedly disavows allegiance to the idea of hereditary aristocracy. But his dominant idea was the courtesy tradition of natural inequalities: "I believe that none but Helvetius will affirm, that all children are born with equal genius. None will pretend, that all are born of dispositions exactly alike,—of equal weight; equal strength; equal

## HOW TO TAME THE TIGER?                                   79

length; equal delicacy of nerves; equal elasticity of muscles; equal complexions; equal figure, grace, or beauty."[17]

Thus "the idea of the 'well-born' . . . is the ordinance of God Almighty, in the constitution of human nature, and wrought into the fabric of the universe." Philosophers and politicians from Theognis and Plato on down through the ages might "nibble and quibble," he told Jefferson, but they could never do away with this truth. Yet he stuck to his guns in denying that the true and important aristocracy was a matter of genealogy. The power of birth lay in the mighty advantages which it gave to some men in the cradle *without* reference to their ancestry. After all, "the son of an excellent man may never inherit the great qualities of his father; this is a common observation, and there are many instances of its truth. Should we not, therefore, conclude that hereditary nobility is a solecism in government?"[18]

Adams was intrigued by the force of beauty as a factor in aristocracy. "You may laugh at the introduction of beauty among the pillars of aristocracy," he wrote Jefferson rather defensively. "But Madame du Barry says *'la veritable royauté, c'est la beauté;'* and there is not a more certain truth." There is a gusto not usual to Adams's writing as he selects a concrete example to prove his point that

> female aristocrats are nearly as formidable as males. A daughter of a greengrocer walks the streets in London daily, with a basket of cabbage sprouts, dandelions, and spinach, on her head. She is observed by the painters to have a beautiful face, an elegant figure, a graceful step, and a *debonair*. They hire her to sit. She complies, and is painted by forty artists in a circle around her. The scientific Dr. William Hamilton outbids the painters, sends her to school for a genteel education, and marries her. This lady not only causes the triumphs of the Nile, Copenhagen, and Trafalgar, but separates Naples from France, and finally banishes the king and queen from Sicily. Such is the aristocracy of the natural talent of beauty.

The same unusual levity is evident in his corollary that "matrimony" is "another source of natural aristocracy." Suppose, he says, "a family of six daughters. Four of them are not only beautiful, but serious and discreet women. Two of them are not only ugly, but ill tempered and immodest. Will either of the two have an equal chance with any one of the four to attract the attention of a suitor, and obtain a husband of worth, respectability, and consideration in the world?"[19]

At the bottom of it all, Adams would say, there is only one mainspring of human action. Men are constituted to live selfishly. Of all the passions of man, there is none "more essential or remarkable, than the *passion for distinctions.*"

> A desire to be observed, considered, esteemed, praised, beloved, and admired by his fellows, is one of the earliest, as well as keenest dispositions discovered in the heart of man . . . This passion, while it is simply a desire to excel another, by fair industry in the search of truth, and the practice of virtue, is properly called *Emulation.* When it aims at power, as a means of distinction, it is *Ambition.* When it is in a situation to suggest the sentiments of fear and apprehension, that another, who is now inferior, will become superior, it is denominated *Jealousy.* When it is in a state of mortification, at the superiority of another, and desires to bring him down to our level, or to depress him below us, it is properly called *Envy.* When it deceives a man into a belief of false professions of esteem or admiration, or into a false opinion of his importance in the judgment of the world, it is *Vanity.*[20]

It is dangerous to trust even the greatest of men. For,

> the most heroic actions in war, the sublimest virtues in peace, and the most useful industry in agriculture, arts, manufactures, and commerce, proceed from such emulations on the one hand, and jealousies, envy, enmity, hatred, revenge, quarrels, factions, seditions, and wars on the other . . . Nature has ordained it, as a constant incentive to activity and industry, that, to acquire the attention and complacency, the approbation and admiration of their fellows, men might be urged to constant exertions of beneficence. By this destination of their natures, men of all sorts, even those who have the least of reason, virtue or benevolence . . . are really thus constituted by their own vanity, slaves to mankind.[21]

It is from this in human nature that the pillars of aristocracy derive their strength. Like Veblen long after, Adams saw that wealth is power simply because *"riches attract the attention, consideration and congratulations of mankind* . . . there is more respectability, in the eyes of the greater part of mankind, in the gaudy trappings of wealth, than there is in genius or learning, wisdom or virtue." This is what leads to luxury and extravagance. The upper classes are no more wasteful than other people, but the wicked way of the world demands that they must always remain a certain degree above the less rich in their displays of power to spend. The same shadow of fault falls across the prestige of birth into an aristocracy: "An illustrious descent attracts the notice of mankind . . . it still attracts the *attention* of the world . . . The pride is as irrational and contemptible as the pride of riches, and no more." Yet again, "Why are the personal accomplishments of beauty, elegance, and grace, held in such high estimation by mankind?" The answer is that "those attractions command the notice and attention of the public; they draw the eyes of the spectators. This is the charm that makes them irresistible . . . beauty and address are courted and admired, very often, more than discretion, wit, sense, and many other accomplishments and virtues, of infinitely more importance to the happiness of private life, as well as to the utility and ornament of society."[22]

Adams regretted the evils of human selfishness and believed that wisdom and goodness could be obtained by those few who would discipline themselves with learning, the worship of God, and a fortified conscience. Where Chesterfield was justifying a program with theory, Adams leaned through temperament to the pessimistic philosophers of his age and through circumstance to the partly rejected patrimony of Puritanism. But the theocratic faith carried with it the counter theory that by grace and self-discipline some degree of salvation from himself is possible to man. Even if liberty itself has most often been the product of the love of power,[23] yet there have been some men who have suffered and sacrificed for others without hope of advantage to themselves. "There are a few, and God knows, but a few, who aim at something more:
> They aim at approbation as well as attention, at esteem as well as congratulation . . . This last description of persons is

the tribe out of which proceed your patriots and heroes, and most of the great benefactors to mankind. But for our humiliation, we must still remember, that even in these esteemed, beloved, and adored characters, the passion, although refined by the purest moral sentiments, and intended to be governed by the best principles, is a passion still; and therefore, like all other human desires, unlimited and unsatiable.[24]

If not the greatest figures known to human history can be fully trusted and "evil . . . lies in human nature,"[25] what can be done to save humanity from the vast power of the inevitably selfish natural gentleman? "There is a voice within us, which seems to intimate, that real merit should govern the world; and that men ought to be respected only in proportion to their talents, virtues, and services," Adams admitted. "The question always has been, how can this arrangement be accomplished? How shall the men of merit be discovered? How shall the proportions of merit be ascertained and graduated?" Over and over he asked, "Who shall be the judge?"—"Ay! there's the rub!" Both history and logic showed that there was no glib or easy answer to be had.

"All that men can do, is to modify, organize, and arrange the powers of human society . . . in the best manner to protect, secure, and cherish the moral, which are all the natural rights of mankind." Government must "check" the power of the gentlemen, and this is only possible in "a mixed form of government." Only by balancing the people against the gentlemen, against the executive power, against the law could "decency, honesty, and order" be hoped for.[26] He wrote to an adherent, William Keteltas, in 1812, "Your last sentence is a jewel, 'a monarchy of justice, an aristocracy of wisdom, and a democracy of freedom.' "[27] Mankind could not well live without the abilities of the gentlemen, yet they could not well live with them unless they were securely restrained by careful balancing of the lines of social force.

John Adams believed with Pope, whom he quoted approvingly,

> Order is Heaven's first law; and, this confess'd,
> Some are, and must be, greater than the rest . . .

## HOW TO TAME THE TIGER? 83

In the pattern of plenitude within the great chain of being, to which Pope referred, order demanded that some be greater than the rest but also that the great try no more to leave their appointed niches than the lowly theirs. Adams was much more afraid of "the few," of "Aristocracy" in America than of the coming of monarchy. And he thought he saw a solution in a government of checks and balances to the threat of the gentlemen:

> The rich, the well-born, and the able, acquire an influence among the people that will soon be too much for simple honesty and plain sense, in a house of representatives. The most illustrious of them must, therefore, be separated from the mass, and placed by themselves in a senate; this is, to all honest and useful intents, an ostracism. A member of a senate, of immense wealth, the most respected birth, and transcendent abilities, has no influence in the nation, in comparison of what he would have in a single representative assembly. When a senate exists, the most powerful man in the state may be safely admitted into the house of representatives, because the people have it in their power to remove him into the senate as soon as his influence becomes dangerous. The senate becomes the great object of ambition; and the richest and the most sagacious wish to merit an advancement to it by services to the public in the house. When he has obtained the object of his wishes, you may still hope for the benefits of his exertions, without dreading his passions; for the executive power being in other hands, he has lost much of his influence with the people, and can govern very few votes more than his own among the senators.[28]

Here is seen clearly the ancient fallacy of asserting that John Adams held that "the rich, the well-born, and the able" ought to govern everyone else. Obviously, Adams said nothing of the sort. What he kept saying was that these men would have a hand in government willy-nilly, and that they should be carefully restrained *lest* they capture it entirely. The immense talent and ability of the gentlemen should not be lost to the state. But they must be restrained in their own group by each other and so balanced by an independent people's legislature and by the executive that they could never break through. The common people must learn without fail "never to trust any part of the executive power to a senate, or, in other words, to the body of the gentlemen."[29] There must be "a democratical branch in the constitution which represents the hopes of the simplemen. And a strong executive is their ally. Much as he might seem to hamper them, they must never attack him, for "the democratical mixture . . . can never be preserved without a strong executive."[30]

Finally, the balanced government must be just. It must protect rich and poor alike, the poor from oppression and the rich from robbery. And it must protect itself from extralegal forces. This was the reason for Adams's hatred of the Society of the Cincinnati,—the Revolutionary army officer's American Legion, which at first proposed to perpetuate itself hereditarily. The organization of this group "is the first step taken to deface the beauty of our temple of liberty,"[31] Adams said. He declared his disapprobation of the new "order of chivalry" even to Lafayette, the leading foreign hero of the group.[32] And the reason for his dislike is not far to seek. Here was a sudden new machine by which those slippery gentlemen, already strong in prestige because they had led a victorious army, threatened to turn themselves into a hereditary aristocracy.

The crux of the Federalist dilemma becomes painfully clear when seen through the eyes of John Adams. Free of Dennie's pettiness and sincerely devoted to the republic as Ames could never be, Adams was still embarrassed by his pessimistic temperament and his New England background. He simply could not believe that men would seek the good and shun corruption if left to themselves. Reared in post-theocratic Massachusetts, he could not believe, either, that the gentlemen would ever cease to command. To him the problem was not how to see that the gentlemen ruled, but how to see that they did not tyrannize and thus corrupt the good that was in them. The main thing was to keep the tiger tamed.

## CHAPTER FIVE

## JEFFERSON AND THE DEMOCRATIC ARISTOI

JOHN ADAMS fathered a line of gentlemen; Thomas Jefferson was the scion of one. In Virginia, frontier chaos and hardship had retarded gentlemen, but with stability and prosperity they raced forward to the goal of likeness with the country squires of Old England. A commercial and cultural intimacy with England, the equal of which few New Englanders had ever wished to enjoy, inspired in Virginia that pure fervor for things from "home" which only colonials can know. Among these was the eighteenth century version of the British gentleman. Virginians too were conquered by the notion of the true, Christian gentleman. But they knew enough of the polite world of England to be aware that grace and gayety could live in the same gentleman with piety and virtue. And they also knew that the polite world held one virtuous till he was proved wicked, but gauche until proved gracefully "accomplished." In America "the mould of fashion was indisputably the Virginian or the Carolinian, celebrated not only for elegance in dress, speech, dining, and sport, but also for that graceful lotus-eating in a land where the abundance of nature had made hard work seem almost an act of ingratitude."[1] And young Thomas Jefferson, wealthy, landed, related to the best families, laughed and danced, fiddled and flirted as well as studied and thought during the distinguished years of glamorous Williamsburg.

## I

That Virginia background comes out from time to time in Jefferson's writings, despite the democratic trend of most of his thought. It gave him a high opinion, for one thing, of the advantages of gentlemanly associations. Orphaned at fourteen, he remembered in later life that he might easily have gone off with the young rakes and fox hunters with whom his youth abounded. But the serenity and dignity of great gentlemen like Wythe, Dr. Small, or Peyton Randolph had so attracted him that he modelled every decisive act on his ideal of them. When he came to design the University of Virginia, he was anxious that similar opportunities be made available to the students. Its faculty must be the best which Europe and America could afford. "No secondary character will be received among them," he wrote. "They will give us the selected society of a great city separated from the dissipations and levities of its ephemeral insects."

What Jefferson meant by "the best," and his way of putting it, show how perfectly he balanced the conflicting theories of Chesterfieldian and Christian gentleman in his time. Of one of those models of his youth he wrote:

> No man ever left behind him a character more venerated than George Wythe. His virtue was of the purest tint; his integrity inflexible, and his justice exact, of warm patriotism, and, devoted as he was to liberty, and the natural and equal rights of man, he might truly be called the Cato of his country, without the avarice of the Roman; for a more disinterested man never lived. Temperance and regularity in all his habits gave him general good health, and his unaffected modesty and suavity of manners endeared him to every one. He was of easy elocution; his language chaste, methodical in the arrangement of his matter, learned and logical in the use of it, and

of great urbanity in debate; not quick of apprehension, but, with a little time, profound in penetration and sound in conclusion. In his philosophy he was firm; and neither troubling, nor, perhaps, trusting, any one with his religious creed, he left the world to the conclusion that that religion must be good which could produce a life of such exemplary virtue.[2]

There is enough in this which could serve as self-portrait to leave little doubt that Jefferson regarded it as ideal.

But virtue meant honor, as well. "Give up money, give up fame, give up science, give up the earth itself and all it contains, rather than do an immoral act," he advised. "And never suppose, that in any possible situation, or under any circumstances, it is best for you to do a dishonorable thing, however slightly so it may appear to you."[3] Jefferson was, in fact, convinced of the truth of the environmentalist adage that evil communications corrupt good manners. It was almost impossible, he said in a famous passage, for a slave-holding people to retain a level of rational and good behavior. Let Virginia beware of the vicious consequences of rearing its children in "daily exercise in tyranny" over helpless slaves.

By many contemporary accounts, Jefferson was a man of brilliant courtesy in the high tradition. He taught a grandson unforgettably, one day, one of the distinctions between manners and courtesy. As they rode out on one of Jefferson's favorite Monticello jaunts, they met a negro who bowed. Jefferson returned the bow in his stateliest fashion, but the boy exercised his Caucasian right of race-prejudice and ignored it. Allowing time for the discrepancy to sink into the boy's mind, Jefferson turned, finally, and asked, "Do you permit a negro to be more of a gentleman than yourself?"[4]

A poor speechmaker in an age of accomplished orators, Jefferson wielded most of his influence through the friends he had won and kept. In part, at least, he won and kept them by his ability to charm people socially. Because the ceremonious pomp surrounding President Washington had dismayed Jefferson, he kept the White House in his own presidency as though it were a private residence of "republican simplicity." Washington ladies on one occasion, the story goes, descended on him one afternoon with the notion of forcibly restoring the neglected presidential levee-day. They caught Jefferson out riding, and they established themselves in the parlors to wait him out. Warned on his return, Jefferson did exactly what he would have done at Monticello. In dusty riding-clothes he went at once to greet his callers, charmed them with his Monticello manner, and succeeded in making the affair a private rather than a public one—and so avoided resuming the embarrassingly aristocratic custom of levees.[5]

This success was based, again, on the high tradition. For Jefferson thought of courtesy as two-fold. It consisted of "good-humor," or the will to make life as pleasant as possible for others; and of politeness, the conventionalized expression of that good will. As he wrote to his nephew Thomas Jefferson Randolph, "It is the practice of sacrificing to those whom we meet in society all the little conveniences and preferences which will gratify them, and deprives us of nothing worth a moment's consideration; it is the giving a pleasing and flattering turn to our expressions, which will conciliate others, and make them pleased with us as well as themselves. How cheap a prize for the good-will of another! When this is in return for a rude thing said by another, it brings him to his senses, it mortifies and corrects him in the most salutary way, and places him at the feet of your good-nature in the eyes of the company."[6] To the philosophical scientist, Dr. Benjamin Rush, he wrote, "What I value more than all things [is] good humor. For thus I estimate the qualities of the mind: 1. good humor; 2. integrity; 3. industry; 4. science. The preference of the first to the second quality may not at first be acquiesced in; but certainly we had all rather associate with a good-humored, light-principled man, than with an ill-tempered rigorist in morality."[7]

In Virginia society there was one other very serious reason for constant formal politeness. There was the code duello. In advising young Thomas Jefferson Randolph of the "prudential rules for our government in society," Jefferson stressed "the important one of never entering into dispute or argument with another. I never saw an instance of one of two disputants convincing the other by argument. I have seen many, on their getting warm, become rude, and shooting one another."[8] Adams might write little sermons against the introduction of duelling in New England; Jefferson was faced with a brutal reality sanctioned by the mores of his people. Caution became particularly necessary when he sent the young name-sake off to study in a capital full of political enemies who might be only too happy to strike at the man whom they were advertising as an atheist, incendiary, and fiend, by procuring a bully or two to quarrel with, challenge, and shoot down his nephew. He would have done away with the duel entirely if he could. In the *Bill for Proportioning Crimes and Punishment in Cases heretofore Capital* which he prepared for the Virginia legislature, he proposed that, "Whosoever committeth murder by way of duel shall suffer death of hanging; and if he were the challenger, his body, after death, shall be gibbetted." And in a footnote he asked, "Quaere, if the estates of both parties in a duel, should not be forfeited? The deceased is equally guilty with a suicide."[9]

Between courtesy and manners, politeness and etiquette, Jefferson distinguished carefully. And as he valued courtesy highly, he intended to deflate etiquette. On returning to republican America from imperial France, he was shocked to find what seemed an entering wedge of monarchy being driven into our governmental procedures from the outset by the adoption of an official etiquette and ceremony brought from Europe. "I never doubted the propriety of our adopting as a system that of pomp and fulsome attentions by our citizens to their functionaries. I am decidedly against it, as it makes the citizen in his own eye exalting his functionary and creating a distance between the two which does not tend to aid the morals of either. I think it a practice which we ought to destroy and must destroy and, therefore, must not adopt as a general thing even for a short time," he wrote. At his inauguration as Vice-President under Adams, unable to predict that Adams would act as simply as he did, Jefferson wrote ahead firmly, saying, "I hope I shall be made a part of no ceremony whatever."[10] When his own party came into power, he rejoiced in the simplicity which made so good a target for young Washington Irving's Federalist man-about-town shafts of wit.

So much for the etiquette of official life; but what about that of the private citizen? Jefferson believed that "The manners of every nation are the standard of orthodoxy within itself. But these standards being arbitrary, reasonable people in all allow free toleration for the manners, as for the religion of others."[11] Accordingly, he advised his friend Madame de Brehan, who was about to visit America, to go and simply be herself. But he wished to see a new standard of etiquette proper to the new republican nation arise within it. American manners, he said, as many Americans were to say after him, ought to be "founded in nature" and adapted to American circumstances.

One thing which led Americans to adopt European manners was the colonial tradition that a sound education was only to be obtained in Europe. Supporting this was the ancient idea that the Grand Tour added an essential final polish to the young gentleman's training. Despite Jefferson's admiration for the manners of the best Europeans, he was as heartily opposed as Royall Tyler to the notion of travelling and living abroad for education. "An American, coming to Europe for education, loses . . . in his morals, in his health, in his habits, and in his happiness . . . Cast your eye over America: who are the men of most learning, of most eloquence, most beloved by their countrymen and most trusted and promoted by them? They are those who have been educated among them, and whose manners, morals, and habits, are perfectly homogeneous with those of the country . . . The consequences of foreign education are alarming to me, as an American."[12] To list all the disadvantages of "sending a youth to Europe . . . would require a volume." At very best, then, travelling "makes men wiser, but less happy." Young men are often ruined by it, and "men of sober age," though they gather useful knowledge, make themselves dissatisfied strangers to all the world. Therefore, "Be good, be learned, and be industrious, and you will not want the aid of travelling, to render you precious to your country, dear to your friends, happy within yourself."[13]

For all Jefferson's utilitarianism, he valued the traditional cultivation in the arts of expression and of living necessary for the gentleman. For its music only he admired France. When he divided up his "professional schools," into law, theology, medicine, war, agriculture, and fine arts, he sent "the gentleman, the architect, the pleasure gardener, painter and musician to the school of fine arts."[14] Nor had he Adams's rather surly suspicion of the minor graces. He advised his daughter that, "The ornaments too, and the amusements of life, are entitled to their portion of attention. These, for a female, are dancing, drawing, and music. The first is a healthy exercise, elegant and very attractive for young people. Every affectionate parent would be pleased to see his daughter qualified to participate with her companions, and without awkwardness at least, in the circles of festivity, of which she occasionally becomes a part."[15] Still, Jefferson's central ideals about the gentleman seem to be expressed in a letter of advice to his grandson, Francis Eppes. After alluding to the necessity of studying hard, he goes on to say:

> But while you endeavor, by a good store of learning, to prepare yourself to become a useful and distinguished member of your country, you must remember that this never can be without uniting merit with your learning. Honesty, disinterestedness, and good nature are indispensable to procure the esteem and confidence of those with whom we live, and on whose esteem our happiness depends. . . . Above all things and at all times, practice yourself in good humor; this, of all human qualities, is the most amiable and endearing to society.[16]

This is Jefferson's gentleman, and it is the Southern gentleman: an excellent blend of the Christian and Chesterfieldian ideals. As Robert E. Lee he may be more nominally Christian than Jefferson was, but he is never a prig. For there is something there of the magnanimity of the Renaissance, and always a touch of the grace of the fine gentleman. Yet it should be observed that there is in the beginning nothing so very distinctively "Southern" about this gentleman. He is an American blend of the traditions, but quite like Cooper's gentleman, as will be seen. It is not until the time of the Civil War and after, in Thomas Nelson Page's or F. Hopkinson Smith's "Cun'ls" that the Southern gentleman begins to seem unique. And is this not because, in concept at least, the Colonels adhered to an agrarian, pre-Jacksonian ideal which most of the nation, including most of the South, had discarded? This suggests that the American gentleman in the South was (and is) a magnificent figure; but that "the Southern gentleman" is a genteel tradition.

## II

Yet the really important fact about Jefferson's deep devotion to the tradition of the gentleman was not that he was in one fashion an archetypal Southern Gentleman. The important fact was that he revolutionized the theory of the American gentleman to conform to the revolutionary situation. As profoundly concerned for the gentlemanly ideal as for the democratic, Jefferson saw that the two could be married—but only after the forced union of gentleman-ideal and gentry-class had been dissolved. He succeeded, in the long run, in destroying the gentry in America, and he initiated the reconciliation of gentlemanliness with democracy. Like Adams, he centered his political thought, with all it has meant to the destiny of America, upon his personal philosophy of the natural gentleman. He also predetermined the future direction of general American thought about the gentleman.

Through all the amities of their twilight correspondence, Jefferson and Adams were never restored to the entire trust of the early years of friendship. Even after their reconciliation in mellowed age there remained an unbridgeable temperamental and intellectual rift which was laid clear when they discussed human nature as the ground of gentility. Jefferson could not accept Adams's pessimistic view of the nature of man. Consequently there was contradiction in Adams's writing that, "You suppose a difference of opinion between you and me on the subject of aristocracy. I can find none. I dislike and detest hereditary honors, offices, emoluments, established by law. So do you. I am for excluding legal, hereditary distinctions from the United States as long as possible. So are you. I only say that mankind have not yet discovered any remedy against irresistible corruption in elections to offices of great power, but by making them hereditary."[17]

Jefferson simply could not believe in "irresistible corruption." Adams's view of man's selfishness had sound support in human behavior: "Self-love," Jefferson conceded, "is the sole antagonist of virtue, leading us constantly by our propensities to self-gratification in violation of our moral duties to others." But it can be subdued "by education, instruction or restraint." Thus far he and Adams are at one: there is a negative tendency in man to sin through selfishness, and this tendency can be checked by conscience and mental discipline. But Jefferson went completely beyond Adams in finding a positive element within man himself which was as strong as evil. "Nature hath implanted in our breasts a love of others, a sense of duty to them, a moral instinct, in short, which prompts us irresistibly to feel and to succor their distresses," he wrote. "I sincerely, then, believe . . . in the general existence of a moral instinct. I think it the brightest gem with which the human character is studded, and the want of it as more degrading than the most hideous of the bodily deformities."[18] This being true, democracy was possible; for all but the morally crippled would be men of good will by their lights—and all could be further enlightened by education. The natural aristocrats could be trusted, for they would feel within their hearts an instinct of well-doing. "We both love the people," Jefferson told a friend, "but you love them as infants whom you are afraid to trust without nurses, and I as adults whom I freely leave to self-government."[19]

Thus Jefferson's theory of democracy was centered about the *aristos,* who had for centuries past been recognized as the natural gentleman. "For I agree with you that there is a natural aristocracy among men," he wrote Adams, "The grounds of this are virtue and talents. Formerly, bodily powers gave place among the aristoi. But since the invention of gunpowder has armed the weak as well as the strong with missile death, bodily strength, like beauty, good humor, politeness and other accomplishments, has become but an auxiliary ground of distinction . . . The natural aristocracy I consider as the most precious gift of nature, for the instruction, the trusts, and government of society. And indeed, it would have been inconsistent in creation to have formed man for the social state, and not to have provided virtue and wisdom enough to manage the concerns of society. May we not even say, that that form of government is the best, which provides the most effectually for a pure selection of these natural aristoi into the offices of government?"[20]

While Jefferson was willing to agree with Adams that "the terms of whig and tory belong to natural as well as civil history" and that "whether the power of the people or that of the aristoi should prevail, were questions which kept the States of Greece and Rome in eternal convulsions, as they now schismatize every people whose minds and mouths are not shut up by the gag of a despot," he thought he saw a new way of reconciliation. If the people could control the *aristoi* by the power of the ballot, not only would the fatal witlessness of hereditary nobilities be avoided, but all the necessity for the strife of classes would be at an end. "I hold it to be one of the distinguishing excellences of elective over hereditary successions, that the talents which nature has provided in sufficient proportion, should be selected by the society for the government of their affairs, rather than that this should be transmitted through the loins of knaves and fools, passing from the debauches of the table to those of the bed."[21] In spite of Adams's fears, strife between natural and artificial aristocrats being what it is, "I think the best remedy is exactly that provided by all our constitutions, to leave to the citizens the free election and separation of the aristoi from the pseudo-aristoi, of the wheat from the chaff. In general, they will elect the really good and wise. In some instances, wealth may corrupt, and birth blind them; but not in sufficient degree to endanger the society."

If there were the all-important *aristoi*, Jefferson recognized that, "There is also an artificial aristocracy, founded on wealth and birth, without either virtue or talents; for with these it would belong to the aristoi . . . The artificial aristocracy is a mischievous ingredient in government, and provision should be made to prevent its ascendancy."[22] Being rich or of good family disqualified no man for the *aristoi;* Jefferson was no bitter, Jacobinic leveller. If a great natural gentleman had also the advantages of wealth and blood, so much the better. But he had been deeply shocked by his observations of the evils of hereditary nobility in Europe. "If anybody thinks that kings, nobles, or priests are good conservators of the public happiness, send him here," he wrote from France. "It is the best school in the universe to cure him of that folly. He will see here, with his own eyes, that these descriptions of men are an abandoned confederacy against the happiness of the mass of the people . . . where, notwithstanding the finest soil upon earth, the finest climate under heaven, and a people of the most benevolent, the most gay and amiable character of which the human form is susceptible; where such a people, I say, surrounded by so many blessings from nature, are loaded with misery . . ."[23] The "hereditary aristocracy" of France, he says again, makes "existence a curse to twenty-four out of twenty-five parts of the inhabitants of this country."[24] He loved to contrast the happiness of life in America's agrarian democracy, "The tranquil, permanent felicity with which domestic society in America blesses most of its inhabitants; leaving them to follow steadily those pursuits which health and reason approve, and rendering truly delicious the intervals of those pursuits."[25]

Consequently he did all he could to make hereditary and artificial aristocracy impossible in the United States. He gloated a little in writing to Adams that, whereas in Massachusetts and

Connecticut "there seems to be . . . a traditionary reverence for certain families, which has rendered the offices of the government nearly hereditary in those families," in Virginia "a Randolph, a Carter, or a Burwell must have great personal superiority over a common competitor to be elected by the people." And he correctly assigned the reasons for the situation in New England to a combination of personal superiority in the representatives of the old families with a theocratic hangover.[26] On another occasion he told Adams:

> You surprise me with the account you give of the strength of family distinction existing in your State. With us it is so totally extinguished, that not a spark of it is to be found but lurking in the hearts of some of our old tories; but all bigotries hang to one another, and this in the Eastern States hangs, as I suspect, to that of the priesthood. Here youth, beauty, mind and manners, are more valued than a pedigree.[27]

Perhaps this account of Virginia does not square with the traditions of the F.F.V.'s because Jefferson had a certain amount of quiet vanity about the success of his efforts to wreck the power of the Virginia planter aristocracy. Threatened with bankruptcy in his old age, he petitioned the Virginia legislature for the right to sell his property by lottery in order to realize enough cash to pay all his creditors. The petition cites some of the major "legislative services" which he had rendered the state. High on the list came "the abolition of entails, which broke up the hereditary and high-handed aristocracy, which, by accumulating immense masses of property in single lines of families, had divided our country into two distinct orders, of nobles and plebeians." Next was the abolition of primogeniture.

In his *Autobiography* Jefferson discussed his work in the Virginia legislature in more detail, describing the principal ideas he submitted to it. "I considered four of these bills, passed or reported, as forming a system by which every fibre would be eradicated of ancient or future aristocracy; and a foundation laid for a government truly republican. The repeal of the laws of entail would prevent the accumulation and perpetuation of wealth, in select families, and preserve the soil of the country

# THE DEMOCRATIC ARISTOI

from being daily more and more absorbed in mortmain. The abolition of primogeniture, and equal partition of inheritances, removed the feudal and unnatural distinctions which made one member of every family rich, and all the rest poor, substituting equal partition, the best of all Agrarian laws. The restoration of rights of conscience relieved the people from taxation for the support of a religion not theirs; for the establishment was truly of the religion of the rich, the dissenting sects being entirely composed of the less wealthy people; and these, by a bill for a general education, would be qualified to understand their rights, to maintain them, and to exercise with intelligence their parts in self-government; and all this would be effected, without the violation of a single natural right of any one individual citizen."[28]

In Jefferson's old age he encouraged his followers by showing that events had proved him right and morbid Federalism wrong. "Only lay down true principles, and adhere to them inflexibly," he advised in 1816. "Do not be frightened into their surrender by the alarms of the timid, or the croakings of wealth against the ascendancy of the people. If experience be called for, appeal to that of our fifteen or twenty governments [of the States, of course] for forty years, and show me where the people have done half the mischief in these forty years, that a single despot would have done in a single year; or show half the riots and rebellions, the crimes and the punishments, which have taken place in a single nation under kingly government, during the same period."[29] History and experience in America had shown, despite all the researches of the Federalists into the histories of petty principalities in Greece, that the people could be trusted. The same history had shown, he told John Adams, that the *aristoi* were not inevitably wicked .Though the American Senate and the upper branches of State legislatures had not functioned according to Adams's plan to fence in the *aristoi*, nothing disastrous had happened.

The key to Jefferson's plan to reconcile democracy and gentlemanliness was his famous scheme for universal education.

It posited that every individual should receive 'the degree of instruction" which his "condition" and talents warranted.[30] That is, he was to be trained for his "order" in life through a sort of hierarchy of education. Seeking, after all, to establish a practical system for the Virginia of the early nineteenth century, Jefferson envisaged three main kinds of schools. The first was the "Elementary school." To this every child must be sent. "The mass of our citizens may be divided into two classes—the laboring and the learned," he wrote. "The laboring will need the first grade of education to qualify them for their pursuits and duties; the learned will need it as a foundation for further acquirements." But this initial education must be the same for everyone. Next come the "General schools," which are necessarily plural in kind; for they train the laboring classes in their callings and the learned classes for either the professions or the independent life of the gentleman. Finally, there are the "Professional Schools," from which the merely wealthy seekers of liberal education retire, for there "each science is to be taught in the highest degree it has yet attained."[31] Though enough to qualify one for usefulness in public or private life might be learned in the general college, it could be assumed that the *aristoi* would go on to learn, as Jefferson had about law, something in "the highest degree."

Since the *aristoi* will as often appear among the poor and "laboring" classes as among the rich and "learned" ones, how are they to be discovered? Jefferson's answer to this bares his whole thought. Naturally the "best," they will easily be recognized in the elementary school. Then they must be cared for and brought forward, proving themselves competitively at each step, by the state which will benefit from their powers in time to come. Jefferson restated his basic idea in various forms over a period of many years. The law he drafted for the educational system of the State of Virginia, never adopted intact, provided for a zoning system throughout the state, with enough elementary schools and a college in each section, all coming to a peak at the State University. For the *aristos* without money, provision was made at each point. "The object," he wrote at another time, "is to bring into action that mass of talents which lies buried in poverty in every country, for want of the means of development, and thus give activity to a mass of mind, which, in proportion to our population, shall be the double or treble of what it is in most countries."[32] But the center of his intent may be seen in the statement that, had his program been carried out, "Worth and genius would thus have been sought out from every condition of life, and completely prepared by education for defeating the competition of wealth and birth for public trusts."[33] Though his program was never fully tried, yet its value to the nation in the working tradition of publicly-supported higher education has been beyond estimation. And there is still much to profit from in his vision of education at once broad in content and scope and sharply steep in standards.

Unlike Adams, Jefferson had not the endless flow of argumentation which creates tomes. Yet the leading of his plan seems clear. Believing in the *aristos,* in the natural gentleman as seen from the point of view of his function, he sought to establish a democratic method by which his services could be made available to society and by which he could be saved from frustration. Adams was afraid of human nature and, in the end, could think of nowhere to turn consistent with theory. Seeing the evil that men do, Jefferson still had faith that democracy which recognizes the innate worth and dignity of every human soul was possible because the masses and the *aristoi* alike had a principle of good as well as one of evil within them, because the people could learn to judge and choose the *aristoi,* because the *aristoi* could in a democratic government learn to find their way to knowledge and to willingness to serve well. In a very real sense, then, American democracy is founded in part upon Jefferson's concept of the gentleman.

### III

Jeffersonian success in scotching a vested, hereditary class of gentlemen in America had a number of important results.

It did make the American measure of democracy in government possible to undistinguished citizens. On the negative side, it removed all blocks except an often feeble public morality from the way to power of such unsavory *aristoi* as plutocratic industrialists, undercover city bosses, gang chieftains, and labor racketeers. To the American concept of the gentleman, nevertheless, Jefferson's thought was tonic. For the first time the ideal of the gentleman was clearly separable from a very fallible class. Emerson found it possible to work out a gentlemanly ideal as personal as religion and as imperative as morality: in a theoretically fluid society there should be neither hindrance to any man's quest for self-perfection nor class alibi for his failures. The concept of the gentleman was now assimilated to the concept of democracy. Howells could preach, in the name of gentlemanliness at its highest, the Utopian social and economic democracy of Tolstoian socialism to accompany Jeffersonian political democracy.

In 1888, working within Jefferson's heritage, President Eliot of Harvard found a way to deny the hard-evolutionist charge that democracy denied the principle of natural selection. On the contrary, he said in Jeffersonian terms, the artificial protection afforded hereditary aristocrats gave unnatural and unwise protection to degeneration. Under democracy the catalogues of the universities, for example, showed that families which handed down intelligence and vigor retained leading places. But only the fit could stay at the top, because equally strong and keen men and women constantly rose to compete with them on even terms. This was, said Eliot, strikingly proved by the ladies and gentlemen abundant in America. "They have personal force, magnanimity, moderation, and refinement; they are quick to see and to sympathize; they are pure, brave, and firm."

Though Eliot believed that America had more such persons proportionately than any other country; at any rate "American experience" showed that "neither generations of privileged ancestors nor large inherited possessions are necessary to the making of a lady or a gentleman." A "gentleman is *born* in a democracy, no less than in a monarchy"; but that is because he must have "natural gifts," that is, "fine bodily and spiritual qualities, mostly innate." With those he must have "early access to books, and therefore to great throughts and high examples." All else necessary is "early . . . contact with some refined and noble person." Men and women who have thus become "the highest types" are "every-day phenomena in American society." What do they prove? That "the social mobility of a democracy . . . is immeasurably more beneficial to a nation than any selective in-breeding, founded on class distinctions, which has ever been devised." This being true, we may expect "that science and literature, music and art, and all the finer graces of society will develop and thrive in America, as soon as the more urgent tasks of subduing a wilderness and organizing society upon an untried plan are fairly accomplished."[34]

Federalist thinking on into the nineteenth century obeyed the normal tendency to blur ancient distinctions, and the ideas of Adams and Ames were blended into a conviction that the structure of society must be maintained, that both society as a whole and his own class expected the gentleman to do his duty, and above all that the checks and balances of the Constitution must be held inviolate. These were the inherited preconceptions of Washington Irving, Bryant, Fenimore Cooper, and Holmes and Lowell, to mention only a few. Though the class of gentlemen as such was negated by Jefferson and finally destroyed by the Jacksonian triumphs, there were fascinating attempts to use again notions which had been intellectually rickety in the time of Dennie and Fessenden to undergird the "American system" of predatory capitalism. By the end of the Jacksonian era that was done with,[35] as was the last vestige of feudal land-tenure in America.[36] The traditional organization of the class of gentlemen was effectively and permanently broken, and the natural gentleman was set free to realize all the highest ideals of merit and function of the traditional concept. Now, in a Jeffersonian democracy, where all was fair and free, the gentleman might give his best to the public good, might conserve for all the richness of the past while he pointed the way to the progress of the future. It was a beautiful possibility,—but like all Jeffersonian thought, though it knew it could overcome the evils of the past, it could not reckon with the incredible mixture of good and evil yet to come from both the industrialization of American culture and nineteenth century science.

# CHAPTER SIX

# THE DEATH OF THE AGRARIAN DREAM: FENIMORE COOPER

WITH mercantile Federalism intellectually dead and the future barred to a national class of gentlemen, there was, before 1830, still chance for the growth of a class of agrarian gentlemen. The sentiment of Adams and Jefferson had favored it, though both opposed any move which, like primogeniture, would establish artificial over natural aristocracy. In America's first significant novelist, James Fenimore Cooper, the agrarian dream of a thriving country-side dotted with spendid yet democratic gentry to lead and serve the people had its most imaginative, energetic, and sincere spokesman. Not to consider for the moment the creative stimulant Cooper found in imagining his characters and situations as gentlemen solving gentlemen's problems, he wrote at least ten novels and three other volumes to clarify and defend the agrarian dream. Whatever part of the Civil War was a cultural struggle in which the South fought for the same dream, that fight was unrealistic; for when America as a whole, the South included,[1] rejected Cooper's ideal and adopted the business ideal of "the

American system," the rationale of planter aristocracy was negated. The *post bellum* agrarianism of the South has been a genteel tradition.

No one has put the agrarian case with more strength than Cooper. Through his wife he was allied to New York State gentry who had participated in the benefits of patroon land-tenure. Some of them had been Tories. From William Cooper, his staunch Quaker-turned-gentleman father, "the mirror of partisan perfection as a Federalist squire,"[2] he inherited not only land and social position but an intense devotion to the ideal of the function of the gentleman. He thought of himself as a gentleman and was able to impress others as being distinguished and eligible for the best society, European or American.[3] Yet with all this went a burning purpose and faith in the ultimate human *rightness* of his ideal which is hard to match.

Fighting the adverse current of American cultural changes, men like the Van Renssalaers were vicious and dishonest because they were frightened; men like Dennie and Fessenden were lugubrious and outrageous because they were bewildered. Cooper was neither. Although the operating margin which supported his gentlemanly way of life depended largely on income from his writing, he calmly shattered his own popularity by neglecting romantic adventure for patrician polemic. When the bitter contemporary political warfare made him a target, he embarked on the most gruelling, self-sacrificing, and brilliant instance of the performance by an American author of the function of the gentleman in a democratic society. In a long series of libel trials initiated and fought through almost alone by Cooper, he spent time, energy, money, and reputation to establish it firmly in American law that no citizen shall be punished by libel for his independence of the opinions of a newspaper editor.[4] Disinterested defender of his concept of the gentleman or not, Cooper was at least intensely sincere.

Distrusting and belittling mercantile Federalism, Cooper believed enthusiastically from the start that a synthesis of his father's agrarian Federalism with Jeffersonian ideals was the rightly destined blue-print for American progress. In 1831 he wrote to Samuel Rogers describing the decline of those American "gentry" who "put themselves in opposition to the mass, after the revolution" and so lost the trust of the nation. Subsequent events had shown how wrong they were. Now "the nation shows all proper deference to education and character," especially when they are "united to money and discreetly used." But this has not come about by accident, he concludes: "Jefferson was the man to whom we owe the high lesson that the *natural* privileges of a social aristocracy are in truth no more than their *natural privileges*."[5] Thus Cooper forged the odd but coherent union of ideas which made him the determined upholder of democracy and the class of gentlemen at the same time. He followed his friend, the master New York politician De Witt Clinton,[6] into Andrew Jackson's party primarily because Jackson was "a gentleman" of high courtesy, "mild and graceful mien," "great dignity," and "perfect good humor."[7] As far as Fenimore Cooper was concerned, agrarian gentility and the truest American democracy were not only compatible but mutually necessary.

I

In this first enthusiasm Cooper took time from writing the already internationally popular adventure tales to block out his notion of an agrarian gentleman's democracy. In conventionally disguised epistolary essays, *Notions of the Americans, Picked up by a Travelling Bachelor,* he sketched out in 1828 the basic scheme which subsequent battle and defeat only slightly modified. Not Cooper's ideas so much as his feelings toward the country he sought to guide changed later under stress. But here, at the beginning, he was thoroughly optimistic, even expansive.

He started in the Jeffersonian tradition by saying that life in America is distinguished by the "simplicity of common sense." The democratic way, joining "the best effects of civilization, with as little as possible of its disadvantages," stimulates clear thought and logical behavior. Therefore, American society possesses "those conventional castes which divide the whole civilized world into classes" because they "are the unavoidable consequences of differences in fortune, education, and manners." Democracy does not "destroy the influence of education, talents, money, or even birth." But if this is all true, is American life democratic? Yes, completely so, said Cooper. For in America these differentiating factors are made subject to democratic control by the abolition of artificial, hereditary aristocracy. Hence "less impassable barriers" separate the gentry from the masses—natural gentlemen are free to rise competitively to the top. And the American gentleman "must be content to enjoy his advantages as a concession of the public opinion, and not as a right," though that makes him no less a gentleman.

No man to blink facts, Cooper was anxious to show how factors which had long remained traditional parts of the concept of the gentleman still survived under republican institutions, and deserved to survive so long as they were kept subject to democratic rules of equal rights and free competition. Safely taken "within limits of reason" in America, it was right that the "sentiment of birth" as opposed to the "prejudice" of blood should continue. Though everyone knows that nature almost never perpetuates the "inequality of her gifts" in one line, still no one should lose the benefits of a good name unless his own delinquency warrants it. But competitive merit is the important thing. In a democracy "it is not enough simply to be the son of a great man; in order to render it of essential advantage, some portion of his merit must become hereditary, or the claim had better be suppressed."

The same is true for the influence of wealth. Hard-headedly one must admit that "when money is united to merit and talent . . . it can do more than when the latter qualities are unsupported." But it is a canard to say that money alone can make an American gentleman. Often one finds distinguished men who are not really rich. Money helps, it can neither make nor break the gentleman. In America "a man can neither buy preferment in church, state, army, navy, nor in anything else, with his dollars. He can give dinners, and he can educate his children, and give them manners, and in this direct and natural manner, advance his own or their importance; but there the benefits of money cease."[8] In the end there must be as delicate a balance as possible between the kindness and fellowship of "true humanity, which is the essence of all civilization" and a state of free individual competition. Thus democracy could best "avail of the talents of the gifted few, while the long train of humbler beings shall have scope and leisure also for the privileges of their mortality."[9] The aristocracy of merit should serve the nation.

The democratic nation and its gentry were, Cooper felt assured, good for each other. The snobbery and arrogance of European aristocrats was impossible in America. A gentleman who tried them would be "in great danger of humiliation"; his "countrymen would not tolerate his airs." Though this has made American manners both "circumspect and reasonable," the net result has been admirable. "Delicacy of demeanour" has resulted from the democratic process of consulting everyone in affairs. The time was at hand, Cooper thought, "when the American gentleman will pride himself . . . on his peculiar simplicity" because it rests not on the hypocrisy of courtiership, but on "the immutable and sacred empire of truth." He has the unique opportunity to live by "that rare and lofty courtesy, in which the party knows how to respect himself, by sacrificing no principle while he reconciles his companion to the stern character of his morals by grace of mien and charity to his weaknesses . . ."[10] At the same time the presence of a proportionately great number of gentlemen in the country has had a decidedly elevating effect on the whole population. There is a whole class of people in an "equivocal" place between gentility and commonness, more in America than anywhere in the world. And from this group, newcomers into the ranks of gentlemen continually arrive.

All this made Cooper crow with nationalistic pride. Twenty years before Emerson's *Representative Men* singled out Napoleon as the symbol of worldly megalomania, Cooper contrasted him with Washington to show that America had produced the great gentleman of the age. Washington "lived for others"; Napoleon lived "solely for himself." Napoleon's glory is in the ephemera of deed and accident—how, Cooper asked, is he better than Jenghis Khan? But the glory of Washington is "in the whole tenor of his life" and its "stern lesson of virtue."[11] This greatness Cooper liked to think an augury of the future of the nation's gentry. Guided by their talents and devotion, America would be supreme. At the end of the *Notions* appears a 'letter' to the British correspondent which embodies at once all Cooper's pride and hope with his fearless assumption that his was the correct plan for the American future:

> Let us suppose these States inhabited by one hundred millions of people . . . Their men of fortune, breeding, and education, have reached the acme of human elevation, (of course no allusion is intended to religion), for a patent of nobility does nothing toward raising the qualifications of its possessor, however it may serve to depress his inferiors. We will suppose some four or five millions of these men, acknowledging, and actually possessing no earthly superior, in full communion with the rest of the world . . . They will claim to be equal to ranks that are admitted to be superior to the immense majorities of other nations. Nor do I see how their claim is well to be denied. They will be quite equal in manners, in wealth, in general elevation of character . . . Now, my dear Somersetshire baronet, what are we to do to maintain our present unquestionable superiority over these gentry?[12]

It was in this belief, though with deepening social and political insight during his seven-year European residence, that Cooper wrote his first thirteen novels, including *The Spy, The Pilot,* and the first three Leatherstocking Tales. For him it was a time of faith and optimism, particularly about the possibilities of the foundation of an agrarian gentry, an aristocracy of merit and virtue, which could carry America to greatness. He spent his years abroad secure in the faith that all was going well under the admired Jackson. But on his return in 1833 he found

America in a condition far from his dream. The Whig counter-revolution was under way, and the "American system" men were hiding their intentions under an emotional, anti-intellectual barrage of "plain-folks" propaganda. Already conspicuous in the newspapers for his comments on French politics, Cooper was a perfect target for Whig papers. He was a Jacksonian and an avowed gentleman. Furthermore, he would stand and fight, giving as good as he got, but making colorful political copy for unscrupulous editors.

In 1835 he published his fantastic-voyage satire, *The Monikins,* in which he blistered the "social-stake" theory together with the traditional Anglophilic, Hamiltonian mercantile notions which underlay Whig dollar-chasing. In 1837 he was involved in the celebrated Three Mile Point case in which the public of Cooperstown sought to restrain him from taking back a part of his patrimony which had been used as a community picnic-grounds. He was viciously attacked by New York Whig papers and next year began to conduct his libel suits against their editors. The prime of his life was to be spent fighting; and it was on his theory of the agrarian gentleman that he rested his fighting philosophy.

Though his travel volumes were edited somewhat to point up his case and there was a separate legal battle over his *History of the Navy of the United States* in 1839, the principal fighting documents were the three issued in 1838 *The American Democrat* was a text-book of agrarian gentility. *Homeward Bound* and *Home as Found* brought the Effinghams home from Europe to conquer as American gentry the pretensions of British aristocrats, the snobbery of Whig parvenus, and the dictatorship of local demagogues. They are fighting volumes, and into them went the energy which was to be expended in the next five years on legal battles. *The American Democrat,* Cooper's major social document, expanded and systematized the earlier ideas. Its tone is that of a man who is dealing as patiently as he can with a perverse audience which he thinks should know all this without having to be told it. Sometimes it rises to heights of persuasiveness. Sometimes it is acutely argued. It is always an abstract effort to persuade by the logical manipulation of facts according to Cooper's agrarian pattern.

Repeating virtually everything he had said before, Cooper in *The American Democrat* seemed most of all to be concerned to have the value of the function of the gentleman made clear. Claiming "to be as good a democrat as there is in America," he admitted freely that democratic imperfections were better than monarchy or aristocracy for the Adamsian reason that only "the body of the nation" could protect itself against the "gross abuses" to which power in the hands of the few would be perverted. Still the function of the gentleman mattered most. "The class to which he belongs is the natural repository of the manners, taste, tone, and, to a certain extent, of the principles of a country," Cooper said. Knowledge is peculiarly his possession. In words the antiquity of whose use to support the class of gentlemen Cooper could hardly have known, he said, "If the head is necessary to direct the body, so is the head of society, (the head in a social, if not in a political sense) necessary to direct the body of society." Those who do not see "the importance of possessing a class of such men in a community, to give it tone, a high and far-sighted policy, and lofty views in general, can know little of history" or of causation.[13]

Cooper was also eager to point out that, after all, membership in the class was competitive and that organized public attack upon gentlemen was a basic violation of democratic, Constitutional rights. Liberty leaves "every man master of his own acts"; it denies "hereditary honors" but never "the inevitable consequences of civilization." No true gentleman wishes to stand upon any "superiority" other than those of "his attainments, practices and principles." The great object of democratic society is to free and to refine its men of talent:

> In a democracy men are just as free to aim at the highest attainable places in society, as to obtain the largest fortunes; and it would be clearly unworthy of all noble sentiment to say, that the grovelling competition for money shall alone be free, while that which enlists all the liberal acquirements and

elevated sentiments of the race, is denied the democrat. Such an avowal would be at once, a declaration of the inferiority of the system, since nothing but ignorance and vulgarity would be its fruits.[14]

With pathetically thin plots and only a moment in the first of exciting sea-adventure, *Homeward Bound* and *Home as Found* are significant for their stiff portraits of Cooper's gentlefolk and for a few new ideas. It is reiterated that the American gentleman can be the world's finest figure. Edward Effingham, whom the Whig papers immediately charged was self-portraiture by Cooper, very nearly realizes the possibility. By contrast, Edward's cousin John Effingham confirms the anti-mercantile bias of *The Monikins* and Cooper's writings in general. He is in every particular a less worthy gentleman because he is sprung from the trading, "English Federalist" branch of the family. Growing impatience with the yapping vulgarity of Cooper's antagonists crops out in the portraits of Editor Steadfast Dodge, Aristabulus Bragg, and their friends and relatives of Templeton. One begins to sense that Cooper's reaction to his warfare will be emotional rather than intellectual. He will hold fast to his ideas but lose hope and zest, fighting ever more grimly until he becomes almost entirely defensive.

## II

In a speech at the literary "Bread and Cheese Club" which Cooper founded in New York, he once said, "Sir, if there be any man in this community who owes a debt to the Muse of History, it would seem to be the one who had now the honor to address you." Certainly no serious reader can fail to be struck by the scope of his interests and the vividness of his sense of history. It was inevitable that he should build a theory of American history and that that theory should be founded on his ideal of the agrarian gentleman. In *Home as Found* the theory is set forth which had informed the conception of *The Pioneers* and the character of Natty Bumppo throughout, which underlay his faith in the future of America and American gentility, and which was to inform all the important novels among the fifteen yet to come, including *Pathfinder, Deerslayer,* and the Anti-Rent Trilogy.

Quite naturally, a historical theory formulated by an American of the early nineteenth century was primarily concerned with the extension of the frontier. "The march of civilization with us has a strong analogy to that of all coming events, which are known to 'cast their shadows before,'" Cooper had written in *The Prairies* "The gradations of society, from that state which is called refined to that which approaches as near barbarity as connection with an intelligent people will readily allow, are to be traced from the bosom of the States, where wealth, luxury, and the arts are beginning to seat themselves, to those distant and ever-receding borders which mark the skirts and announce the approach of the nation, as moving mists precede the signs of the day."[15] With this frontier of light the Leatherstocking was always associated as he kept, generation by generation, ahead of its horizontal progress westward. Cooper keenly appreciated the drama of that movement; but he was, as a social theorist, more concerned for the vertical cultural process by which frontier communities became the seats of civilization in the highest sense—when they began to produce gentlemen.

As he saw it, the process had three distinct stages. At the "commencement of a settlement" everything is fluid; everyone, gentleman and commoner, meets and lives equally on the lowest plane of "mere animal force." Hard work, community of effort, and danger make these years "the happiest of the first century of a settlement . . . Good-will abounds; neighbor comes cheerfully to the aid of neighbor; and life has much of the reckless gaiety, careless association, and buoyant merriment of childhood." But the very success of this comradeship destroys it. As soon as physical stability is attained, a period of competition sets in: "struggles for place, the heartburnings and jealousies of contending families, and the influence of mere money." Here the able and the wealthy forge to the front, institute the inevitable "gradations of society," and fight against "the rudest assaults of the coarse-minded and vulgar" who are the more determined because of "the late *pele-mele*." This is "the least inviting condition of society" in a so-called civilized country, but it must be endured until the coming of the third period. In the end the gentry will assert themselves. Virtue and talent will win out. The community will have "a civilization that conforms to that of the whole region . . . with the division into castes that are more or less rigidly maintained, according to circumstances."[16]

Here Cooper has a principle by which he can explain various seemingly contradictory elements in American life. A frontier settlement must be expected to differ from a settlement in another period. He is provided with a ready explanation for the fact that there seems to be bitter opposition to the gentleman in many parts of America, particularly in the section in which he happens to live: they are simply passing through the second stage! Thus he explained in a letter written in self defense to the New York *Evening Post* on November 22, 1838, that "the scene of *Home as Found* was transferred to the Templeton of *The Pioneers,* in order to show the difference which half a century has made in the appearances and usages of an American village."[17] Here was hope for the eventual supremacy of the American gentleman with all the vast good he could do his country, when at last the passions of period two were worn out and he had come into his own. And here was an excellent chance to explain the variations in men born with the innate capacities of gentlemen. Perhaps those who had failed to realize their potentialities had been handicapped by the times in which they lived.

Absorbed in fighting through litigation, Cooper did not return to his social theme proper until *Afloat and Ashore* and *Miles Wallingford,* really two halves of the same novel, in 1844. By then the victory for principle, for Cooper personally a Pyrrhic one, was established in the courts. But Cooper was psychologically on the defensive. Miles Wallingford, whose wooing and winning of a Hudson Valley heiress is constantly reminiscent of Cooper and Susan De Lancey, is put through agonizingly involved lessons in the natures of true and false gentility and the conditions under which a young natural gentleman may rise to the head of the class of gentry. Though there are moments of moving incident, there is a dragging argumentativeness about the novel which pulls the substance out into two books and the reader's patience at least as fine.

*Satanstoe* and *The Chainbearer* of the Anti-Rent Trilogy remain excellent as long as Cooper travels about in the social history of New York and his own romantic wilderness. They also become annoying with painful multiplications of fortified argument on behalf of the Cooper gentleman. So defensive is Cooper now that he misunderstands the Anti-Rent controversy, pleads for the Van Rensselaers on irrelevant grounds, and ends up in *The Redskins* with Littlepages, Effinghams all over again, engaged merely in intensified strife with the disappointed vulgarians of *their* village in the throes of its second period.

Cooper loved agrarian gentlemen. He believed wholeheartedly in the rights of property on which he centered his defense of the patroons. It seems clear that he got himself on the wrong side in the Anti-Rent War (though little good his Trilogy did) because he was now so hurt, defensive, and disillusioned at the rejection of the agrarian dream that he could see the controversy only in his own familiar but now unreal terms.

His last novels, *The Sea Lions* and *Ways of the Hour,* show incidentally that Cooper held his idea of the gentleman firm to the end. But the last work centered on the Cooper dream, a book wholly disillusioned in tone, is *The Crater*. Mark Woolston, a powerful natural gentleman, creates an ideal society on a South Pacific isle, sees it ruined by second period materialists, levellers, and sectarian fanatics, and is himself ostracised and exiled just in time to see a volcanic eruption blow the whole sinful lot to smithereens. Yet, until his last illness perhaps,[18] Cooper never lost faith in the possibilities of the gentleman in America, however much American behavior distressed him. In *The Sea*

*Lions,* his next to last novel, he commented that the American average still remained high: "the direction is onward, and though it may take time to carve on the social column of America that graceful and ornamental capital which it forms the just boast of Europe to possess, when the task shall be achieved, the work will stand on a base so broad as to secure its upright attitude for ages."[19]

### III

With his strong mind and assertive personality, Cooper had definite, positive ideas about the attributes of the ideal, essential gentleman. It is a paradox that, taken partially, these attributes excited his creative imagination, while most of his gentlemanly characters are as lifeless and typical as dummies in a store-window. One reason for this is that rounded gentlemen do not enter the books until Cooper had begun his fighting period. Then they are not people with fictional lives of their own but illustrations for *The American Democrat*. Some of the earlier gentlemen have a certain life. Judge Temple does in *The Pioneers;* and there are stirrings in *The Pilot's* gentlemen and those of *Lionel Lincoln*—in military and sea-going gentlemen about their proper business in general. But in the later volumes the only characters who seem to breathe are the first-person narrators Miles Wallingford and Corny Littlepage, both natural gentlemen coming up. Nevertheless Cooper packed his books full of little pronouncements about the main elements of ideal gentlemanliness. And his ideas seem never to have changed significantly.

With a vehemence surpassed only by Twain, Cooper attacked Sir Walter Scott as dangerous to American readers for his "deference to hereditary rank," to the prejudice of "mere feudal and conventional laws, which had their origin in force, and are continued by prejudice and wrong." Justice and democracy demanded the practical recognition only of the innate aristocracy of talent and intelligence. Yet Cooper felt free, as we have seen, to recognize the "sentiment" of birth. Consequently he might refer to characters as of gentle birth or make use, like Emerson and Holmes in the future, of the Spanish proverb "it takes three generations to make a gentleman." But he always intended to be understood as being proud that good family in America meant "ancestors who have been chosen to fill responsible stations," not hereditary aristocracy.[20] The only important criterion of birth was personal quality judged by the "standard which brings the individual himself to the ordeal of the public estimation, paying as little deference as may be to those who have gone before him."[21]

From *Notions of the Americans* through *The Crater,* Cooper held that "property is the base of all civilization" and particularly necessary to the refinements which mould the gentleman.[22] But the only good source of wealth was the land. "God protect the country that has nothing but commercial towns for capitals!" he wrote Mrs. Cooper in 1839, and he exulted when Jackson broke Nicholas Biddle's National Bank. Devotion to commerce, he said, "made whole communities degenerate into a mass of corruption, venality and cupidity." [23] Boom times became in *The Monikins* a celestial eclipse of Principle by Interest to the moral ruin of the entire Leaplow nation.[24]

Everywhere in Cooper's fiction he celebrates the fitness, joy, social good, intellectual peace, and moral health of life as an agrarian gentleman. And everywhere there is the recognition that wealth was merely the gentleman's tool. It gave him leisure and opportunity to strive for education and cultivation; it could of itself give him neither of those things; nor could it give him the indispensable inward "gifts" of the gentleman. There was no denying that families rose into or sank from gentility because of the vicissitudes of economics; but the sympathy of the world was always rightly on the side of "the quiet ascendancy of better manners and ancient recollections" over "the fussy pretensions of the vulgar aspirant, who places his claims altogether on the almighty dollar."[25] No schoolboy would think of according "distinction" to money alone.[26] To be accepted and then forgotten in the face of more significant factors, money was "the great accident, with its customary advantages," nothing more.[27]

The best advantage of wealth for the gentleman was education. "The parent of all that is excellent and great in communities, no less than individuals," Cooper said, "is intelligence." Education should aim directly at the production of leaders of civilization. "The fruits of knowledge are not to be weighed by the credit they reflect on the searcher after truth, but by the influence they produce on the mass of society."[28]

The gentleman must be soundly educated; the best college training was none too good. Cooper lamented any diminution of intellectual stature in American colleges. With the birth, the character, the habits, and "the general notions of the caste," Andries Coejemans, the Chainbearer, was not quite a gentleman. In the last analysis his being "but indifferently educated" disqualified him; for "we must all admit how necessary a certain amount of education has become . . . to make a gentleman."[29] Yet Cooper did not accept the tradition that the holder of a college degree was automatically a gentleman. Pedantry he thought as vulgar as ignorance.[30] Provincialism and petty "silver-forkism" were the great dangers of America, and they could be overcome only by association with distinguished people.

Contrary to Jefferson, Cooper thought travel to Europe immensely valuable for the young American. If he is a fool, European adventurers will do for him at once. But if he has the possibilities, the shock of the facts of life in Europe will make him "an intellectual man" and "he will finally return home, conscious alike of the evils and blessings, the advantages and disadvantages, of his own system and country—a wiser and it is to be hoped a better man."[31] The ideal, as ever, was Edward Effingham. He had been well taught, had travelled, observed and thought for himself in the quiet of "intellectual retirement." As a result, "while hundreds were keener, abler in the exposition of subtleties, or more imposing with the mass, few were as often right, and none of less selfishness, than this simple-minded and upright gentleman."[32]

More important than wealth, or training, or enabling gifts of birth to the Cooper gentleman was "a creditable moral elevation of character" which led him to "elevated views." [33] Entire candor of act and word sprang from "the honor of a gentleman," whose word is superior to an oath. [34] Yet this honor is not metaphysical. It is simply a blend of ethics and delicacy, of moral purity and truth directed by good taste. The gentleman's very honor, Cooper thought, kept him above duelling as it did above petty trickery and malicious gossip: they were all in about the same category. Though Cooper early lost interest in the dramatic possibilities of the duel, the saccharine Denbigh of *Precaution* and John Paul Jones, the magnificent *Pilot,* scorned the challenges of crude opponents. Cooper admitted ruefully that in America duels were more frequent and fatal than anywhere else. But he could exult that Americans were "the only people among whom I have found gentleman-like men who have openly laughed at the gross folly of the usage, and who, it was understood, considered themselves too rational to be guilty of so great an act of folly." [35]

If there is any genetic shift in Cooper's ideal of the essential gentleman, it is in the relationship of gentlemanliness to religion. He inclined to the tradition of the Christian gentleman. His heroes are calm but firm Christians. This is true of Judge Temple, of the Effinghams, of the Littlepages, of Miles Wallingford, and Mark Woolston. No Cooper gentleman is guilty of even venial sins. Yet there is a marked variation of comment on the question. In *Notions of the Americans* Cooper identified gentlemanliness with the Golden Rule, though he qualified it by recognizing the necessity of social competition. But in *The Chainbearer* he shows the influence both of his love of precisian logic and his deepening orthodoxy. Because of the significant things it says about Cooper's ideal of the gentleman, the passage is worth quoting at length:

> ... I repeat, there is no *necessary* connection between the Christian and the gentleman, though the last who is the first attains the highest condition of humanity. Christians, under the influence of their educations and habits, often do things that the code of the gentleman rejects; while it is certain that

gentlemen constantly commit unequivocal sins. The morality of the gentleman repudiates meannesses and low vices, rather than it rigidly respects the laws of God; while the morality of the Christian is unavoidably raised or depressed by the influence of the received opinions of his social caste. I am not maintaining "the ten commandments were not given for the obedience of people of quality," for their obligations are universal; but, simply, that the qualities of a gentleman are the best qualities of man unaided by God, while the graces of the Christian come directly from his mercy.

Nevertheless, there is that in the true character of a gentleman that is very much to be respected. In addition to the great indispensables of tastes, manners, and opinions, based on intelligence and cultivation, and all those liberal qualities that mark his caste, he cannot and does not stoop to meannesses of any sort. He is truthful out of self-respect, and not in obedience to the will of God; free with his money, because liberality is an essential feature of his habits, and not in imitation of the self-sacrifice of Christ; superior to scandal and the vices of the busy body, inasmuch as they are low and impair his pride of character, rather than because he has been commanded not to bear false witness against his neighbor. It is a great mistake to confound these two characters, one of which is a mere human embellishment of the ways of a wicked world, while the other draws near to the great end of human existence. The last is a character I revere; while I am willing to confess that I never meet with the first without feeling how vacant and repulsive society would become without it; unless, indeed, the vacuum could be filled by the great substance, of which, after all, the gentleman is but the shadow.[36]

On the whole, the gentleman's "unequivocal sins" seem to be those of unbelief, for surely Cooper has nowhere a gentleman with sins of commission.

In *The Ways of the Hour*, Cooper's last novel, he attacked a bishop "who has lately been defining a gentleman" and has described "a 'Christian' rather than a 'gentleman.' This notion of making converts by means of enlisting our vanity and self-love in the cause, is but a weak one at best." [37] In his usual uncomfortable fashion he had struck the spot weak in the tradition of the Christian gentleman from its beginning. What seems to have happened is that Cooper, increasingly absorbed through the latter years of his life in uncompromisingly exact, orthodox Anglicanism, [38] found cause for rebellion against the sentimental Christian gentleman. Both ideals were violated. Christianity was entangled in petty this-worldliness. The gentleman was diverted from his proper earthly objects, and the way was opened for a levelling onslaught upon him from people who had no better claim than piety. Crotchety and acrid after battling the whole length of a gainsaying generation, Cooper let the shift in religious thought which came with the years modify his concept of gentlemanliness. But for most of his life, and for all of his heroes, especially those of the late books, upright Christian character was the most important element in the ideal Cooper gentleman.

The courtesy which is the outward flower of the character of the gentleman was a constant stimulant to Cooper. Too empiric to worry about platonic definitions, he thought of courtesy as compounded of common sense, consideration for the feelings of others, and sound morality. False courtesy which substituted "the seemly, for the right" annoyed him. Gentlemen ought to depend upon "the inherent sense of right, . . . which becomes conscience in moral things . . . as the safest means of regulating the deportment of the different castes in society towards each other." [39] We have seen how he valued the "rare and lofty courtesy" which reconciles others to the "stern character" of a gentleman's morals. Yet most etiquette, he believed, was sound because it was "usually derived from very rational and sufficient motives' which the intelligent man could readily perceive. [40] And these would produce the beauty of modest delicacy which was "gravely considerate of the feelings" [41] of others.

For "bland courtesy" which "elevates others" without degrading the gentleman, Cooper's praise was always ready. [42] He thought of courtesy as dividing naturally into manners and manner: or, as he put it, into "breeding" and an "air." Manner is of the utmost importance to a gentleman. It marks him out at once, so that all the world recognises him and other gentlemen are drawn to him. It takes life-long intimacy with gentlemanly ways to give one "the air," and that is one of the things which rising natural gentlemen can hardly have.

Gentlemen become "grave as they become thoughtful," and the "natural feeling of gentlemanly reserve" should be one's guide. Yet care must be taken to express delicacy as well as dignity and poise. Not only the gentleman's actions, but his manner also, must display "that graceful semblance of living less for oneself than for others, and to express, as it were, their feelings and wishes" which is the mirror of delicacy. Thus the mysterious Mary Monson of *Ways of the Hour* shows "the air, manners, countenance and finesse of one accustomed, from infancy, to good company. The reader may smile at this," says truculent Cooper, "but he must pardon us if we say that the smile will betray ignorance, rather than denote the philosophy that he may fancy controls his opinions." [43]

By good breeding Cooper meant the cool yet well-intentioned adaptation of deportment to the demands of ideal delicacy on the one hand and fashions in manners on the other. A successful writer almost without having intended it, he was extremely sensitive to diction and locution. He prescribed for "the utterance of a gentleman" at length in *The American Democrat*,[44] and, as might be expected, provided Edward Effingham with "a voice, intonation, utterance, and manner . . . eminently those of a gentleman; without pretension, quiet, simple, and mellow, while on the other hand, they were feeling, dignified, distinct, and measured." [45]

It was thus as the organic expression of good sense, of the fine taste which also made the gentleman the devotee of the arts, and of full discipline of mind and personality that Cooper conceived of good breeding. The "crowd of genteel vulgar" are full of "fussy pretensions" because their ideas of manners are "obtained at second-hand, as the traditions of fashion, or perhaps in the pages of a novel." [46] They always over-do things, like Muir, the villainous quartermaster of *The Pathfinder,* whose fine-gentleman ways are obviously artificial. They are made suspicious and uneasy by "the simplicity and natural ease" of ladies and gentlemen whom they think should be all "fuss and pretension." [47] The French correspondent's portrait of John Cadwallader, Cooper's first full drawing of an ideal American gentleman, shows his ideal of good breeding in miniature. Cadwallader is said to be:

> ... an educated and a gifted man, with a simplicity of, thought, as well as of deportment, that acted like a charm on my exhausted feeling ... He is saturnine by nature, and, a Frenchman might add, taciturn to a fault ... Still, I find great equanimity of temper, and the same calm, deliberative manner of considering things, as if he deemed himself already removed from most of the great and moving interests of the world ... this calm, reasoning American, so fresh, so original in his ways of treating things, which long use had rendered, to my imagination, fixed and unalterable as the laws of nature themselves, and so direct in his application of all his opinions to the practices of the world ... [48]

Among the many folk-definitions of the gentleman (ribald and otherwise), one of the most intriguing is that the gentleman can look any man in the world straight in the eye and tell him to go to hell. Cooper would have admired that. The democratic gentleman, he thought, having conceded the right of all others to participate in political power and to compete with him for social eminence "will proudly maintain his own independence of vulgar domination, as indispensable to his personal habits. The same principle and manliness that would induce him to depose a moral despot would induce him to resist a vulgar tyrant." [49] When the Whigs began to turn the tables on the Jacksonians and to cry down "aristocrats" while they cried up log cabins and hard cider, Cooper replied that evidently "it takes an aristocrat to make a true democrat." In the character of Miles Wallingford he went on, "Certain I am, that all the real, manly, independent democrats I have ever known in America have been accused of aristocracy, and this simply because they were disposed ... not to let that imperious sovereign, 'the neighborhood,' play the tyrant over them." [50] Exclusiveness in society and a complete independence of thought for the gentleman were absolutely essential to the maintenance of democracy and the progress of civilization.

The word most often used by Cooper to explain special abilities, attitudes, or ideas, is "gifts." He explains the Leatherstocking as the exemplification of "white gifts" in savage situations.[51] The word is often in Natty's own mouth. He has "a white birth and white gifts,"[52] he says of himself; and to extenuate almost any action he observes that "the man acted according to his gifts."[53] The psychological doctrine upon which this usage is based, a doctrine which seems to apply to all of Cooper's characters and which certainly aids in the understanding of his concept of the gentleman, is made clear in Natty's words as follows:

> A natur' is the creatur' itself; its wishes, wants, idees, and feelin's as all are born in him. This natur' never can be changed in the main, though it may undergo some increase or lessening. Now, gifts come of sarcumstances. Thus, if you put a man in a town, he will get town gifts; in a settlement, settlement gifts; in a forest, gifts of the woods. A soldier has soldierly gifts, and a missionary preaching gifts. All these increase and strengthen until they get to fortify natur' as it might, be, and excuse a thousand acts and idees. Still the creatur' is the same at the bottom . . . Herein lies the apology for gifts; seein' that you expect different conduct from one in silks and satins from one in homespun . . .

This is not "ra'al missionary doctrine," Natty observes,—that is, it will not square with orthodox Christianity—but it is a sound practical observation.[54]

Preceding discussions of birth and education explain much about the bearing of this psychology upon Cooper's theory of the gentleman. Birth, in the sense of the innate potentialities of the human being, is nature. The differences made by it invalidate "the celebrated proposition contained in the declaration of independence" for all but political rights.[55] As a great Indian chief, Eaglesflight, puts it:

> The Great Spirit makes men differently. Some are like willows, that bend with the breeze, and are broken in the storm. Some are pines, with slender trunks, few branches, and a soft wood. Now and then there is an oak among them . . .[56]

Mr. Howel, a friend of the Effinghams, is a case in point. "Nature had done more toward making Mr. Howel a gentleman than either cultivation or association," says Cooper, and a gentleman he was.[57] The power to be correct in all the aspects of gentility is in part "obtained from education, but far more from the inscrutable gifts of nature." [58] There is an indispensable "instinct of propriety." [59]

In America the lack of proper educational facilities has created almost a special class for those who have the natures of gentlemen but have never been able to acquire all the "gifts." The dashing young Dutchman of *Satanstoe* is one of these. He is not quite a gentleman, though he should be, for "nature intended Guert Ten Eyck for better things than accident and education, or the want of education, have enabled him to become." [60] Worse difficulties crippled Aristabulus Bragg, the pettifogger of *Home As Found*. He had risen to prominence from an unfavorable start. He was "bold, morally and physically, aspiring, self-possessed, shrewd, singularly adapted to succeed in his schemes where he knew the parties, intelligent after his tastes, and apt," Cooper says. "Had it been his fortune to be thrown earlier into a better sphere, the same natural qualities . . . would have conduced to his improvement, and most probably would have formed a gentleman, a scholar, and one who could have contributed largely to the welfare and tastes of his fellow-creatures." [61]

Cases like those of Guert and Aristabulus reveal the need for the cultivation of "gifts" as much as the initial need of a gentlemanly nature. And Cooper has much to say about the influence of the "gift." It is a result in part of experience and long habit. More significantly, it is likely to be produced by culture-patterns. "What is a warrior without his traditions?" dignified old Leatherstocking asks the hostile Sioux chief in *The Prairie*.[62] He distinguishes again and again between white men and red on the basis of "gifts" which are part of the heritage of each. "Revenge is an Injin gift, and forgiveness a white man's." [63] "A king's soldier will swear, and he will drink, and it is of little use to try to prevent him," says Natty in *The Pathfinder*. "A gentleman likes his delicacies, and a lady her feathers . . ." Therefore Chingachgook must be allowed to follow his "Indian's nature and gifts." Indeed, his doing so when "he is a lone man in this world" is honorable, "honest and respectable"; it is gentlemanly.

Though gifts are "only skin-deep" and depend upon experience and education, they must be carefully controlled. They may through long habit alter character. Natty is careful to explain in time of war that he has not the true gifts of the soldier—"bloodshed and war are not my real gifts, but peace and mercy." Again, he refuses in *The Deerslayer* to join in the infamous and disastrous scheme of Hurry Harry and Tom Hutter to slay Indian women and children for the scalp-bounty. "My gifts are not scalpers' gifts," he says indignantly, ". . . I'll not unhumanize my natur' by falling into ways that God intended for another race." [64]

The main significance of the "gift" to the concept of the gentleman is the importance it gives to his rearing, education, and associations. To validate his political ideas Cooper had to get away from the old notion of hereditary gentility. His "gift" psychology creates a new basis for exclusiveness which is to be reconciled with democracy only in his own highly technical sense. Only life-long association with members of the class of gentlemen can produce their gifts. And if the perfection of all the qualities which make gentility possible must await the slow acquisition of such environmental gifts, then the perfect weapon has been forged with which the encroachments of the leveller can be beaten back by gentlemen of good conscience.

Cooper was determined that the "gifts" of the American gentleman should be home-grown. He scorned Americans who were in danger of being carried away by European, particularly British, influences. He deplored especially the unfortunate Mr. Howel in *Home As Found*. An untravelled resident of Templeton, Howel "dreamed away his existence in an indolent connection with the current literature of the day. He was fond of reading, and being indisposed to contention or activity of any sort, his mind had admitted the impression of what he perused, as the stone receives a new form by the constant fall of drops of water . . . and, as all his reading was . . . confined to English books, he had gradually, and unknown to himself, in his moral nature at least, got to be a mere reflection of those opinions, prejudices and principles . . . that it had suited the interests or passions of England to promulgate by means of the press." [65] It was a sad day for Howel when the much-travelled Effinghams returned to their old haunts. They spend hours, it seems to the reader of the last half of the novel, stripping the poor man of his little illusions.

Few readers of Fenimore Cooper can help liking him for his candor, his courage, his integrity. His ideal of the forthright, high-minded, agrarian gentleman and his whole class of wheel-horses for democratic government and the progress of American civilization has something of the same attractiveness. Yet in the theory there is a chilly snobbery which somehow Cooper's warm personality overcame in himself. The actualities of history were passing Cooper by. The swelling materialism he hated so cordially shunted his agrarian dream down the sidings of history with the rest of the genteel traditions. There had to be freedom for the exploitation of the American earth: room for millions of immigrants and for the Robber Barons.

It was not, after all, any ordinary democracy in which Cooper believed but a complexly rationalized gentleman's society. Perhaps he was deceived by Jacksonianism. Certainly that movement of urban laborers and frontiersmen had no intention of setting any class of gentlemen in the saddle. It represented the new dominance in American life of a levelling force which was forever to turn the gentleman out of his class function. He might yet lead, but he would lead as a citizen, not as a gentleman. By the time of Cooper's death, Americans had ceased to think of the class of gentlemen and turned to the Jeffersonian pattern. The gentleman became simply a member of the democratic community. His talents and training were at the service of the community with the reservation that he serve on terms not repulsive to his ethics, courtesy, and taste.

## CHAPTER SEVEN

## THE GENTLEMAN AS THE SUBSTANCE OF ART: COOPER'S NOVELS

As A WRITER Cooper was richly stimulated by his ideal of the gentleman. Though the American novel had been concerned for the true gentleman from its Richardsonian beginnings, Cooper's was the first significant literary mind stirred by the philosophy of gentility. His novels can be understood as he understood them himself, and from a critical viewpoint never steadily taken before, when they are examined in terms of that philosophy. For Cooper could hardly write without reference to it. Virtually all his characters are imagined within its interpretive scope; and the most important of them all, Natty Bumppo, takes on intellectual respectability for the first time when he is seen framed within Cooper's social structure. Cooper visualised his fictitious people as placed on both the psychological and the social planes which the theory of the gentleman drew for them. Our seeing his creations as he did must be a part of that effort to understand literary work totally which makes enlightened criticism possible.

## I

With all Cooper's great interest in history, it was inevitable that there should be figures from the actual history of the country whom he praised as notable American gentlemen. In the days when Americans thought of themselves as citizens first of a state, then of the United States, it was natural that Cooper should concern himself with distinguished New Yorkers. In *The Chainbearer,* Mordaunt Littlepage, present at the siege of Saratoga, praises "a New York gentleman" with outstanding "air, position, and deportment . . . This was Philip Schuyler, so justly celebrated in our annals for his wisdom, patriotism, integrity, and public services." Another great Yorker was John Jay, with whose family Cooper was intimate. "I scarcely remember to have mingled with any family, where there was a more happy union of quiet decorum and high courtesy than beneath the roof of Mr. Jay," he wrote. "The venerable statesman himself is distinguished, as much now, for his dignified simplicity, as he was, formerly, for his political sagacity, integrity, and firmness." Jay had to an unusual degree "those little acts of bland courtesy" which, "while they elevated others, in no way subtracted from his own glory." [1]

Not all gentlemen lived in New York, however. In researching for the magnificent sketch of the Battle of Bunker Hill around which *Lionel Lincoln* is centered, Cooper was much taken by the character of Joseph Warren. In Boston during its long siege by the Americans, "Lionel heard the name of Warren mentioned oftener than any other in the circles of Province-House, and with the sort of bitterness which, even while it bespoke their animosity, betrayed the respect of his enemies. This gentleman, who until the last moment had braved the presence of the royal troops, and fearlessly advocated his principles, while encircled with their bayonets, was now known to have suddenly disappeared from among them, abandoning home, property, and a lucrative profession; and by sharing in the scenes of the day in Lexington, to have fairly cast his fortunes on the struggle." Warren also became one of the model American gentry in *Notions of the Americans*. Cooper praised him as "distinguished for his high moral intrepidity" and felt that his death on Bunker Hill was a disaster far greater than the technical defeat of the troops who were forced to abandon the position for which they had exacted many British casualties: "The exceeding merit and unquestionable patriotism, no less than the high rank which this gentleman was destined by his countrymen to fill, induced them to consider his loss ... the greatest calamity which befell them on that day." But the premier American gentleman was still George Washington. Even disguised as Mr. Harper in *The Spy* "his whole appearance was so impressive and so decidedly that of a gentleman" that he received instant notice. In *The Pilot* his most ardent British antagonists remembered him as "quite a gentleman." That Cooper thought him the noblest, most virtuous product of "the age" we have already seen.

## II

The seriousness with which Cooper took his conception of the inevitability of gentlemen in any civilization crops out in the American aborigines for whose portraits he became internationally famous. He is careful to give lip-service to the most respectable historical traditions of the innately primitive and inferior culture of his Indians. Yet often they are his most convincing gentlemen. Cooper admitted that he knew very little about red men at first hand. He never saw them in their pristine state or on their native grounds.[2] Whatever little contact he may have had with "real" Indians other than the disinherited waifs of the New York woods was with parties travelling to treat with the government in Washington. Even this small observation was colored by the preconceptions which he had absorbed from his reading, especially of the Moravian missionary Heckewelder.

Admitting his debt to such sources, Cooper rejected "realistic" criticism of his Indians by saying frankly, "it is the privilege of all writers of fiction, more particularly when their works aspire to the elevation of romances, to present the *beau ideal* of their characters to the reader." [3] Since he was idealizing Heckewelder, it may be interesting to glance briefly at some of the ideas about the Indians which he got from the missionary and which are relevant to a concept of Indian gentlemen. Heckewelder had noted, for instance, that the Indians were governed purely by their class of gentlemen, "by the mere force of the ascendency which men of superior minds have over those of a more ordinary stamp; by a tacit, yet universal, submission to the aristocracy of experience, talents, and virtue." Heckewelder Indians were naturally courteous, too. "It is a striking fact," he observes, "that the Indians, in their uncivilized state, should so behave towards each other, as though they were a civilized people . . . they often meet for the purpose of conversation, and their sociability appears to be a recreation to them, a renewal of good fellowship."

Cooper's Indians thus hold to a number of the elements of his concept of the gentleman. They believe in the innate inequalities of men, perhaps transmitted from father to son. Yet their leaders are chosen on the basis of individual merit. Indian chiefs "were divided into two classes; those who were mainly indebted for their influence to physical causes and to deeds and arms, and those who had become distinguished rather for their wisdom than for their services in the field."

The best combined both powers. Such were Chingachgook, who appears in all but one of the Leatherstocking Tales, Magua of *The Last of the Mohicans,* Mahtoree of *The Prairie,* and Scalping Peter of *Oak Openings.* The Indian leader has the "courtesy of one trained in high society . . . in all things he is dignified and quiet." His delicacy is of "a refinement in politeness that would be looked for in vain" in most "civilized" groups. Even marauding Mingo Chiefs can display to poor crazy

Hetty Hutter "an ease and deference of manner that would have done credit to men of more courtly origin." Indians of the United States proper are notable, moreover, for a typical "chivalrous honor," which they expect from others as readily as they exercise it themselves. Intellectually the best Indians are marked by "a liberality and candor" that would do credit to the best-educated white gentleman. So perfect and imposing was the manner of the Indian, finally, that even a second-rate Tuscarora like Arrowhead of *The Pathfinder* could overawe a blustering British sea-dog like Charles Cap by the mere "quiet superiority of his reserve."

The greatest of Cooper's Indian gentlemen is Chingachgook. Though as Indian John in *The Pioneers* he is as often futile and sordid as he is admirable, in the other three novels in which he appears he is a truly distinguished figure. Even chauvinistic and race-prejudiced Cap says that he is "a gentleman for an Injin." He has a natural "delicacy of . . . native refinement" and an unusual share of "liberality and candor." To Natty Bumppo, "the Sarpent is, indeed, a wise and virtuous chief; and any white man might covet his gifts." [4] On one occasion Natty explains that it is Chingachgook's immense self-respect which prevents him from succumbing to the curiosity about other people's affairs which is likely to tempt even "a white gentleman. The Sarpent, here," he continues, "would turn his head aside if he found himself unknowingly lookin' into another chief's wigwam . . . I'll be bound, Judith, you wouldn't get the Sarpent there to confess there was another in the tribe so much greater than himself as to become the subject of his ideas, and to empl'y his tongue in conversation about his movements, and ways, and food, and all the other little matters that occupy a man when he's not empl'y'd in his greater duties." [5] The independence of the gentleman so significant to Cooper is maintained among his Indians, at least.

The finest Indian gentleman in Cooper, the most highly idealized character he ever drew, is Uncas, the reflection of

Chingachgook. His portrait is sketched early in *The Last of the Mohicans*:

> The travelers anxiously regarded the upright, flexible figure of the young Mohican, graceful and unrestrained in the attitudes and movements of Nature. Though his person was more than usually screened by a green and fringed hunting shirt, like that of the white man, there was no concealment to his dark, glancing, fearless eye, alike terrible and calm; the bold outline of its high, haughty features, pure in their native red, or to the dignified elevation of his receding forehead, together with all the finest proportions of a noble head, bared to the generous scalping tuft. It was the first opportunity possessed by Duncan and his companion to view the marked lineaments of either of their Indian attendants, each individual of the party relieved from a burden of doubt as the proud and determined, though wild expression of the features of the young warrior forced itself on their notice. They felt it might be a being partially benighted in the vale of ignorance, but it could not be one who would willingly devote his rich natural gifts to the purposes of wanton treachery. The ingenuous Alice gazed at his free air and proud carriage as she would have looked upon some precious relic of the Grecian chisel, to which life had been imparted by the intervention of a miracle: while Heyward, though accustomed to see the perfection of form which abounded among the uncorrupted natives, openly expressed his admiration at such an unblemished specimen of the noble proportions of man.

Uncas's most triumphant moment comes when he affirms the greatness of his birth. He has been captured by a group of wandering Delawares who do not know him, and they are about to burn him at the stake when they notice the royal tortoise tattooed on his chest. "For a single instant Uncas enjoyed his triumph," Cooper writes, "smiling calmly on the scene. Then motioning the crowd away with a high and haughty sweep of his arm, he advanced in front of the nation with the air of a king, and spoke in a voice louder than the murmur of admiration that ran through the multitude. 'Men of the Lenni Lenape!' he said, 'my race upholds the earth! your feeble tribe stands on my shell! What fire that a Delaware can light would burn the child of my fathers,' he added, pointing proudly to the simple blazonry on his skin; 'the blood that came from such a stock would smother your flames! my race is the grandfather of nations!'" Cooper was trying hard to make Uncas a magnificent personage.

Uncas's courtesy is as high as his pride. For the ladies whom he escorted through the forest he executed "all the little offices within his power with a mixture of dignity and anxious grace that served to amuse Heyward, who well knew that it was an utter innovation on the Indian customs, which forbid their warriors to descend to any menial employment, especially in favor of their women." But in the name of hospitality these services were correct. Throughout the book Uncas shows off his "instinctive delicacy" toward "the females," until Cora is so drawn to him that only the tragic deaths avert what must have been to Cooper the unthinkable tragedy of their actually falling in love. Chingachgook's elegy for Uncas makes the most effective ending Cooper ever wrote for a novel:

> "Why do my brothers mourn?" he said, regarding the dark race of dejected warriors by whom he was environed; "Why do my daughters weep? that a young man has gone to the happy hunting ground, that a chief has filled his time with honor! He was good, he was dutiful, he was brave. Who can deny it? The Manitoo had need of such a warrior, and he has called him away."

A third Indian gentleman is Susquesus, who appears in the Littlepage Manuscripts, or The Anti-Rent Trilogy. He is referred to repeatedly as "a gentleman," even by the later Littlepages' English butler! His mind, Cooper says, "had ever possessed much of the loftiness of a grand nature, left to its native workings by the impetus of an unrestrained, though savage liberty." Susquesus lived to an immense age in the service of the Littlepages. They had known from the beginning that there was some secret reason why he had left his tribe to join forces with them. And in the third generation of the family and the last book of the trilogy Cooper revealed the highly romantic story of Susquesus. Indians who travel many miles to see the old chief relate the tribal legend of his nobility which is too reminiscent of Sarah Wentworth Morton's *Ouâbi*.

Susquesus left his tribe with a broken heart. The greatest man in the tribe, he had fallen in love with a captive girl who belonged to the lout who had happened to take her. Though she returned his love, her captor would not release or sell her to Susquesus. So great was the integrity of Susquesus that he would not use his mighty powers to take the girl or to crush his rival. Instead he sacrificed love, power, and prestige to uphold justice and the laws of the tribe. This parable of the true gentleman of Cooper made the capstone of his trilogy.

In the magnificence of the Indian gentlemen lies part of the secret of the glamor of Cooper's novels and their international popularity as vivid escape literature throughout the past century. Much more of that glamor, though, springs from the figure who in the wilderness outdid any Indian at anything and with "white man's gifts" was morally nobler than the finest of them. Natty Bumppo—the Deerslayer, Hawkeye, Pathfinder, and Leatherstocking—was Cooper's bid for immortality. He is still a major American myth. Is this most vital of Cooper's creations, the figure which has kept his reputation green throughout the Western world, a "major vulgarian" in the midst of Cooper's gentlemen?[6] Hardly, for as Cooper conceived of him, Natty was a great natural gentleman. He served, according to Cooper's theory of historical progress, an indispensable function as a sort of knight of the wilderness who made the way smooth before the oncoming edge of civilization.

"Few knew the Pathfinder intimately without secretly coming to believe him to be one of extraordinary qualities," said Cooper.[7] He was an "innate gentleman."[8] As Natty himself asks, "In the sense of reality why may not a beaver hunter be as respectable as a governor?"[9] That is, discounting the acquired "gifts" of the gentleman, why may an untutored individual not be recognized for the true gentility within him? Certainly Natty had "much of the innate and true feeling of the gentleman."[10] His character was superb. When Mabel Dunham gently rejected his suit for her hand, she told him, in all sincerity, "if courage, truth, nobleness of soul and conduct, unyielding principles, and a hundred excellent qualities, can render any man respectable, esteemed or beloved, your claims are inferior to those of no other human being." [11] Beautiful Judith Hutter, who had been flattered by the attentions of many a British gentleman, was amazed by Natty's "dignity and high principle." "So much honesty—such obstinate uprightness" intrigue and rather frighten her until she asks Hetty, "But we are not altogether unequal, sister—Deerslayer and I? He is not altogether my superior?" Yet Natty gently declined when Judith proposed to marry him. His "untaught, natural courtesy," equal to any occasion, was founded upon the only proper grounds: "the duty of the strong to protect the weak," [12] and upon "habitual deference for the rights and feelings of others." [13] His taste in social relationships was well formed. From association with gentlemen he understood their wants and needs. An "instinctive discrimination" led him to seek out the best associates, entirely indifferent to "all distinctions which did not depend on personal merit." [14]

Natty's liberality was entire. He was completely fair, modest to an extreme, generous in word and deed. His sense of honor was unshakable. Rather than violate the parole given him by the Mingoes in *The Deerslayer,* he chose to return to them and the probability of death by torture. Natty displayed *noblesse,* the willingness of the gentleman to sacrifice himself for others more conspicuously than any of Cooper's characters. In *The Pathfinder* Natty intentionally allowed Jasper Western to win their shooting match because he knew Jasper. When he must finally give Mabel up to Jasper after she had refused the offer of his own love, he sends them away with his unselfish blessing. "Well, Jasper, she is yours"; he said, "and though it's hard to think it, I do believe you'll make her happier than I could, for your gifts are better suited to do so . . ." The most magnificent gesture came when twice Natty volunteered to give himself up to the Mingoes in exchange for Uncas.

Though Natty became more and more glamorous as Cooper developed him,[15] it is certain that at best he is not the sort of gentleman who would have graced the drawing room of Edward Effingham in its more worldly moments. Yet certainly he is some kind of gentleman. What kind becomes clearer when one looks at his function in Cooper's world. He is the advance agent of civilization in the great American wilds. It is he who first pushes out "those distant and ever-receding borders which mark the skirts and announce the approach of the nation." [16] He holds to his "white gifts" in contrast to a typical white renegade gone native, like Captain Sanglier, because he is a builder, not a killer and destroyer. "I'm form'd for the wilderness"; he says, "if ye love me, let me go where my soul craves to be . . ." But he is no mere skulking hunter. Like Daniel Boone, he "penetrated the wilds" only to draw a stifling multitude to what he had secured, so that he must move on again. When frontier civilization, the first period in Cooper's historical scheme, made his woods untenable, he went out on the plains "far towards the setting sun,—the foremost in that band of Pioneers, who are opening the way for the march of the nation across the continent." [17]

To the Temples and the Effinghams he seemed "a noble shoot from the stock of human nature which never could attain its proper elevation and importance for no other reason than because it grew in the forest . . ." [18] In itself this disposes of the "major vulgarian" charge. But in the perspective of Cooper's thought, Natty is not to be held down to the level of Aristabulus Bragg or Guert Ten Eyck. He is a special creation, formed for the wilderness. As noble as the noblest Indian, he is yet superior to him. For he is the advance agent of American civilization, the knight of the wilderness.

### III

This concept of Natty as a special gentleman whose calling was to break the trails for the coming of civilization throws some light on one of Cooper's more puzzling novels, *The Pioneers*. Part of its obscurity undoubtedly rises from the fact that it was only Cooper's third attempt. He had not yet clearly formed his historical or social theories. Yet there are two clear conflicts in the book. One is that of Natty against Judge Temple. They are two gentlemen with functions which inevitably clash. The other is that of the two gentlemen together against a lout and a pseudo-gentleman together.

A former Quaker, Marmaduke Temple had come to the New York frontier to found the establishment of a country gentleman. He had not lost the philanthropy of the Friend in becoming a gentleman, as indeed true courtesy would not have permitted. Cooper is careful to measure justly his willingness to invest cash and energy in his pioneer experiment. Both in character and in the sense of responsibility, he is in direct contrast to his cousin Richard Jones. Jones is a braggart, a timid bully, a little man who would like to be a gentleman but who does not know how.

Natty, at his least attractive in *The Pioneers*, has still many of the characteristics which make him the knight of the wilderness. He has all his usual candor and integrity. His gift for spectacular action appears when he rescues Elizabeth Temple from a wildcat and a forest fire. In spite of the accent placed on his vulgarities of diction and manner, he has much of his inherent dignity and courtesy. The person in his own group with whom Natty clashes is Billy Kirby, the plundering woodsman. The conflict is over the proper use to be made of the abundance with which God has stocked the wilderness. Natty maintains that the law of the woods, the law of God, is that men may use anything which they need but may not waste or wantonly destroy as Kirby does. This is the law of Adam which, since Natty is a type of Adam, he observes throughout Cooper's works. On this issue, as on most others, the Judge concurs with Natty, and Richard Jones with Billy Kirby.

The battle between the Judge and Natty is joined on the same ground. The Judge attempts to create and to enforce game laws for the good of the settlement, and Natty will have nothing to do with them. To Natty, the Judge's attempt to prevent him from using the good things of the forest, especially venison, whenever he needed them was contrary to God's law. He would not obey the Judge's law. "I hold to a white man's respecting white laws, so long as they do not cross the track of a law comin' from a higher authority," Cooper makes him say in *The Deerslayer*. He is not opposed to law; he is not a leveller or a rampant materialist. He simply insists upon living by the ancient law of the forest which is made obsolete by the Judge and his civilization.

The Judge holds that civilization must have the powers necessary for its survival, though he values Natty personally. Even Elizabeth, who owes life and happiness to Natty, is made to comment, "Neither were we so silly as to wish such a thing, could we convert these clearings and farms, again, into hunting-ground, as the Leatherstocking would wish to see them." There is nothing for Natty to do but wish civilization well, leave his friends with their difficulties resolved by the marriage of Elizabeth and the original Edward Effingham, and disappear into a new wilderness. In one sense, then, *The Pioneers* is a historical epic. It shows two great gentlemen in a necessary conflict in which neither is morally wrong. They are agreed on the necessity of using the gifts of nature wisely. But they clash because Natty is the knight of the wilderness and Judge Temple belongs to the class of true gentlemen whose business is the furthering of civilization. Natty's law is right in its time and its place, and the Judge's law in its. The progress of civilization and the process of history are greater than either of them, though they serve that process equally. But Cooper thinks that Natty must give way before the Judge just as greater gentlemen must someday come to displace Marmaduke Temple and the pioneer period in their turn.

## IV

Some understanding of the other novels may be gained from the observation that they display a hierarchy of gentlemen. This starts with the false or anti-gentleman, and it rises, through a number of interesting partial gentlemen, to the level of that man "without a worldly superior," the true American gentleman. Accusing his Whig attackers of secretly wishing to be gentlemen while they hypocritically extolled the common man, Cooper poured out his bile upon them. "No meanness is impossible to a demagogue—a pretender to things of which he has even no just conception—a man who lives to envy and traduce; in a word, a *quasi*-gentleman," he said.[19] These are "the monstrous off-spring of peculiar circumstances . . . a species of gentry perfectly *sui generis*," he said. "I compare the gentlemen of no country to these philosophers.[20] These are the men who take advantage of the chaotic circumstances of the second period of American history to set themselves up for gentlemen, though they have none of the true elements of "the character." They slander and oppose true gentlemen.

Perhaps the worst of these was the editor Steadfast Dodge, of *Homeward Bound*. He was hopelessly below the gentlemanly level "in principles, manners, character, station, and everything else." He was "a demagogue and hypocrite in his ordinary practice; one whose chief motive was self, and whose besetting passions were envy, distrust and malice." It was he who worked to make life in Templeton unbearable for the Effinghams on their return. Almost as bad was Jason Newcome, the Yankee schoolmaster who with his vulgar descendants represented villainy in the Anti-Rent Trilogy. Though it was "impossible" from the start to accept him as a gentleman, he did his best to worm himself into the society of the Littlepages. Failing, he retired to the frontier community which they had founded in upstate New York. There he turned envy and chicanery into a way of life. It was this which led to the upsurge of the Anti-Rent War against the Littlepages.

The second group is made up of men who were born with the potentialities of gentlemen but who never acquired the true gentleman's gifts. These are of all ranks. The most humble, perhaps, was the bee-hunter of *Oak Openings,* Benjamin Boden. Out courting, "he spoke with a simplicity and truth that imparted to his manner a natural grace that one bred in courts might have envied . . . with a delicacy that few in courts would deem necessary . . ." Aristabulus Bragg's indeterminate character we have already noticed. Blessed at birth with the potentialities of a gentleman, he had received no further advantages at all. And his education in the school of Steadfast Dodge had nearly ruined him. Guert Ten Eyck had not been spoiled by Dodgeism. "All the books in the world could not have converted Guert Ten Eyck into a Jason Newcome, or Jason Newcome into a Guert Ten Eyck . . . Nature had . . . drawn broad distinctions between them. All the wildness of Guert's impulses could not altogether destroy his feelings, tone, and tact as a gentleman; while all the soaring, extravagant pretensions of Jason never could have ended in elevating him to that character." [21] Andries Coejemans, the older and wiser Chainbearer, was sounder than giddy young Guert. Of good family, gentlemanly instincts, and some knowledge of the respectable world, he was handicapped only by lack of education. In character he had few peers.

The third class, genuine gentlemen, is made up of those who, out of the second period struggle, have proved their qualities and risen into the magic sphere. Cooper never set a novel in the tranquillity and security of his accomplished dream. His books had to have action and struggle.

*The Sea Lions* takes Cooper far away from the frontier, land-bound situation for which his historical theory was invented. Yet it shows how any young man starting with the character and instincts of the gentleman but little wealth, education, or polish can prove himself by grasping at great chances, and emerge a gentleman. Instead of going to an agrarian frontier, Roswell Gardiner sails to the Antarctic to hunt seals. He has courage and hardihood, like the "magnanimity" which Elizabethans admired. He goes to sea, moreover, with "a little case that contained about a hundred volumes of different works" by which his education is considerably improved. When his unscrupulous rival, Daggett, is shipwrecked in the Antarctic, with winter impending, Roswell shows the stuff of the gentleman. He risks disaster to help Daggett get his ship refitted and is then forced to delay while Daggett avariciously tries to make up for the lost catch. Daggett, realizing that Roswell is "a spirited and generous-minded man," skilfully appeals to his sense of honor by throwing himself on Roswell's mercy, thus forcing a delay until the fearful Antarctic winter has closed down upon them. With poetic justice, however, Daggett loses his life during the winter, and Roswell returns in the spring with an immensely valuable cargo which makes it possible for him to marry and found a family.

A somewhat similar case is that of Mark Woolston. It is he who founds the model society of *The Crater*. Shipwrecked on a barren crater, he and a lone friend transform it into a burgeoning garden. Eventually he is rescued and returns to the United States to bring out colonists to his little Eden. Naturally, he is then made governor of the settlement. Woolston's story, of course, is skilful special pleading. Here is a lad of good family, some education, and extraordinary talents. He improves a plot of barren rock into a perfect home for man. Thus he gains great wealth, which, added to his personal talents, gives him political power and prestige. Why, asks Cooper, should not such a man, granting him a concern for the welfare of the community, be its governor? Who is there fitted so well to perform the task? Have not our gentlemen created much of our prosperity, established most of our civilization?[22] American history is fed to the reader of *The Crater* in capsule form. And the ultimate catastrophe is Cooper's warning that if Americans persecute their gentlemen individually and deny them their proper place of leadership as a class, there will be a social catastrophe as terrible as the eruption of the hidden volcano beneath the crater. As a gentleman-character in his own right, Woolston is a complete failure. From the time he ceases to be the breezy young sailor and pioneer whom Cooper could do well, he is simply a stuffed allegory.

A third young sailor, Miles Wallingford, started higher and became more securely a great gentleman than either Gardiner or Woolston. More significantly, he faced the turmoil of second period America and won out. Though he achieved manhood and wealth on the sea, his real battle was against commercial materialism and artificial gentility, rather than against mere levellers, and it was fought on land. His great problem was to win the love of Lucy Hardinge, a girl with whom he had been reared but who was a step above him on the social ladder. Fortunately, Miles had a chance to benefit from association with the cultivated Mertons during a long voyage which included a period of shipwreck. He returned from the sea much more the man of the world than when he embarked. Having also improved his financial situation and gained the habit of command as a successful sea-captain, he was well prepared to sustain himself against the foolish notions of Lucy's brother, Rupert, and his servile imitation of things British.

By the end of the second novel, Miles has been completely justified. Lucy has taken him as a true gentleman over a foppish friend of Rupert's. Rupert, having turned out to be a puerile Lovelace, has jilted Miles's sister, broken her heart, and absconded with as much of Lucy's inheritance as he could lay his hands on. Miles and Lucy between them, however, have made their place the finest in a notable country gentleman's society. They shed peace, joy, and prosperity upon a whole countryside and are, of course, founding a family of immense promise. Admitting that no romantic writer like Cooper confines himself to the dull planes of actual biography for long, Miles is pretty much a self-portrait. With his origin in the country gentry, his early flight to sea and view of the sordid side of London, and his marriage a step above himself in the social scale, he matches Cooper much more closely than does, for instance, Edward Effingham.

The greatest of Cooper's gentlemen are those who reverse the process of history. They come out of assured position as gentlemen into the struggles of a first or second period situation. This is the story of Judge Temple of *The Pioneers,* the Effinghams of *Homeward Bound* and *Home as Found,* and the Littlepages of the Anti-Rent Trilogy. Although Corny Littlepage denies at length that his family is equal to great gentry such as the Morrises of Morrisania and the DeLanceys, they are unquestionably gentlemen. Corny is given a college education. After he has saved the life of the girl he loves, he is thanked by her father with words that indicate a respect far above that called for by gratitude, especially when they come from so great a man as Herman Mordaunt: " 'I am thankful that the debt of gratitude I owe you, my young friend,' he said . . . is due to the son of a gentleman I so much esteem as Evans Littlepage. A loyal subject, an honest man, and a well-connected and well-descended gentleman, like him, may well be the parent of a brave youth, who does not hesitate to face even lions in defense of the weaker sex.' "

By founding the great estate at Ravensnest, Corny participates in a first-period situation. But he passes on to his son, Mordaunt Littlepage, an impregnable gentility. Mordaunt can add to his father's heritage the great wealth of Herman Mordaunt, the vast estate of Ravensnest, social position without peer gained from his mother, and, more intrinsically, the almost perfect character and training which the combined superiority of his father and mother have given him. Consequently, Mordaunt is able to consolidate himself at Ravensnest when it enters period two despite the worst efforts of Jason Newcome and his henchmen *(The Chainbearer).* And his son, Hugh Littlepage, stems the highest tide of the whole levelling crew, the arson plot attendant on the anti-rent war, with comparative ease *(The Redskins).*

All the Littlepages have character, talent, and courtesy. They are all well-educated both in books and the world. The most important fact which Cooper wanted to show about them, however, was that by their talents, wealth, good-will, social and political power they had created in the American wilderness the possibilities of civilization. They inaugurated the familiar first period and prevented the second period from engulfing the possibilities of civilization in ruthless materialism and envious levelling. There was much to be hoped for from them when the final period of their dominance had been reached and they were free to shed prosperity and tranquillity forever upon their inferiors.

So much more is said of the personal excellence of the Effinghams as gentlemen that it seems clear that Cooper's aim with them was different from his purpose in creating the Littlepages. The view of the Effinghams is microscopic compared to the wide binocular sweep over the field of American social history which we get in the Littlepage Manuscripts. In *Homeward Bound* and *Home as Found* Cooper was fighting for the recognition of the right of the gentleman to be valued for his personal excellence by a society which attacked him for daring to be different from the mob. This is why the portraits of Edward and John Effingham are in Cooper's terms the most brilliant of his gentlemen. They illustrate every outstanding quality of "the caste." John is "a man of cultivated mind, of extensive intercourse with the world," of an impeccable, if somewhat cold manner, and of too vigorous a personality.[23] Where John is acrimonious, Edward, while not pliant, is calm and tolerant. He is without peer for courtesy, cultivation, integrity, and beauty of taste and speech.[24]

For the matter of the Effingham participation in the historical process one must hark back to *The Pioneers*. There they appear upon the first period scene as gentlemen, unite themselves with the family of Judge Temple, and so come through the pioneer period on the very top of the heap. There is no suggestion that their influence as members of the class of gentlemen can be nullified by Steadfast. Dodge. The books in which they figure as gentlemen standing off the encroachments of competitive levellers are essentially protests against the undervaluation of them by a society blinded by struggle.

What the conjunction of all these true Cooper gentlemen with the historical process seems to prove is that Cooper read history in such a way as to achieve a faith that no matter how long and bitter the struggle the gentleman would always emerge victorious. The warning he principally conveyed to his countrymen was that if they struggled too long and too hard against the gentleman, they would set back the flowering of their civilization by unnecessary years or generations. But that Cooper misread the images in his historical crystal ball is now much less important than the fact that the intensity of his concern for the agrarian gentleman stimulated him to write many of his novels.

# CHAPTER EIGHT

## DR. HOLMES AND THE BEST SOCIETY VIRUS

THE LOSS of the class of gentry, the rise of plutocratic wealth, and the dominance of middle-class and competitive attitudes in America all contributed to the emergence of the notion of society-page Society. Fundamentally this has been a prestige-system which hinges upon the belief that a line, supposed to be metaphysical but often financial, could be drawn between 'acceptable' and 'unacceptable' people. At worst it has degenerated into the "social game" stingingly summarized by Dixon Wecter in the "Blue Book" chapter of his *Saga of American Society*. Its bathetic *Iliad* is Ward McAllister's pudgy *Society as I Have Found It* (1890). Some of its practitioners fumbled intellectually with the tradition of the gentleman. But for the most part they were defenseless against the tonic attacks of the 1920's on the fuzzy semantics and petty hypocrisies of their effort to rationalize Success into Good Society. And despite the twenties, the drive for distinctions however small has carried the 'Best Society' virus deep into American life. The inhabitant of Whistlestop, Michigan, says in all seriousness of his friend from the neighboring crossroads, "He belongs to the aristocracy of East Whistlestop."

Of all the hundreds of literary carriers of the 'Best Society' virus, the most charming was Oliver Wendell Holmes, the Autocrat of the Breakfast Table. Post-bellum Boston "had a silver age of urbanity and culture," says Harry Hayden Clark, "and Holmes, the laureate of banquets, was its mouthpiece." [1] Holmes was one of the most successful of diners-out on record: a supremely articulate one who produced high quality *vers de societé* at the drop of a perfumed invitation into his mail-box. In Emerson's terms, if one forgets about an adequate function for the gentleman, Holmes's was the apotheosis of Society's Gentleman.

With every suspicion of vice Bostonized away, Holmes was back at the fine gentleman again. "What constitutes a gentleman?" he asked himself in his character of the Professor. The answer was a little list "adapted to particular classes of questioners"—incipient cads:

    a. Not trying to be a gentleman.
    b. Self-respect underlying courtesy.
    c. Knowledge and observance of the *fitness of things* in social intercourse.
    d. £. s. d. (as many suppose) [2]

Or again, the gentleman is characterized by,

    Good dressing, quiet ways, low tones of voice, lips that can wait, and eyes that do not wander,—shyness of personalities, except in certain intimate communions,—to be *light in hand* in conversation, to have ideas, but to be able to make talk, if necessary, without them,—to belong to the company you are in, and not to yourself,—to have nothing in your dress or furniture so fine that you cannot afford to spoil it and get another like it, yet to preserve the harmonies, throughout your person and dwelling.[3]

There are important elements of the tradition here. Especially there is the urge to urbanity and grace of living. But it is the grace of the "beautiful but useless begonia." It condoned the disinclination of the dominant plutocracy to assume its social and cultural responsibilities.

There are several obvious reasons for Holmes's having become the spokesman for such a position. His post among the delights and distinctions of Boston mercantile society was gained the hard way. The scion of a scholarly, clerical, Cambridge family, he won access to the gracious life of the hub of the universe only by tugging himself up to literary celebrity and by his extraordinary conversational technique.[4] His success was complete, but the concentration necessary to it made him what W. D. Howells called extremely Boston-minded.[5] The Boston which monopolized his attention was only that segment directly related to his great social adventure. Out of sympathy with reforming, idealistic Boston, he seems hardly to have known that proletarian, immigrant, Irish Boston existed. His was Proper Boston.

I

As a scientist as well as an adherent of the best society, Holmes was repelled by the wooliness of transcendental idealism. Commonsense treatment of facts as facts, whether in the sickroom or the drawing room appealed to Dr. Holmes. The question to him was not how gentlemen *ought* to be recognized but how they actually were in the Back Bay. And as an early adherent of Darwinian theories of natural selection, Holmes was fortified in his admiration of the local aristocracy. The fittest, who had climbed to the top competitively, had good heredity and the best of environments to help keep them on top. Perhaps there was something to the old idea of blood after all. If some fell and new ones rose to take their places, well and good—in time the new ones would match the best of the old.

Medical professor Holmes's genetic theories made him repudiate the notion of individual responsibility for evil. They profoundly affected both his Unitarian revolt against his father's hell-fire Calvinism and his precedence of Clarence Darrow and Harry Elmer Barnes in preaching amoral criminology. They also stimulated his writing, particularly the "medicated novels"—*Elsie Venner, The Guardian Angel, A Mortal Antipathy.* In *Elsie Venner,* alongside the Gothic notion that venom prenatally absorbed by the heroine makes her want to act like a rattlesnake, runs the tale of true love between Helen Darley and Bernard Langdon, each of whom can tell at a glance that the other is gently born and bred. It was for Langdon that Holmes coined the phrase which has since been corruptly extended to all genteel Boston: "the Brahmin caste." Langdon's actions throughout the novel were largely given to proving that he was a special sort of gentleman. Though Holmes admitted that sometimes Brahmins became allied to plutocrats, he mocked "a critic in ground-glass spectacles" who called the Brahmins a "bloated aristocracy." Really, said he, "they are very commonly pallid, undervitalized, shy, sensitive creatures, whose only birthright is an aptitude for learning."[6]

What is the Brahmin caste of New England? It is a "harmless, inoffensive, untitled aristocracy" of scholars. In contrast to New England's fleeting plutocracy, usually genteel poor three generations after it becomes *nouveau riche,* the Brahmins are a caste, even a race, because "aptitude for learning" is "congenital and hereditary" and scholars are the sons of scholars.[7] In his best scientific manner Holmes described the species in his life of Emerson, whom he considered a choice specimen:

> We have in New England a certain number of families who constitute what might be called the Academic Races. Their names have been on college catalogues for generation after generation. They have filled the learned professions, more especially the ministry, from the old colonial days to our own time. If aptitudes for the acquisition of knowledge can be bred into a family as the qualities the sportsman wants in his dog are developed in pointers and setters, we know what we may expect of a descendant of one of the Academic Races. Other things being equal, he will take more naturally, more easily, to his books. His features will be more pliable, his voice will be more flexible, his whole nature more plastic than those of the youth with less favoring antecedents. The gift of genius is never to be reckoned upon beforehand, any more than a choice new variety of pear or peach in a seedling; it is always a surprise, but it is born with great advantages when the stock from which it springs has been long under cultivation.[8]

Out of the usual tradition and far from the theocracy which had bred that race of "minister's boys"[9] to which Holmes himself belonged, nothing is said of Brahmin stewardship or of gentlemanly function in life for them. They are expected to be, not do (there is one of the cords that bound Henry Adams). It is enough if among them appear the "half a dozen men, or so" who carry in their brains as "rudimentary ideas or inchoate tendencies" the *"ovarian eggs* of the next generation's or century's civilization."[10]

Yet if this was true for Brahmins, it was true for gentlemen as a group. Holmes recognized cultural sports—natural gentlemen —as well as biological ones. The law of physiology expressed itself in New England in "pitch-pine Yankees and white-pine Yankees . . . a native aristocracy, a superior race." And the "last born nobleman I have seen . . . was pulling a rope that was fastened to a Maine schooner loaded with lumber." The right series of "felicitous crosses" might even produce a natural Brahmin— "the large uncombed youth who goes to college and startles the hereditary class-leaders by striding past them all" with the fresh virility he brings from the soil.[11] "That," Holmes snapped, "is Nature's republicanism; thank God for it, but do not let it make you illogical."[12]

Heredity counts in the long run. One could even be born a cad. The best blood comes from the soil, no doubt. But, "as a general thing, you do not get elegance short of two or three removes from the soil." Let us admire a "self-made man whittled into shape with his own jack-knife," said Holmes; but *"other things being equal,* in most relations of life, I prefer a man of family." The most precious "republican privilege" was "the right of strict social discrimination of all things and persons, according to their merits." For the man of family was surrounded by helpful environmental factors like good society, the knowledge of distinguished ancestry, family portraits, a library, silver, and a fine residence.[13]

Admiring the Brahmins was all very well; most of what Holmes could say about them applied more or less to himself. But as a disciple of the Boston plutocracy who could be proud of having won himself a plutocratic competence for the keeping up of appearances, Holmes was perfectly candid. In spite of the hypocrisy and all the "silly stuff" of frivolous moralists, he often said, what we have in America is a "chryso-aristocracy." The thing that counts is money.[14] He loved all the little comforts and rituals of opulence, listing in his poem "Contentment" all the luxuries he was ready to forswear—in moderation! As the Poet at the Breakfast-Table he made another such list and commented, "For the life of me I cannot see anything Satanic in all this."[15]

Fine clothes well kept are throughout his volumes an index of gentlemanliness. In *A Mortal Antipathy* the most rustic characters can tell that a gentleman has come to board with them by his appreciation of "good cookin'" and by the quality (observations made on wash-day) of his underwear. Bourgeois pettinesses and efforts to be genteel in reduced circumstances made his snubbed nose wrinkle. Let the fires roar and live expansively, or go back to the farm, he said.[16] From his Parisian experience as a medical student he wrote his family that he must have $1200 a year to have "a certain degree of ease connected with my manner of living," short of extravagance, or come home.[17] This is not out of the main tradition of gentlemanly liberality and excellence in living: unless Holmes protests too much.

He was devoted to the Gospel of Success. In *Elsie Venner* the Professor told Bernard Langdon on his leaving medical school:

> You are made for the best kind of practice . . . When a fellow like you chooses his beat, he must look ahead a little . . . Go for the swell-fronts and south-explosure houses; the folks inside are just as good as other people, and the pleasantest, on the whole, to take care of. They must have somebody, and they like a gentleman best. Don't throw yourself away. You have a good presence and pleasing manners. You wear white linen by inherited instinct. You can pronounce the word *view*. You have all the elements of success; go and take it. Be polite and generous, but don't undervalue yourself. You will be useful, at any rate; you may just as well be happy, while you are about. The highest social class furnishes incomparably the best patients, taking them by and large.[18]

And in an author's aside Holmes brilliantly resolved the Gospel of Success into its prime elements of ego-preening appeal. "A young man, using large endowments wisely and fortunately, may put himself on a level with the highest in the land in ten brilliant years of spirited, unflagging labor. And to stand at the very top of your calling in a great city is something in itself—that is, if you like money, and influence, and a seat on the platform at public lectures, and gratuitous tickets to all sorts of places where you don't want to go, and, what is a good deal better than any of these things, a sense of power, limited, it may be, but absolute in its range, so that all the Caesars and Napoleons would have to stand aside, if they came between you and the exercise of your special vocation."[19]

Two contradictory ideas keep Holmes's thought clear of Horatio Algerism. Wealth strengthens gentility by creating the special environment which confirms heredity and passes it on more powerful than before, he thought. Wealth is untrustworthy, often immoral; and its possessors almost always lose it in three generations.

Regardless of where it comes from, Holmes says, in his bedside manner again, "money kept for two or three generations transforms a race . . . in blood and bone." The children get "air and sunshine" with "good nursing, good doctoring, and the best cuts of beef and mutton." When they grow up their wealth will allow them to "afford the expensive luxury of beauty" in their mates and raise "the physical character of the next generation." Beauty, suavity, and sensibility are almost a monopoly of the rich.[20]

The only way to reconcile that exaltation of the chryso-aristocracy with Holmes's other assumptions about the influence of wealth is to see that his good gentleman is good for nothing in particular. To him beauty has come at the price of the sapping of his whole character. And though Holmes suggests that,[21] he would hardly have been willing to defend it very long. Partly he was caught between two wishes. He loved to admire

Boston plutocrats, whose virtue could be taken for granted. He snapped and snarled at the "accursed" poison of "mercantile materialism" which produced the gigantically menacing millionaires of the American mainland psychologically so remote from Holmes.[22] "The spiritual standard of different classes I would reckon thus," he said once:
1. The comfortably rich.
2. The decently comfortable.
3. The very rich, who are apt to be irreligious.
4. The very poor, who are apt to be immoral.[23]

From the irreligious very rich, he surmised during the first bitter industrial strife of the nineteenth century, only a well-administered scheme of *"Richesse oblige"* could save the country. Otherwise they would drive it into chaos.[23] He never took the idea any further. But he did, paradoxically, think that three generations of spending and inheriting money reduced it to " scanty competences for . . . ancient maidens." [24] The result was the decaying gentility so congenial to his contemporaries the Local Colorists. Holmes called them "slack-water gentry";[25] but he never thought to explain why the personal superiority of blood and bone given the rich by their wealth did not empower them to stay rich through the successive generations. It would, as Cooper could have told him, have been hard to explain.

When there was no need to apologize, Holmes came back gratefully to the Brahmins. There he played on his home court. They showed what it meant to have family traditions and "the cumulative humanities of at least four or five generations," to have tumbled about a library as a child.[26] The truth, he once said, about the problem of determinism was that man's free will was like a drop of water imprisoned in a ball of crystal. "The fluent, self-determining power of human beings is a very strictly limited agency in the universe. The chief planes of its enclosing solid are, of course, organization, education, condition . . . Education is second only to nature."[27] To dramatize that, one could contrast Achilles with James Russell Lowell. Achilles was "a very noble gentleman in point of courage, lofty bearing, courtesy, but an unsoaped, ill-clad, turbulent, high-tempered young fellow" rather like John L. Sullivan. But Lowell shows that " 'self-made' is imperfectly made" and that it takes "the union of exceptional native gifts and generations of training to bring the 'natural man' of New England to the completeness of scholarly manhood."[28] It takes a full, literary, liberal education and the cultivation of all the arts of the beautiful to produce the right sort of gentleman. Holmes himself was especially fond of "good old gentlemanly reading" like the odes of Horace.[29]

## II

Ardently in love with the exquisite balance and sensitivity of the best Bostonians, Holmes went back almost directly to Chesterfield for his theories on courtesy. Repeatedly through his writings he thought up new images and new settings in which to say that the best manners were the normal expression of good will. Like Cooper he never tired of showing how simple and free from pose and fuss these natural manners are. And Holmes also fell into the trap of all the panting little books on etiquette in discussing the conventions of society and its need for smoothness. "Good-breeding *never* forgets that *amour-propre* is universal," he pontificated.[30] Therefore the desire to be courteous in society makes us liars "—not absolute liars, but such careless handlers of the truth that its sharp corners get terribly rounded."[31] Physician and amateur psychologist, Holmes approached the insights of Freud in observing how the "thin film of politeness separates the unspoken and unspeakable current of thought from the stream of conversation."[32] After all, he wrote, swooping back to the tradition of the fine gentleman, "Good-breeding is *surface-Christianity.*" It excludes from social intercourse everything that might possibly cause pain.[33]

Though Holmes would have bristled at the suggestion of anything out of keeping with the famous Boston morality, this view of courtesy is morally dangerous. Where does one draw the line which makes morality possible? When does he stop lying and why? With Beacon Street virtue to count on, he had no need to worry about such problems, perhaps; but other people did. Further, that way led the pressing futility of a genteel tradition. Seeing more truly than Emerson, perhaps, the state of gentlemen in America deprived of their class, Holmes made the fatal error of the empiricist and allowed his ideal concept to become merely a description of the average facts. No such description is valid long. The ideal which sifts out the more promising facts and seeks to shape the future in an ideal direction may be more valid later than when it was written.

At any rate, Holmes saw that in his America outstanding men had all been "decanted off from their historic antecedents and their costume of circumstance into the every-day aspect of the gentlemen of common cultivated society."[34] Like the fine gentleman of the eighteenth century *beau monde,* he decided that success in that fashionable society was an end in itself. Such success came, he knew, in a struggle as ruthlessly competitive as that for biological survival. Young ladies must learn 'that the 'struggle for life' Mr. Charles Darwin talks about reaches to vertebrates clad in crinoline, as well as to mollusks in shells, or articulates in jointed scales, or anything that fights for breathing-room and food and love in any coat of fur or feather!"[35] That is why fashionable society requires "rich natures" and "vitality above all things." He gloried in dash and dandyism shining at exclusive affairs.[36] The only repulsive fine gentleman he ever drew was one who tried to take a nice girl off into the "misery of semi-provincial fashionable life" with its social round of petty ennui and materialism.[37] That was wicked, not because it was worldly, but because it was unsuccessfully so. The question Howells and more and more Americans were to raise was the intensely American "So what? What does all this come to in the end?" Stripped of all but glitter, Best society eventually stripped itself of all significance for the American mind.

From his soul a rebel against evangelical Calvinism, Holmes repudiated very coolly the tradition of the Christian gentleman.

To be sure, a gentleman should have his religion. But he should folow the "lines of social cleavage," be an Episcopalian or Unitarian, and "be a gentleman in his hymns and prayers."[38] Smugly he wrote pious Harriet Beecher Stowe that he could not imagine how anything in the conversation reported between Jesus and Nicodemus could have been unfamiliar to "a 'master in Israel.' After all, love and obedience must be formed in the character somehow, before it is fit for the *best company*." The conversion experience so central to American evangelism, he held, was for the lower classes only. Members of the upper classes had a "kind of congenital conversion" through birth and education which brought them to "the most elevated . . . moral and religious standard."[39] He might "reluctantly" find Byron guilty of a certain *"vulgarity."*[40] But it was easy to smile and admit how easily "Timidity, and after her Good-nature, and last of all Polite-behavior" chip the sparkling cubes of truth down to dingy spheres of falsehood.[41]

Though not for Cooper's reasons of social good, Holmes agreed with him that the gentleman had to be independent of society at large. Thus he excused himself from participating in the Boston mania for reform. Self-respect and self-determination were together the badge of gentlemanliness and the key to Western civilization, he said.[42] It would be interesting to compare his historical gentlemen with those of Emerson. Holmes liked dandies who had pluck, men of "audacious self-esteem with good ground for it": Wellington, "Brummel and D'Orsay and Byron," Alcibiades, Aristotle, Marcus Antonius, Sir Humphry Davey, and Lord Palmerston.[43] Emerson might have rated Aristotle as God's Gentleman, or he might not; Wellington Davey and Palmerston as fair to middling Society's Gentlemen; the rest could have been only run-of-the-mill or even spurious. But Holmes loved his dandies.

Howells, who wrote that Holmes had a tendency to look at other people over the broken bottle-tops set in his garden wall, remembered that he "liked his fences" and had deliberately made him feel their presence. Holmes enjoyed exercising h "democratic liberty of choice" and being socially exclusive.⁴⁴ Proud self-respect and audacious dandyism he thought a fine thing—until they were extended to him. Then he struck out with normal resentment. A lady who "nips off the end of a brittle courtesy, as one breaks off the tip of an icicle, to bestow upon those whom she ought cordially and kindly to recognize, proclaims the fact that she comes not merely of low blood, but of bad blood," he said. ". . . An official of standing was rude to me once. Oh, that is the maternal grandfather—said a wise old friend to me—he was a boor."⁴⁵ He recalled with pain "the social knee-action I have often seen in the collapsed dowagers who lifted their eyebrows at me in my earlier years."⁴⁶

The same need of a competitive little man for props to his ego appears in his love of the *code duello*. He had none of the opportunities of Jefferson or naval officer Cooper to understand the murderous realities of "the code" which had quite disappeared from Boston. A bantamweight with a typical admiration for men who could assert themselves violently and a yen to see other men do so, he exulted in the Civil-War records of upper-class Bostonians, especially his own thrice-wounded son. "I don't believe in any aristocracy without pluck as its backbone," he said. These men had vindicated Boston.⁴⁷ Duelling he thought would do the same thing, when there were no wars, and thus give New England a true aristocracy.⁴⁸

The same ignorance of the limitations of physical courage made Holmes unique as an interpreter of the tradition of gentlemanliness who retained his boyish faith in the moral and social efficacy of the sock-in-the-jaw. He praised young gentlemen who sparred to show their supremacy to "this white-blooded degeneration" he saw overcoming Americans in the days before general participation in sports.⁴⁹ He liked to show his fictional gentleman slugging it out with some blackguard. Brahmin though Bernard Langdon was, he thrashed a bigger and stronger butcher's boy who was his unruly pupil with ease, after tuning up the evening before with a pair of dumbells.⁵⁰ The Professor at the Breakfast Table cheered lustily while the rising young clerk with a heart of gold thrashed the boorish "Koh-i-noor."[51] Holmes's personal weapon, of course, was satire at two removes.

Because Holmes's mind was as atomistic as a charge of buckshot and because he was given to the gospel of success in Best Society, he failed to understand the ancient validation of the gentleman in his function as a leader who conserves the good heritage of the past and hastens the good progress of the present and future. He ignored the special insistence of American theorists that the success of democracy must come from its discovery and use of its natural gentlemen. Believing himself a thorough democrat, he said, "I go politically for *equality* . . . and and socially for *the* quality,"[52] with no apparent sense that there should be any connection. Holmes's mind was in a variety of ways a queer mixture of irreconcilable ways of thinking.[53] His concept of the gentleman remained a self-contradictory rationalization of the dominant but doomed trend of his times.

The distinctions which singled out the Best Society were real, Holmes maintained. Indeed, "of all the facts in this world that do not take hold of immortality, there is not one so intensely real, permanent, and engrossing as this of social position." He enjoyed rehearsing the old tale of the inevitability of strata in society and poking sarcasms at the petty genteel whose ignorance and energy led them into absurdities.[54] With the unction but not the wit which produced his *mot* that Boston was the Hub of the universe, he was sure his Boston gentleman was "the finest sight our private satellite has had the opportunity of inspecting on the planet to which she belongs."[55] Holmes himself inspired Leslie Stephen to write that he had proved "that refinement was compatible with democracy, and that a thorough American might also be the most polished of gentlemen."[s] But the notion which Holmes sponsored, the ideal of the festive glittering, feckless dancing partner, became a poisonous virus to the American concept of the gentleman.

Far from Jefferson's *aristos* or Emerson's gentleman, "the truth's man," the old fine gentleman had degenerated into Rake-Hellism and "the code," swagger instead of courtesy brutality in place of service. The new fine gentleman sank swiftly into inanity. With no function in the life of his times, he dropped into the unmatched vulgarity of Gilded Age conspicuous waste. Or if he had brains and integrity enough to stay clear of that, he drifted into the futilitarian self-pity and bewilderment of a genteel tradition which is portrayed in George Apley, Oliver Alden, and the dozens of imitations and emendations of them. Filtered down to American society as a whole, the daily competitiveness over meaningless and picayune details stimulated by such thinking created a moral atmosphere in many an American town so thick that the literary *sans-culottes* of the 'twenties thought only a thorough breaking of windows could freshen it. Gentlemanliness dissociated from class power and privilege could be assimilated to democracy. Gentlemanliness dissociated from social responsibility could only rot.

## CHAPTER NINE

## GOD'S DEMOCRATIC GENTLEMAN: RALPH WALDO EMERSON

THE vulgarization of the concept which Cooper and Holmes had feared would attend the destruction of the class of gentlemen was no mere phantom of conservative despair. A sub-tradition was growing up which identified snobbery and fine-gentlemanly wickedness with pretenders to the class, and true-gentlemanly virtues and courtesy with the poor and untutored but naturally noble common man. In the Oddfellow's *Casket* which was printed in the Ohio newspaper office of William Dean Howells's family in 1853-54, typical beginnings of that vulgarization may be seen. Really a school-paper of the neighboring Kingsville Academy, the *Casket* carried contributions by the adolescent Howells (not a student), local ministers, and the pupils. In the carefree custom of the day, it plagiarized freely from other publications a steady stream of little items concerning gentlemanliness. These dilute and vulgarize the high tradition of the gentleman for two apparent reasons: they wish to inculcate virtue and courtesy in citizens who can never acquire the traditionally prerequisite disciplines; they are determined to stamp out nostalgia for the class of gentry.

The most illuminating example in the *Casket* of the sort of writing which was appearing all over the country was a double-barrelled sketch entitled "Which Was The Gentleman?" which had been lifted from the *Nashua Telegraph*. The first part describes a snippy young man with "gloved fingers, curling locks, and expensive broadcloth" who jostles a child in the crowded doorway of a lecture hall, crushing her bonnet, and refusing to give her room. When a kindly farmer intervenes, the dandy tells him, "I look out for number one." So the farmer throws him down the stairs: "Which was the gentleman?" The second tale is of a poor girl who is so ogled by a brace of fine gentlemen as she leaves a store that they bring "the color to her cheek and the tear to her eye" and so put her out of countenance that she slips on the ice outside and spills all her groceries on the ground. At this mishap "the two gentlemen burst into a loud laugh"; but a noble youth "whose hands showed that he was accustomed to labor, and whose coarse, well-patched coat, indicated that he was the child of poverty," leaped forward to help her up "with a bow and a smile that would have graced a drawing room." It concludes with admonitions to the boys, who "are all ambitious to be considered gentlemen," of course, that they must never presume on wealth, family, or position, but always be kind, considerate, respectful, and affable.[1]

In themselves there is nothing to be said against such tales except that they are based upon fragmentary considerations. But they herald the onset of the great American success story. In the mode deathlessly labelled "Horatio Alger" it became a principle that the poor boy, if he minded his mother, was always superior to the snotty little rich boy; and that all he needed was luck and pluck to bring him wealth, the banker's daughter, and a chance to outshine his humiliated rival in conspicuous waste. The success story does come from the traditions of the true, Christian gentleman and of the natural gentleman, corrupted and vulgarized to pulp-paper idealizations of acquisitiveness.

Yet Algerism and High Society snobbery did not dominate American thinking about the gentleman entirely. The keepers of the American conscience were also free to work with a major ideal of human excellence no longer compromised by necessary association with political and economic privilege. And Ralph Waldo Emerson, America's foremost prophet of cultural idealism, showed how the ideal of the gentleman could become a living part of the loftiest democratic dream. Something less than philosophy and something more than history or politics to him, thinking about the gentleman suited Emerson's intellectual and temperamental bent. The new freedom of the theory fitted his love of abstract morals and manners. The Protean possibilities which sprang from the extraordinary complexities of the gentlemanly configuration fitted his reluctance to do violence to his worship of intuition by thinking systematically. Interestingly, the gentleman appears almost everywhere in Emerson's prose but seldom in his poetry. It moved him to thought but not to song. And there seem to be no significant turns in Emerson's thought about the gentleman from one end of his career to the other. Evidently he, like Cooper, only elaborated his concept of the essential gentleman through the years.

I

As to the existence of the gentleman Emerson had no doubt. His own historical era, he said in "Manners," would be characterized by the word "gentleman" as much as by the word "Christian." Half the drama and all the novels, from Sidney to Scott, in English literature are devoted to painting this "self-constituted aristocracy, or fraternity of the best" which "is a spontaneous fruit of talents and feelings . . . It is made of the spirit, more than of the talent of men, and is a compound result into which every great force enters as an ingredient, namely virtue, wit, beauty, wealth and power."[2] In a typically Emersonian phrase, the respect paid to "this idea of the Gentleman" came from that "secret homage to reality and love which ought to reside in every man."³ It was simply a *fact,* "as commanding a feature of the nineteenth century and the American republic as of old Rome, or modern England."⁴ That current conditions and usages had made "equivocal . . . all the words in use to express the excellence of manners and social cultivation" was only a cause for careful thought about them:

> The word *gentleman* has not any correlative abstract to express the quality. *Gentility* is mean, and *gentilesse* is obsolete. But we must keep alive in the vernacular the distinction between *fashion;* a word of narrow and often sinister meaning, and the heroic character which *the gentleman* imports . . . The gentleman is a man of truth, lord of his own actions, and expressing that lordship in his behavior . . . beyond this fact of truth and real force, the word denotes good-nature or benevolence: manhood first, and then gentleness. . . . But personal force never goes out of fashion. That is still paramount today, and in the moving crowd of good society the men of valor and reality are known and rise to their natural place.⁵

Emerson confided to his *Journal* in 1839 that he doubted a perfect gentleman could be found "anywhere among the privileged classes." Forty-one years later he recorded that "A gentleman, English, French, or American, is rare; I think I remember every one I have ever seen."⁶ Yet he had no trouble reconciling gentlemanliness and democracy. He rejoiced that Concord tradesmen and farmers had manly dignity and courtesy. "If there is grandeur in You," he insisted, "you will detect grandeur in laborers and washer women." And he held to democratic government as well as to the democratic faith in the individual personality. Although he declared, in anger at "underlings" in Washington who "take the law from the dirtiest fellows," that "any form of government would content me in which the rulers were gentlemen," he had no desire to return to aristocratic government. Like Jefferson, he trusted democratic processes to discover and empower the naturally best men more often than any other system. A travelling American might study the beauties of English aristocracy, but he must always remember that it degraded the "underprivileged classes" and had demonstrated that Birth and Caste could not give society "the benefit of the best leaders." Hence his word to young Americans was both challenging and hopeful. "Let us have our leading and our inspiration from the best,"[7] he cried. "I call upon you, young men, to obey your heart and be the nobility of this land."[8] It was America's destiny to provide the world with the great modern agent of civilization:

> The flowering of civilization is the finished man, the man of sense, of grace, of accomplishment, of social power—the gentleman. What hinders that he be born here? The new times need a new man, the complemental man, whom plainly this country must furnish.[9]

This call for the new, democratic gentleman seemed to Emerson not extreme. Natural aristocracy, he thought like Jefferson, was "a part of the order of Providence." To his *Journal* he said in 1824:

> There are some men, wittily called Nature's Gentlemen, who need no discipline, but grow straight up into shape and grace and can match the proudest dignified demeanor and the gentlest in courtesy. Of these the line in the old song is a thousand times quoted, "My face's my fortune, Sir, she said."[10]

He found examples in persons as different as Napoleon and Plato. Bonaparte was so organically related to his time and place that "the land and sea seemed to presuppose him. He came unto his own, and they received him." And Plato's patrician tastes made him see rightly that the basis of culture is the doctrine of the organic character of caste. In society these distinctions seemed natural and inevitable. Every man finds himself at one time or another in the presence of a personality which commands his own will. He finds in himself the same capacity for domination. On the evidence of his journals this was a persistent belief for Emerson, one which his social experience verified throughout life.

Nature's gentleman had his real superiority from energy and force of will, "Power first, or no leading class."[11] Strength issuing in versatile leadership was his work. As Emersonian Henry Thoreau put it, Sir Walter Raleigh was "one of nature's noblemen" because he had "not a profounder or grander, but so to speak, *more* nature than other men."[12] Nature's gentleman might be a pirate or a politician, a soldier or a scholar, a lawyer or a prince, saint or lumberjack: in any case he was a strong man and a leader. That Homer and Alfred were as great as Goethe and Washington showd that cultural milieu meant little or nothing. "A little additional force of Will in the individual" made all the difference, Emerson thought.

For Emerson even more than for Cooper, self-reliance was the badge of the natural gentleman. For the good of society he must treat it with the same tender high-handedness with which one medicates a child. For his own good he must have the courage to go apart and grow into his rightful stature, serving not precedent or history but his own perception of the beautiful and good. Emerson congratulated mankind on the example of Napoleon, "who took occasion by the beard, and showed us how much may be accomplished by the mere force of such virtues as all men possess in less degrees."[13] In the crisis of the dismayingly long semi-convalescence of his own young manhood he called the courage of the gentleman to his aid, addressing himself:

> Die? pale face, lily liver! go about your business, and when it comes to the point, then die like a gentleman.[14]

He urged the true poet to accept the new nobility of groves and pastures which the opportunities of the art presented. He must leave society and pass "for a fool and a churl for a long season," until his greatness is known. From the first sentence of the essay Emerson equated gentlemanliness and "Heroism." It was the state of the soul at war, suffering all things, attempting all things. For the sake of truth and justice it worked perhaps in contradiction to the voice of society and to the voice even of the great and good, in obedience to its own secret and sacred impulses.

The third mark of Nature's gentleman is his universality He is the man of the common sense, never provincial. Emerson could hardly overemphasize the point; he returned to it constantly:

> Money is not essential, but this wide affinity is, which transcends the habits of clique and caste and makes itself felt by men of all classes. If the aristocrat is only valid in fashionable circles and not with truckmen, he will never be a leader in fashion; and if the man of the people cannot speak on equal terms with the gentleman, so that the gentleman shall perceive that he is already really of his own order, he is not to be feared. Diogenes, Socrates, and Epaminondas, are gentlemen of the best blood who have chosen the condition of poverty when that of wealth was equally open to them. I use these old names, but the men I speak of are my contemporaries. Fortune will not supply to every generation one of these well-appointed knights, but every collection of men furnishes some example of the class: and the politics of this country, and the trade of every town, are controlled by these hardy and irresponsible doers, who have invention to take the lead, and a broad sympathy which puts them in fellowship with crowds, and makes their action popular.[15]

This affinity is best expressed in service. The great man typifies and illustrates his country, making it loveable to all. Plato was "a great average man" who clarified, interpreted, and made useful the dreams and half-thoughts of other men. The use of universal men is that they see through "federal errors" to the wider more permanent reality and preserve us from our contemporaries and ourselves.[16]

Active service, what Emerson called "Gentilesse," is required also. He urged heroic persistency in sympathy and well-doing by which those who enjoyed ease and plenty might prove by generosity and the experience of personal sacrifice their true sympathy with the down-trodden. Echoing John Cotton on the "Calling," he informed the gentleman that "to live without duties is obscene." Nor could these duties be nominal or superficial charities. "The basis of all aristocracy must be truth—the doing what elsewhere is pretended to be done."[17]

The manners and elegance of society are created by the natural gentleman. They are matters not of breeding or of rules but of innate character. Nature's gentleman finds his way into the most exclusive circles and from them excludes the oldest patrician who has lost his "intrinsic rank."[18] "Genius," Emerson explained, "invents fine manners, which the baron and the baroness copy very fast, and, by the advantage of a palace, better the instruction. They stereotype the lesson they have learned, into a mode." In such a way Nature's gentleman makes the rules of society after his own image and attributes. What his own good sense and character dictate are correct.[19] Restraint, poise, and serenity, self-repose beside which the Alleghanies seem like drifting sand, are the qualities of nature's gentleman and the intention of etiquette. Thus Samuel Hoar of Concord, "that true New England Roman," as Dr. Holmes called him, was described by Emerson as "a model of those formal but reverend manners which make what is called a gentleman of the old school, so called under an impression that the style is passing away, but which, I suppose, is an optical illusion, as there are always a few more of the class remaining, and always a few young men to whom these manners are native."[20]

Toward Abraham Lincoln, Emerson's feelings changed, as did those of many Americans, during his Administration. In 1863 Emerson wrote of him rather sourly:

> We must accept the results of universal suffrage, and not try to make it appear that we can elect fine gentlemen. We shall have coarse men, with a fair chance of worthy and manly ability, but not polite men ... You cannot refine Mr. Lincoln's taste, extend his horizon, or clear his judgment; he will not walk dignifiedly through the traditional part of the President of America, but will pop out his head at each railroad station and make a little speech, and get into an argument with Squire A. and Judge B. He will write letters to Horace Greeley, and any editor or reporter or saucy party committee that writes to him, and cheapen himself.
> But this we must be ready for, and let the clown appear, and hug ourselves that we are well off, if we have got good nature, honest meaning, and fidelity to public interest, with bad manners,—instead of an elegant *roué* and malignant self-seeker.[21]

He knew Lincoln was no fine gentleman, but Emerson was New England Brahmin enough rather to sigh for John Quincy Adams. Two years later he had begun to correct his reckoning. Then he saw Lincoln as truly one of Nature's gentlemen well on his way, when his spirituality (what Emerson called *morale*) has been recognized, to becoming God's gentleman:

> Why talk of President Lincoln's equality of manners to the elegant or titled men with whom Everett or others saw him? A sincerely upright and intelligent man as he was, placed in the Chair, has no need to think of his manners or appearance. His work day by day educates him rapidly and to the best. He exerts the enormous power of this continent in every hour, in every conversation, in every act;—thinks and decides under this pressure, forced to see the vast and various bearings of the measures he adopts: *he* cannot palter, he cannot but carry a grace beyond his own, a dignity, by means of what he drops, e. g., all pretension and trick, and arrives, of course, at a simplicity, which is the perfection of manners.[22]

The gentleman, then, was a natural fact to Emerson. Like any other merely natural fact, he was capable of good or evil. If Socrates and Shakespeare were beneficent, Napoleon was pernicious. Therefore Nature's gentleman must be brought under the operation of Emerson's radical ameliorating Law. He must live out a process of transformation through which he moves first to the plane of the Understanding, the worldly level on which the separate facts of life can be rationally shuffled and arranged. There he becomes Society's Gentleman. Ultimately he must discover the plane of the Reason, that high peak whereon the purposes of the universe are grasped; there he may come to be God's Gentleman.

## II

The practical manifestations of Society's Gentleman in society, Emerson said, were "too good for banning, and too bad for blessing."[23] With some hopes for fashionable American society, Emerson was scorching toward its dilettantism, its empty conventions, and its materialism. No one has been more contemptuous of gentility which was outworn, unnatural, irrelevant to the inward vitality of human nature. He felt it his mission to search out for the true leaders of New England the embodiment of their peculiar values in ideals which were real, modern, and able to restore the lost meaning and force of Puritan thought. Understanding the nature of genteel traditions, he saw that Napoleon's appeal in France had come from his representing reality and modernity against a "small class of legitimates, secluded from all community with the children of the soil, and holding the ideas and superstitions of a long-forgotten state of society." Fashionable society he thought "a hall of the Past" where the sons of the great reap the harvest of privilege sown by their fathers: but *their* sons in turn "must yield the possession of the harvest to new competitors with keener eyes and stronger frames."[24]

The superficiality of outworn gentility he resented particularly. The idleness of English aristocrats seemed criminal. He flouted Scott's efforts to play the fine gentleman, saying "we know very well the height of that doll." His contempt for genteel pretentiousness was packed into the phrase describing a novel of George Sand which "shivers the porcelain chesstable of aristocratic contention." Genteel irresponsibility was vicious. Pepys, Swift, Barnet, and Bacon had recorded the illusion amounting to insanity which is the history of English aristocracy. To the time of Victoria the scandals and corruption continued: "sycophancy and sale of votes and honor . . . lewdness, gaming, smuggling, bribery, and cheating; the sneer at the childish indiscretion of quarreling with ten thousand a year; the want of ideas."[25]

Even in America he saw the fatal divorce between faith and morals which Santayana scorned in "the genteel tradition." Cultivated men had become as sedulous to avoid their duties as once they had been to fulfill them. Sentimentalism was blotting out the sense of reality. Perhaps it was himself Emerson flagellated for scorn of men who worked with their hands. "Have you a title to sit in judgment on industrious, effective, producing men," he asked in his *Journal,* men "who have not indulged themselves by sitting in a corner year by year surrounding themselves with new screens from dust, and light, and noise, and vulgarity, but have exposed themselves by labor in the open air to your inspection and criticism? . . . Once these were your mates. Now you are a gentleman. Away with you!"[26]

With the shame of the Fugitive Slave Act stinging him, he analyzed the gentlemen of New England and found them wanting: a judgment he reversed when the war came. But it shows how acutely he perceived and suffered from the evils of that particular genteel tradition and how much of his theory was devoted to finding ways to restore truth and vitality where smugness, unreality, shallowness, and viciousness were. In his *Journal* for 1851 he wrote:

> There are or always were in each country certain gentlemen to whom the honour and dignity of the community were confided, persons of elevated sentiments, relieved, perhaps, by fortune from the necessity of injurious application to arts of gain, and who used that leisure for the benefit of their fellow citizens in the study of elegant learning, the learning of liberty, and in their forwardness on all emergencies to lead with courage and magnanimity against any peril in the State. I look in vain for such a class among us, and that is the worst symptom in our affairs. There are persons of fortune enough and men of breeding and of elegant learning, but they are the very leaders in vulgarity of sentiment. I need call no names. The fact stares us in the face. They are full of sneers and derision, and their reading of Cicero and of Plato and of Tacitus has been drowned under grossness of feeding and the bad company they have kept. It is the want, perhaps, of a stern and high religious training, like the iron Calvinism which steeled their fathers seventy-five years ago. But though I find the names of the old patriots still resident in Boston, it is only the present venerable Mr. Quincy who has renewed the hereditary honour of his name by scenting the tyranny in the gale. The others are all lapped in after-dinner dreams and are as obsequious to Mr. Webster as he is to the gentlemen of Richmond and Charleston. The want of loftiness of sentiment in the class of wealth and education in the University, too, is deplorable. I am sorry to say I predict too readily their feeling. They will not even understand the depth of my regret and will find their own supercilious and foppish version. But I refer them back to their Cicero and Tacitus, and to their early resolutions.[27]

More even than ossified gentility, Emerson feared the materialism of modern life. It poisoned Nature's Gentleman and Society's Gentleman alike. Very early he saw how thoroughly modern history is the product of the ruthless warfare between the conservative *haves* and the hungry *have-nots*. Yet because genteel traditions were weakly wicked, he saw no reason to give way to cynicism. What our present age has been relearning out of total warfare Emerson puts thus: "That is the fatal quality which we discover in our pursuit of wealth, that it is treacherous, and is bought by the breaking or weakening of the sentiments." Bonaparte it had brought to moral destitution. It is not hard to find a handful of modern parallels. Napoleon was a liar and megalomaniac who would steal, slander, assassinate, drown, or poison as his interest dictated. He substituted hatred and selfish vulgarity for generosity and stooped to cheating at cards and opening other people's mail. Toward women his manners were coarse and of a low familiarity. He treated those who did have ethical standards as contemptible "ideologists" whose ideals made convenient weapons against them. "In short, when you have penetrated through all the circles of power and splendor, you were not dealing with a gentleman, at last; but with an impostor and a rogue; and he fully deserves the epithet of *Jupiter Scapin,* or a sort of Scamp Jupiter." The materialism of England has made its aristocracy, if less lurid, little better. Let America take heed. "As long as our civilization is essentially one of property, of fences, of exclusiveness, it will be mocked by delusions. Our riches will leave us sick; there will be bitterness in our laughter; and our wine will burn our mouth. Only that good profits which we can taste with all doors open, and which serves all men."[28]

With all that could be said against it, fashionable society was still too good for banning. "I will," said Emerson, "neither be driven from some allowance to Fashion as a symbolic institution, nor from the belief that love is the basis of courtesy." There is always, he said, "within the ethical circle of good society," a concentration of its true goodness in its leaders. This group is "constituted of those persons in whom heroic dispositions are native, with the love of beauty, the delight in society, and the power to embellish the passing day." By them Nature's

Gentleman is inducted into practical society there to prove and to polish his genius. "Scipio, and the Cid, and Sir Philip Sidney, and Washington, and every pure and valiant heart who worshipped Beauty by word and by deed . . . The theory of society supposes the existence and sovereignty of these."29

Mankind, Emerson would say, tends to cohere socially around certain men. These are Society's gentlemen whose very natures "point at and imply the existence and well-being of all the institutions and orders of a state." Though champions of a rabble, such men are aristocrats. Such were Luther, Milton, and Burke. The love of mankind for whatever "affirms, connects, preserves" gives them their power. As Emerson sketched Society's gentleman,

> One man appears whose nature is to all men's eyes conserving and constructive; his presence supposes a well-ordered society, agriculture, trade, large institutions and empire. If these did not exist, they would begin to exist through his endeavors. Therefore, he cheers and comforts men, who feel all this in him very readily.30

There is a heroism about the social gentleman, but it depends upon his action in the name of service and that alone. What is done must be done for love and to raise "the standard of civil virtue among mankind." This applied in Emerson's mind to himself and his neighbors. "I know no reason," he observed, "why a gentleman, who is, I take it, a natural formation, should not be true to his duties in Boston in 1850, as haughtily faithful, and with as sovereign superiority to all hazards, as his fathers had in 1770 or as Mr. Hampden or Mr. Eliot in London in 1650, or Arundel, or More, or Milton."31

Society's gentleman both conserves and creates the good life or culture. The greatest point in the favor of the English aristocracy was to Emerson that they had been themselves poets, philosophers, scientists, and the patrons of genius, art, and learning. The gentleman should extend everywhere the tastes for the best which all men possess but few can afford:

> . . . A reference to Society is part of the idea of Culture,— Science of a gentleman, Art of a gentleman, Poetry in a

gentleman;—intellectually held, that is, for their own sake, for what they are, for their universal beauty and worth, and not for economy, which degrades them; but not over-intellectually, that is, not to an ecstacy, entrancing the man,—but redounding to his beauty and glory.[32]

Also the gentleman contributes importantly to social progress. A leader by innate right, he promotes the broad, consistent movement of nature to higher and better things. The best result of aristocracy had been that the whole middle class came to share what had formerly been its distinctions. Education had become cheap, and the poet and the scientist were maintained not by patrons but by the public. In 1858 Emerson's concern for abolition made him draw a strong contrast between the true social gentleman devoted to progress and the false type:

> It is impossible to be a gentleman, and not be an abolitionist. For a gentleman is one who is fulfilled with all nobleness, and imparts it; is the natural defender and raiser of the weak and oppressed, like the *Cid*. But these are snobs. In the Southern country, their idea of a gentleman is a striker. There are abundance of their gentlemen garroting in New York streets.[33]

More than deeds, Society's gentleman contributed the sense of manners which created the "social church": "Politeness is the ritual of society, as prayers are of the church, a school of manners, and a gentle blessing to the age . . ."[34] The sense of manners was nearly everything; it required fine perceptions; it paid homage to beauty wherever found. If it did not equal in ultimate importance the moral Law, the human eye, after all, customarily saw only the surfaces of reality. *"Tournure, urbanité, entregent,"* said Emerson, "this is the trinity which makes the creed and the *cultus* of society."[35] Such was the first commandment of good manners, and the second was like it. "If you wish to be loved, love measure." Upon "the discrimination of fit and fair" depend both beauty and the unity of society. "You must have genius, or a prodigious measure of usefulness, if you will hide the want of measure." Reserve and a calm, "creole" smoothness of manners were prescribed. The ingredients of good manners might be summed up as follows:

> Besides [having] personal force and so much perception as constitutes unerring taste . . . good nature,—expressing all degrees of generosity, from the lowest willingness and faculty to oblige, up to the heights of magnanimity and love . . . a certain heartiness and sympathy . . . the favorites of society, and what it calls *whole souls,* are able men and of more spirit than wit, who have no uncomfortable egotism . . .[36]

On this worldly level, manners were to Emerson the organic expression of good will which Locke long ago imagined. If they were not yet God's gentleman's expression of spiritual love, they had their worldly uses. As a railroad track smooths the way, banishing obstructions and "leaving nothing to be conquered but pure space," manners "aim to facilitate life, to get rid of impediments, and bring the man pure to energize." Like Henry James after him, Emerson saw that perfect manners freed one's humanity. The finest English aristocrats showed that. Emancipated from effort and ambition, from tension and stress, they possessed "a pure tone of thought and feeling." As Howells said of Holmes, Emerson rather liked his fences, and the "vast convenience" of manners appealed to him hugely. "The perfect defence and isolation which they effect makes an insuperable protection," he confided to his *Journal.* "Though he wrestle with you, or swim with you, lodge in the same chamber, sleep in the same bed, he is yet a thousand miles off, and can at any moment finish you. Manners seem to say, 'you are you, and I am I.' "[37]

Occasionally Emerson, who thought in his old age that he could remember every gentleman he had even seen, gazetted one shining individual as notably a gentleman. One who represented Society's gentleman at his very best and had many an outreach toward God's gentleman was John M. Forbes of Naushon, Massachusetts, a self-effacing but strong-minded Boston merchant and Civil-War diplomat. To Emerson he seemed to forecast the better American of the future:

> Our gentlemen of the old school, that is, of the school of Washington, Adams and Hamilton, were bred after English types, and that style of breeding furnished fine examples in

the last generation; but, though some of us have seen such, I doubt they are all gone. But Nature is not poorer today. With all our haste, and slipshod ways, and flippant self-assertion, I have seen examples of new grace and power in address that honor the country. It was my fortune not long ago, with my eyes directed on this subject, to fall in with an American to be proud of. I said never was such force, good meaning, good sense, good action, combined with such domestic lovely behavior, such modesty and persistent preference for others. Wherever he moved, he was the benefactor . . . he was the best talker, also, in the company: what with a perpetual practical wisdom . . . and in the temperance with which he parried all offence and opened the eyes of the person he talked with without contradicting him. Yet I said to myself, how little this man suspects, with his sympathy for men and his respect for lettered and scientific people, that he is not likely, in any company, to meet a man superior to himself. And I think this is a good country that can bear such a creature as he is.[38]

To professional idealist Emerson, Society's gentleman was of course not the highest. "I know," he confessed, "that a comic disparity would be felt if we should enter the acknowledged 'first circles' and apply these terrific standards of justice, beauty and benefit to the individuals actually found there . . . Fashion has many classes and many rules of probation and admission; and not the best alone." Nevertheless, he insisted that the ideal rested upon reality. "For fashion," he said, "is not good sense absolute, but relative: not good sense private, but good sense entertaining company." [39] Society's gentleman was to Nature's gentleman as the Understanding was to natural objects. If Nature's gentleman was the individual, outrageous fact, Society's gentleman was the common sense, practical use of him and his talents in organizing the best life for the greatest number of people on the practical level. There was yet God's gentleman in the higher realm.

### III

In Emerson's youth De Tocqueville, assaying democratic society, had complained that there was no class in America "in which the taste for intellectual pleasures is transmitted with hereditary fortune and leisure and by which the labors of the intellect are held in honor. Accordingly, there is an equal want of the desire and the power of application to these objects." [40] Like Holmes who found the name for them—Brahmins— Emerson knew De Tocqueville's error. There was an intellectual class in New England if not in America. It did not have hereditary wealth; but it did, because of the heritage of scholarly prestige from the ancient theocracy, have sound training, intense respect for learning, and assured security. Insisting that "the Scholars are an organic caste or class in the State," Emerson placed the scholar as gentleman somewhere between Society's and God's gentlemen. Like the gentleman the scholar is a fact of nature, "an organic agent . . . in the knitting and contexture of things." [41] If he uses his natural powers truthfully, "the scholar is to be a new potentate," with the gentleman's power and obligation to serve.[42] He can take his place among "the robust gentlemen who stand at the head of the practical class" without hesitation, for "a master likes a master." [43] His manners, too, single him out. When our higher faculties are in harmonious order, do we not act naturally and agreeably? As soon as the places in society are vacated by faded lions and punctured nine-day's wonders, the artist, the scholar, and "in general, the clerisy," re-place them.

As well as the responsibility to serve *(gentilesse)*, the scholar shares the gentleman's universality: "the triumph of culture is to overpower nationality, by importing the flower of each country's genius into the humanity of a gentleman." [44] By the same token the scholar is opposed to materialism and conspicuous waste. "Against the absurdity of expense, we set up the beauty of manner. They think it becoming in a gentleman to spend much for his dinner. We think it becoming to spend little for his dinner, much for his brain," said Emerson. And this the scholar could do commandingly. For the essential nobility of any man or group could be measured by the depth and richness of its ideas. "Knowledge is the only elegance." [45]

The contribution of the scholar to society was that of equilibrium. He filled the eternal want of "one sane man with adequate powers of expression to hold up each object of monomania in its right relations." His appearance on the mental scene meant the expansion of the mind, the description of a wider and freer circle of intellectual experience.

Emerson appreciated Brahminism, hereditary scholarship. Observing that many a scholar had lost "on ruder companions" those boyhood days which alone could have confirmed in him a true, religious esteem of literature, he though that "the chance for appreciation is much increased by being the son of an appreciator, and that these boys who now grow up are caught not only years too late, but two or three births too late, to make the best scholars of." [46] Yet the dry-rot which turned Brahminism into a genteel tradition appalled him. Some scholarly friends he found taking to Ivory-Towerism, sacrificing ends to means and to conservative timidity, prostituting their minds to a tinsel self-indulgence. When "N———[Norton?]" came to see him with his "fine perceptions, his excellent instincts, his beautiful learning, his catholic mind," he was nevertheless begrudged the time he took. Emerson complained:

> He has become the spoiled child of culture; the *roué* of Art and Letters; *blasé* with too much Plato, Dante, Calderon, and Goethe; tickled with music; pampered by his narrow society; amused by ballets; reading novels 'like my Bible'; and so jealous of partialism, so fearful of losing the level of life, that he has not written for three years, . . . but lies like a bit of bibulous paper . . . Farewell my once beautiful genius! I have learned a sordid respect for uses and values: I must have them. I must send him a peat-knife. Are we to say, man shall not go out to the shed to bring an armful of wood, lest this violence of action hurt the balance of his mind? [47]

Though Emerson once rebuked himself for the literary shallowness of the book, which did nothing but "parrot echoes" of the literati, he had already faced the problem of uniting scholarship to reality in *Representative Men*. Goethe, like Napoleon, had opposed the creative impatience of nature to the "*morgue* of conventions." His lesson was simple and direct: to pierce to the truth; to suffer no pretense; "to honor every truth by use." [48] Plato represented the synthesis perfectly. "An original mind in the exercise of its original power," he united abandon and precision, imagination and facts, gentility and reality. "His patrician polish, his intrinsic elegance, edged by an irony so subtle that it stings and paralyzes, adorn the soundest health and strength of frame." [49] He was the scholar as gentleman so far as any human being had yet approached the ideal Emerson expressed in his poem "Culture":

> Can rules or tutors educate
> The semigod whom we await?
> He must be musical,
> Tremulous, impressional,
> Alive to gentle influence
> Of landscape and of sky,
> And tender to the spirit-touch
> Of man's or maiden's eye:
> But, to his native centre fast,
> Shall into Future fuse the Past,
> And the world's flowing fates
> in his own mould recast.

## IV

When Emerson, devotee of the absolute, cast about for some expression of a still more exalted ideal for the gentleman, he found himself recalling the theocracy. True greatness, he remembered, came out of the ages of faith. The beauty and power men covet "rise out of the mountains of rectitude" so that "any extraordinary degree of beauty in man or woman involves a moral charm." [50] Though there has never been true and pure theocracy, still the influence of a Jesus or a Swedenborg has caused the idea to flame periodically. In Emerson's lexicon, to raise a nation to greatness by greatness of character, by the might of the pure in heart, was theocracy; and he believed it could be achieved in his own America by men who would rely purely upon God—Emerson's God. He who depends completely on "his original perceptions of the true and the beautiful . . . is God's gentleman and a new argument to the stoic." [51]

But this self-reliance was not the bumptious egotism partial readers are fond of ascribing to Emerson. It was of his concept of the highest gentleman that Emerson wrote, "The fountains of thought are in the deeps of man, a beauty which reaches through and through, from the manners to the soul; an honor which is only a name for sanctity, a self-trust which is a trust in God himself." [52] The true gentleman would, by and by, be found to mean the man of Conscience; for "only by the supernatural is a man strong; nothing is so weak as an egotist. Nothing is mightier than we, when we are vehicles of a truth before which the State and the individual are alike ephemeral." [53]

Distinguished like Socrates, Herbert, Wordsworth, Milton, and Michael Angelo (sic) by the spiritual power to create which Emerson called the *"morale,"* God's gentleman was not merely ethereal. "Real service," he proclaimed, "will not lose its nobleness. All generosity is not merely French and sentimental; nor is it to be concealed that living blood and a passion of kindness does at last distinguish God's gentleman from Fashion's." [54] Towering morality, not the brutish violence of the duelling bully, is the source of gentlemanly character:

> It is a vulgar error to suppose that a gentleman must be ready to fight. The utmost that can be demanded of the gentleman is that he be incapable of a lie. There is a man who has good sense, is well informed, well read, obliging, cultivated, capable, and has an absolute devotion to truth. He always means what he says, and says what he means, however courteously. You may spit upon him;—nothing could induce him to spit upon you,—no praises, and no possessions, no compulsion of public opinions. You may kick him;—he will think it the kick of a brute; he is not a brute, and will not kick you in return. But neither your knife and pistol, nor your gifts and courting will ever make the smallest impression on his vote or word; for he is the truth's man, and will speak and act the truth until he dies. He is truth's Thug, and goes willingly to ruin for his Thuggee. Is he not a gentleman? [55]

This moral integrity based on religious thought gave the ideal gentleman peculiar powers. He had a sort of magnetism with which to accomplish things. His higher nature overpowered lower ones as a man charms down the resistance of animals, thwarting and benumbing them. So doing, he was given the opportunity to instill his character into the lower nature by the law of the moral universe. Emerson phrased it on his principle that the laws of physics translate the laws of ethics:

> The will of the pure runs down from them into other natures, as water runs down from a higher into a lower vessel. This natural force is no more to be withstood than any other natural force.[56]

His friend, Francis Cabot Lowell, was "a native gentleman," Emerson said, and he came close to being God's gentleman. Though he had opinions and was true to them, he was frank, considerate, and kind. He had practical ability where it was needed. A man "of quiet inward life," he impressed Emerson most with his moral integrity and strong will. He held his own course gently but inexorably. With all he was "scrupulously," almost "romantically honest." Independent, and with "perfect simplicity" of manner, "he was the friend in need, silent but sure, and the character of the giver added rare value to the gift, as if an angel brought you gold." Emerson saw this Lowell's gentlemanliness exemplified in his generosity. He tied Lowell in closely with the ideal gentleman when he said:

> I am forced to add that the cultivated person must have a moral determination. There will be a certain toleration, a letting be and letting do, a consideration and allowance for the faults of others, but a severity to his own. Sportive in manner, inexorable in act. Then in one of my truest gentlemen is an impossibility of taking an advantage. He will not foreclose a mortgage. Such is Frank C. Lowell.[57]

The two main things which Lowell lacked and which were essential to God's gentleman were prophetic saintliness and intrepid cultural leadership.

After all, the real aristocracy is the one in which "each member contributes something real . . . because he is to receive an equivalent in virtue, in genius, in talent, from each other member." [58] This is that dream society of men of good will in which community would be on a level of freedom and affirmation so high that no defenses would be needed. In the days of the Know-Nothing precursors of the twentieth century's Ku Klux Klan, Emerson told young Americans: "If a humane measure is propounded in behalf of the slave, or of the Irishman, or the Catholic, or for the succor of the poor; that sentiment, that project, will have the homage of the hero. That is his nobility, his oath of knighthood, to succor the helpless and oppressed; always to throw himself on the side of weakness, of youth, of hope; on the liberal, on the expansive side, never on the defensive, the conserving, the timorous, the lock-and-bolt system." [59] And of crude, mighty John Brown he said,

> All gentlemen, of course, are on his side. I do not mean by 'gentlemen,' people of scented hair and perfumed handkerchiefs, but men of gentle blood and generosity, 'fulfilled with all nobleness,' who, like the Cid, give the outcast leper a share of their bed; like the dying Sidney, pass the cup of cold water to the dying soldier who needs it more. For what is the oath of gentle blood and knighthood? What but to protect the weak and lowly against the strong oppressor? [60]

This was to "fall into the divine circuits" and be enlarged.[61]

Thinking on the levels of philosophic idealism which seemed almost native to Emerson's mind, he had no difficulty repudiating Cooper's objection to equating saint and gentleman. He who could resist the eminent and polite in the interests of the lowly and do it with sweet temper and good spirit, who could wait cheerfully twenty years for his vindication, was God's gentleman [62]—and a saint. His gentility was of that love which endureth all things. And to it the gentleman's function and courtesy were the same:

> Everything that is called fashion and courtesy humbles itself before the cause and fountain of honor, creator of titles and dignities, namely, the heart of love. This is the royal blood, this is the fire, which, in all countries and contigencies, will work after its kind and conquer and expand all that approaches it. This gives new meanings to every fact. This improverishes the rich, suffering no grandeur but its own. What *is* rich? Are you rich enough to help anybody? To succor the unfashionable and the eccentric? rich enough to make the Canadian in his wagon, the itinerant with his consul's paper which recommends him 'To the charitable,' the swarthy Italian with his few broken words of English, the lame pauper

hunted by overseers from town to town, even the poor insane or besotted wreck of man or woman, feel the noble exception of your presence and your house from the general bleakness and stoniness; to make such feel that they were greeted with a voice which made them both remember and hope? What is vulgar but to refuse the claim on acute and conclusive reasons? What is gentle, but to allow it, and give their heart and yours one holiday from the national caution? Without the rich heart, wealth is an ugly beggar.[63]

To find synthesis of the elements of gentility in a single great principle, the principle of love, was natural to Emerson, the ex-minister, the Transcendentalist. "For it is—is it not?" he asked, "—the essence of courtesy, of politeness, of religion, of love, to prefer another, to postpone oneself, to protect another from oneself. That is the distinction of the gentleman, to defend the weak and redress the injured, as it is of the savage and the brutal to usurp and use others." [64] There is no higher definition.

Finally, "the Gentleman regards only beauty"; [65] it is the atmosphere of all his action and thought. There are manners which exhilarate and refine the onlooker like the perception of beauty itself. But they "must be inspired by a good heart" and express the "wish to scatter joy and not pain around us."[66] Spurning the false, God's gentleman looks to the true, moral beauty, functionally related to his good works. Emerson hated sham and decoration. The benevolent self-repose of the best manners came from the perception of beauty. The essence of the greatness of God's gentleman, one of the most attractive expressions of what it means to be a gentleman, is in the saying credited by Emerson to a wise friend: "When you come into the room, I think I will study how to make humanity beautiful to you." [67]

Emerson knew that God's gentleman must belong to " theoretic peerage" far beyond the moral grasp (or even the will) of most men. 'It would be ignoble, would it not?" he answered, "to draw our sketch from any body necessarily so impure as any that can contrive to exist amidst so much vice injustice, and imbecility as we all confess in our times." Ye dealing with the freed ideal of the essential gentleman, already in jeopardy of entire vulgarization, he acted upon "a regard for the behoof of the race that there should be model men, that we should all have true pictures of such, and, if possible living standards." [68]

Emerson's concept of the gentleman seems to express the very heart of American idealism. There is nothing so thorough, candid, or exalted among either American or British gentlemanly credos. He is in accord with the main tradition from earliest times. The gentleman is initially a product of nature. He is called upon to serve the good of mankind before his own good, and civilization cannot proceed without his services. He should show in his own character the worth of the highest potentialities of the human mind and soul, and he needs an intense culture if he is to rise to all this expectation.

The division, for purposes of understanding the gentleman, into the ascending orders of Nature's Gentleman, Society's Gentleman, and God's Gentleman, necessarily sharpened in focus by such a study as this, clarifies an easily muddled subject. Emerson's approach to courtesy is superlative: "When you come into the room, I think I will study how to make humanity beautiful to you." Finally, he has provided what might be a key to our emergence from the glowering revelations of the depravity of human nature in contemporary psychology. The essence of gentlemanliness, of courtesy, of religion, of love, is to learn to "postpone" ourselves for the well-being of others, to protect others from ourselves. Americans must see that there are values in peace and in the fragile continuity of civilization so great that, far from repressing ourselves, we may learn to release and use well all our energies for their sakes. The breath and penetration of Emerson's influence in his own day and since remains a bright sign of hope for that enlightenment.

## CHAPTER TEN

## THE GENTLEMAN AS SOCIALIST: WILLIAM DEAN HOWELLS

THE rebels of the 1920's and some of the professional proletarians of the '30's labelled Howells a prissy Western renegade who had stiffened the senile grip of Holmes's 'genteel tradition.' Nothing shows more clearly how glibly wrong such critics were than Howells's ideal of the gentleman. It is true that he was in a sense a native Brahmin, a mutative sport in the Midwest whose early photographs show all the characteristics which physiognomist Holmes ascribed to the Brahmin caste of New England. Held above the vulgarization of gentlemanliness going on all about him, he was drawn into the whirl of 'Best-Society' in Columbus, Ohio, and then into that of Boston. But the idealism of the abolitionist Western Reserve and of his gentle Swedenborgian father drew him from the start toward Emersonian and Christian concepts of the gentleman. Eventually, crystallizing at Howells's "conversion" to Tolstoi, those almost congenital values brought him to one of the logical termini of the tradition of the Christian gentleman dissociated from class in America. He constructed a socialist

Utopia in which the basic standards of life and thought were derived from the ideal of the gentleman.

I

To this day the Howellses are remembered by their Ohio neighbors as pleasant but somewhat exasperatingly different people, rather out of touch with the prevailing commercial realities. With no real background in the class of gentlemen, the family had been "gentle in their thoughts and tastes" on the Ohio frontier. Part of this was inspired by literary preoccupations, but much of it came from a simple determination to meet the best standards.[1] On young "Will" was impressed a sense of duty which was reinforced by the steady reading, permeated by gentlemanliness, which made the boy into a "literary creature." Some of the reading was like the materials we have seen from the Odd-Fellow's *Casket*. Yet he had a very early literary passion for *Don Quixote*. And as an adolescent he began the constant reading of Shakespeare which made him the leading American literary user of Shakespearian references. There was also Thackeray and his "mundane splendor," and the Tory literary quarterlies from England. Adolescent burning for personal distinction called up "impossible dreams of that great world of wealth, of fashion, of haughtily and dazzlingly, blindingly brilliant society." [2]

But such time-worn reactions of the small-town youth were not alone in his mind. His father, William Cooper Howells, had deserted ancestral Quakerism for the magnificent visions of Swedenborgianism which were deeply influencing speculative America minds. The father was also an abolitionist so sincere that he had abandoned editorial security in pro-slavery southern Ohio to come to the Western Reserve where he could run a newspaper in good conscience. His *Ashtabula Sentinel* supported abolitionist national representatives like Joshua Giddings and Benjamin Wade, and printed a fairly steady run of radical-Jeffersonian effusions on the right of rebellion, the political healthiness of periodic governmental over-turns, and the equal distribution of wealth. Understanding his gifted son, he guided his mind and reading with considerable success, though the son never really became politically minded or more than short periods. At any rate, Howells remembered in the home of his youth "a social liberty and equality which I long hoped to paint as a phase of American civilization worthy the most literal fidelity of fiction."[3] The democracy of that life made him think that "wherever life is simplest and purest and kindest, that is the highest civilization."[4] At the beginning of William Cooper Howells's career he had printed and published a little book on gentlemanliness. He was not the man to diminish or reject the ideal. But he wove ineradicably into the texture of his son's mind the conviction that social justice and democracy as a way of life are primary values.

On his own in the great world as a newspaper man in Columbus, Howells was at first hungrily adolescent. To his sister he wrote, "I am proud, vain, and poor. I want to make money, and be rich and grand."[5] Though he made little money, he laid the foundations for both literary and social success in Columbus. Invited first to Thanksgiving dinner by Salmon Chase, then governor of Ohio, he soon won *entrée* into the cultivated circle of the town. Before long he was writing home that at the latest party he had been told that "no young gentlemen but those of the first-chop-est description were invited and that the party was extremely aristocratic. I was presented to Mrs. Parsons," he went on, "who, I am told, affects the *bon*-est possible *ton;* but who was certainly gracious to me."[6]

Such experiences did Howells good. He learned that one could get his fill of that sort of thing and that it was not essential to him. Writing, for instance, was more important. And he did profit from the refinement of the place, learning most successfully how to conduct his shy self. As he remembered Columbus society in after years, it had blended the "wilding grace" of the West with the cultivation of East and South. Its manners were informal but pleasant, innocent, and as democratic as any exclusive society could be. And the kindness, high character, and beauty which distinguished the best homes not only prepared him adequately for Boston but confirmed the idealistic bent of his gentlemanliness.[7]

Howells returned to America from his four years' consulate in Venice, and took the post of assistant editor of the *Atlantic Monthly* in the winter of 1866. He could well feel that he had arrived both socially and professionally. In Cambridge the local literati had formed the perfect home for his soul. The words for life there, he wrote, were *"Intense and simple."* Intellect, personality, and character counted in Cambridge, not money.[8] Even if manners were stiff and a little formal, still they were genuine. The instinctive subtlety and delicacy of Howells's perceptions[9] made it easy for him to adjust to the intricate relationships of the place. And he was the more welcome after his Venetian experience and his writings on Italy and her literature. He could join the local game centered in Longfellow's Dante Club of pretending that they were all wealthy Italian *dilletanti* in a world of rich, warm color, rather than hardworking professors, writers, and magazine editors struggling to create a literary culture in the midst of continental booms and busts.

Howells always felt that the Cambridge of those years was the ideal time and place of all the ages for him.[10] By the time he left, both he and it had changed. But just then it proved, and for him, what he had said in his first important book: that "a gentleman" is not "a person born to wealth or station, but any man who has trained himself in morals or religion, in letters, and in the world."[11] With typical self-consciousness, Holmes had given him the accolade:

> I must congratulate you on the brilliant and commanding position you have fairly won for yourself. You have brought us an outside element which Boston needed, and have assimilated all that Boston could do for you (if you can be said to have needed anything) so completely that it seems as if you had cheated some native Esau out of his birthright.[12]

But it was not Holmes and his Boston which finally attracted Howells. He went into Boston society and later plutocratic New York and the international set—and soon tired of them when they were not literary.[13] The superficiality, the pharisaism, the snooty coldness, and the running to seed of Boston aristocracy were steadily apparent to him. He scarcely knew whether to laugh or weep when even the historian Parkman entirely missed the main point of *The Rise of Silas Lapham* because he was preoccupied with disliking the implication of the sub-plot that Silas's rise was "the achievement of social recognition." Howells "had supposed the rise to be a moral one."[14] He could enjoy the fading Boston which had made patricians of literary men,[15] but it was to Cambridge and to James Russell Lowell that he gave his heart.

Lowell, the Lowell whose humanitarian writings had been so intensely admired at home, who in accepting poems for the *Atlantic* had given him first national recognition, whose interest and advice had followed him through the fallow years when nobody else seemed interested, became Howells's friend. Nor was it that acquaintanceship "through the palings" which he had with Holmes. As the letters between the two show, from the middle of 1869 at least until Lowell went abroad on ambassadorial appointments which Mrs. Howells's relationship to President Hayes helped to get, the two were intimates.[16] Howells found Lowell changed—more conservative, cooler, more mannered—on his return from England after 1885. The still admiring essay in *Literary Friends and Acquaintance* shows his disappointment that Lowell should be retrogressing just when Howells was being converted to Tolstoi. He remembered that a "blend of . . . patrician qualities and democratic principles . . . made Lowell anomalous even to himself." But just when there was no cloud at all on the sky of friendship, Lowell was ready to point Howells's ideal of the gentleman down the way of the highest American concept.[17]

In those years Lowell was engaged in fighting toward intellectual stability in a distressing world. And he was finding in the major ideal of the American gentleman an answer to the problem of human weakness, corruption, and disorganization which had disrupted his wartime dream of democratic perfection.[18] Increasingly he found himself turning to his Puritan and Federalist ancestors, upholders of moral and social responsibility, and to the tradition of the Christian gentleman. Emerson, for whose philosophic pretensions he had little respect, began to appeal as a social theorist. In himself, Lowell said, Emerson was America's conclusive answer to the question "whether America could produce a gentleman."[19]

Eventually Lowell was preaching that the hope of the nation lay in the endeavor of the universities to produce something very much like the Emersonian God's Gentleman: "not a conventional gentleman, but a man of culture, a man of intellectual resource, a man of public spirit, a man of refinement, with that good taste which is the conscience of the mind, and that conscience which is the good taste of the soul."[20] The great friend, guide, and helper of Howells's Cambridge years, Lowell was himself intensely concerned for the best concept of the gentleman he could work out. Allowing for his father's ever present influence toward equality and social democracy, Howells's notion of the gentleman is essentially the same lofty Emersonian ideal as Lowell's. It runs all through his novels, more organic to his art even than Cooper's ideas to his in that Howells was the more concerned with character as such. It never changes in any fundamental way, though Howells did find a radically new application for it.

Through all his long literary life, Howells never altered his conviction that cultivation of mind and personality, not money, counted.[21] His father's liberalism and his own experience combined to make him acutely conscious of the tradition of the natural gentleman. After all, he himself refuted Holmes's theory that it took three generations to polish a gentleman for Boston society. Whatever the literary amenities of the Howells household, it had not been Beacon Street. Throughout Howells's novels runs a recurrent theme. A naturally gentle but socially inexperienced person encounters a person established in society from birth. The character from Best Society always has either a defect of sensibility or a snobbish mental block which makes him permanently or temporarily inferior. This is the conflict which Howells himself described to Henry James as an experiment in "confronting two extreme American types: the conventional and the unconventional." [22] Usually they are lady and gentleman in love. The unconventional, naturally gentle one always turns out to be superior at what Howells liked to call the end of the ends.

The conventional-unconventional formula Howells repeated at least ten times. It forms the sub-plot of his best known novel, when Penelope Lapham, natural lady, and Tom Corey, hereditary Boston gentleman, take the hurdles of true love together in *The Rise of Silas Lapham*. Most interestingly, Howells's preoccupation with showing the superiority of the naive Westerner to the Boston socialite was strongest during the decade of the seventies when he has often been supposed most abjectly devoted to Bostonism. In this period came *A Chance Acquaintance* (1873), the play *Out of the Question* (1877), and *The Lady of the Aroostook* (1879). A repetition of the conflict appeared as central to *The Minister's Charge* (1887) where the farm-boy Lemuel Barker proved himself to Bromfield Corey, the blown rose of Boston gentlemanliness, and to the artistic lady, Miss Carver, to whom he became affianced. *The Quality of Mercy* (1892) and the sequel to its sub-plot, *The Story of a Play* (1898), show playwright Brice Maxwell gradually rising to his true gentlemanly stature and opening the eyes of initially snobbish Louise Hilary. *Ragged Lady* (1899), *The Coast of Bohemia* (1893), *The Landlord at Lion's Head* (1896), *The Kentons* (1902), and *The Vacation of the Kelwyns* (1920) are also built around that conflict.

Of all these the most revealing is the playlet, *Out of the Question*. Nowhere else does Howells declare himself so flatly. At the typical Howells summer resort, the Ponkwasset Hotel, Leslie Bellingham, a blossom of Boston's highest society, is attracted to handsome and very gentlemanly Blake, a Midwestern inventor and sometime steamboat engineer. Leslie's mother and her aunt, Mrs. Murray, who detect an indefinable lack of polish in Blake, summon Leslie's brother Charles, the boon companion of Bromfield Corey. Blake saves Leslie from a horrid tramp, and when Charles arrives it is discovered that he also owes his life to Blake, who had rescued him during the War. Eventually the whole thing settles down to a debate over the nature of gentlemanliness. Charles holds to the idea that Blake is "one of those natural gentlemen that upset all your preconceived notions of those things." He has, Bellingham says, "made me think the Creator was still—active."[23]

Leslie and her mother are shaken by Blake's unfailing tact, refinement, and deep courtesy in meeting all the tests, including that of never hinting at all they owe him. But Mrs. Murray staunchly represents the 'Best Society' forces of evil, insisting that gentlemanliness consists of wealth, formal education and, above all, social position. "His goodness and greatness have nothing to do with it," she announces. The questions are of "station and breeding" and whether Blake could ever be presented to Leslie's circle at home.[24] Put off especially by the fact that Blake had once worked with his hands (Howells had, too) and by Mrs. Murray, Leslie and her mother waver through most of the play. At its climax, Mrs. Bellingham commands Charles to tell Blake he is not worthy of his sister. Filially Charles tries to violate his own beliefs and is failing badly when Leslie sweeps in to end the scene and accept Blake, hoping poor Charles has "not said one word unworthy of you—unworthy of a gentleman!"[25] On Mrs. Murray's final appearance, Charles ironically makes her judge of the rightness of his decision to turn Blake off. When she still maintains that it is her judgement and that of Society that his decision was "exactly right," he turns to beg Blake's pardon and exclaim, "Confound society!"[26]

Given the natural powers, energy, intellect, and sensitivity, anyone could be a gentleman, Howells thought. Into Blake's mouth he puts his rebuff of someone who sounds very much like Holmes. "He believed that you couldn't be a gentleman unless you began with your grandfather . . . I remember shivering over it, for it left me out in the cold, though I couldn't help liking the man; he was a gentleman in spite of what he said,—a splendid fellow, if you make allowance for him." You always have to remember that "it isn't safe to judge people by their circumstances . . . you are a gentleman if you choose to be so." [27] Such were Brice Maxwell, and especially Lemuel Barker who came up the hard way through some of Howells's most successful realistic sketches of his trials and hardships in *The Minister's Charge*. "Why, the boy's an Ancestor!" Bromfield Corey told Charles Bellingham. "All you have to do is to give him time, and he'll found a fortune and a family, and his children's children will be cutting ours in society . . . Look at the Bluebook, where our nobility is enrolled; it's the apotheosis of farm boys, mechanics, insidemen, and I don't know what!" [28] Even Corey's own line was saved from decline by the fact that in his son Tom reappeared the vigor of "the old India merchant" who had founded it, and Corey found it instructive to compare Tom with Barker.[29]

One of the most interesting of Howells's novels is *The Landlord at Lion's Head* in which there is a complex of conventional-unconventional conflicts on a series of levels. The central figure and *raisonneur*, Westover, is a natural gentleman from the West who has at length become a member of good Boston society. On the high moral level of the usual conflict, he gradually perceives that the Yankee farm-girl Cynthia Whitwell is a natural lady from "the spiritual effect" he had painted into a prized portrait of her. By the end of the book they are married. Westover's perception of Cynthia's quality is retarded by the usual hurdles on the course of true love. But the situation is given an amount of tension rare but exciting in a Howells novel by the two conflicts which center around Jeff Durgin, the handsome blackguard son of the proprietors of the summer hotel at Lion's Head. Jeff, a would-be natural gentleman who is only natural, becomes involved in an affair with Bessie Lynde, daughter of an aristocratic Boston house which is rotting into alcoholism in her brother and bored intrigue in

Bessie. When Jeff is a "jay" at Harvard he visits Bessie and proves his caddishness by kissing her "as she had happened to see one of the maids kissed by the grocer's boy at the basement door," [30] the closest Howells ever came to writing a part for Clark Gable. Her self-respect gone, Bessie retains enough of her traditions to turn Jeff away for good. But she has shown that in the Lyndes Boston gentility has lost its basis in character and become the withered formalism of a genteel tradition.

If Jeff is a little inferior to degenerate gentility, he is thoroughly equal to the other set which contrasts to Westover and his Cynthia, the plutocratic Vostrands. To them Jeff "seems very gentlemanly" [31]; and they are willing to take him into the family even after, at their request, Westover has revealed the course of Jeff's boorish treatment of both Bessie Lynde and Cynthia Whitwell (with whom he had crudely broken off a high-school engagement). Lacking every part of the character and courtesy of a gentleman, Jeff is able by energy and cynical maneuvering to enter the Vostrands' international set, turn the old boarding house into a swank resort, and swagger through all the seeming outwardness of gentlemanliness without possessing any portion of its inward virtue. But Westover and Howells are sure that the moral law of the universe is against him. "It's dead sure, pitilessly sure," says Westover. "Jeff Durgin sowed success, in a certain way, and he's reaping it . . . But he sowed evil, and he must reap evil. He may never know it, but he will reap what he has sown. The dreadful thing is that others must share in his harvest." [32] Added to the typical fineness of line in characterization and steady sweep of good talk from major and minor people alike, the tensions Howells set up in his novel by incarnating the conflicting states of gentlemanliness in New England gave him in *The Landlord at Lion's Head* what may yet prove to be his best work.

The courtesy of a gentleman, Howells thought, must be a blend of exquisitely emphatic kindness with conscience. Good manners come from a good heart, and bad from a wicked one. He remembered that great gentlemen like Longfellow, Lowell, and Charles Eliot Norton were distinguished by their kindness. The coolness and distance which Cooper had put into the manner of his Effinghams in *Home as Found,* to help them keep vulgar gate-crashers out, amused Howells because the author was so unconscious of the true vulgarity of these "exemplary people." [33] But kindness must be balanced by conscience; "they cannot be civil where they are not just; honesty and courtesy go together." [34] Therefore, like Emerson he argues that "manners . . . ought to be the flower of morals." [35]

The most interesting because it is the most extensive study of courtesy in Howells's fiction is the original conventional-unconventional novel, *A Chance Acquaintance.* The conventional one here is Miles Arbuton, one of the few Howells heroes who fail at romance. The reason for his failure is that his consciousness of Mrs. Murray's Boston code makes him a poor gentleman. He lacks the vital spark of courtesy; he has no kindliness. On a steamer bound from Niagara to Quebec, he meets accidentally and falls in love unintentionally with Kitty Ellison, a natural lady from a small town in western New York State—the first of Howells's successful portraits of the high-spirited, intelligent, beautiful, and personable American girl.

Kitty has been reared in the Jefferson tradition that "a belief in any save intellectual and moral distinctions was mean and cruel superstition." A cultivated lady, "she had never suffered slight save from the ignorant and uncouth; she innocently expected that in people of culture she should always find community of feeling and ideas; and she had met Mr. Arbuton all the more trustfully because as a Bostonian he must be cultivated." [36] She was shocked to find that Arbuton "seems to judge people according to their origin and locality and calling, and to believe that all refinement must come from just such training and circumstances as his own." By his criteria, she seemed "wanting in every civilized trait, and my whole life coarse and poor, and all my associations hopelessly degraded." [37] She found such his attitude, "hard and narrow" and false.[38] But she was given pause by the real goodness in him, the "scrupulously true" character, and the sense of "something really *high* about him" as a whole.[39] Accordingly she set out on an experiment, complicated yet sharpened by growing love, to prove whether he could be gentleman enough to be worthy of her truly gentle spirit.

It did not take very long to discover the essential flaw in Arbuton. As Kitty expressed it to her aunt in one of those feminine conferences men shudder to think of, "I don't think there's much between his heart and his manners. They seem to have been put on him instead of having come out of him. He's very well trained, and nine times out of ten he's so exquisitely polite that it's wonderful; but the tenth time he may say something so rude that you can't believe it . . . for the tenth time, it's certain his training doesn't hold out, and he seems to have nothing natural to fall back upon."[40] In short, he lacked the essential grace of kindness. " 'It's with his politeness as it is with his reading,' Kitty continued, 'he seems to consider it something that's due to himself as a gentleman to treat people well; and it isn't in the least as if he cared for *them* . . .'—and here Kitty's laugh grew more natural, and she gave a subtle caricature of Mr. Arbuton's air and tone as she spoke,—'I can't help feeling that it's a little—vulgar.' "[41]

Yet dormant under Arbuton's glacial Bostonism lie the instincts of a gentleman. His love for Kitty is crystallized when he saves her, unaware of her danger, from a vicious dog. He has the magnanimity to refrain from telling her, and in the first moment of self-forgetfulness of his career he is able to give himself somewhat freely to love. Perceiving those first glimmerings of life, Kitty hesitantly accepts his proposal. In this first instant of humanity, Arbuton is suddenly faced by the necessity to leap over convention, to do the joyful, natural thing instead of the formal. He balks miserably at the barrier and everything is lost.

Only a few minutes after Kitty has accepted his proposal in a picturesque spot outside Quebec, he is hailed by two ultrafashionable ladies from Boston. Etiquette demands that he shall not force the acquaintance of an unchaperoned young woman on these ladies. The natural and truly courteous thing would be to introduce Kitty as his fianceé and to let the Boston ladies huff away if they wished. But his code is too strong, his freedom too recent. He allows these friends to elevate their noses and draw him skilfully away from Kitty into a half-hour's promenade of small-talk while she sits alone in disconsolate humiliation. When at last they dismiss him to her, she sends him away with tearful determination. Then Arbuton wakes suddenly to the moral: "He saw it with paralyzing clearness; and, as an inexorable fact that confounded quite as much as it dismayed him, he perceived that throughout that ignoble scene she had been the gentle person and he the vulgar one. How could it have happened with a man like him!"[42] Howells's first problem novel, written in the fullness of his immersion in the life of Cambridge, contrasts Boston society with the humane West and brings the latter out in obvious triumph.

Another case of false, because selfish, courtesy is that of *The Son of Royal Langbrith* (1904). James Langbrith did have a certain warm emotional foundation for his attempt to set up as the squire of a small New England village. His plutocratic father had died before James could know him, and he sought with "a tender, chivalrous longing to champion his forgotten father, to rehabilitate this vanished personality."[43] After he had allowed his desire to glorify himself and his house, in a town which his father had really dominated by cruelty and fraud, to lead him to torture his mother and twist the life of good Dr. Anther, he brought his house of cards tumbling about his ears. Attempting to express "the noble nature and magnanimous ideals of Royal Langbrith," he enforced "a general contempt" for the uncle, John Langbrith, who had long cared for the family business.[44] Maddened by such treatment, John told him the sordid truth about his father, and he was left to face the facts of his own meanness and essential vulgarity, to be rescued from ruin only by the magnanimity of his mother and his fianceé, the daughter of the man his father had most wronged.

Though his complex and mystical family religious background never assumed personal vitality for Howells, it joined with the ideas of both God's gentleman and Boston's to demand high and positive character. To the practiced beholder, it was Jeff Durgin's want of "spiritual distinction" which instantly gave him away as no gentleman but "a prehistoric man that the barbers and tailors had put a *fin de seticle* surface on." [45] Conscience which made the taking of any personal advantage unthinkable and also required the full performance of duty was indispensable to the gentleman. As in Basil March's "holy war" against the vulgar plutocrat Dryfoos, who tried to force Basil to punish the socialist Lindau for his opinions by discharging him from the magazine March published for Dryfoos, the gentleman's conscience might also expose him to real sacrifice for the sake of principle.[46] Products of that conscience are the breathtaking adherence to truthfulness which absorbs Howells heroines and gentlemen both; the magnanimity lacking which, the Coreys taught Tom, one was "less than gentlemanly";[47] the entire uprightness and honesty of mind and act which characterize Howells's real and fictional heroes alike.

It was appropriate to his Quaker, Swedenborgian, and Jeffersonian backgrounds as well as to the Brahmin tradition that he should hold character as the gentleman's first and indispensable badge. The Brahmin scholar John Codman Ropes, he said, was a man so high of soul and sweet of nature that "his whole life was a monument of character." If the term had not been smutched by some of its associations and were worthy of the man, he went on, "I should say he was one of the most perfect gentlemen I ever knew." [48]

Self-educated so successfully that he was repeatedly offered chairs of literature at various universities, even Longfellow's and Lowell's professorship at Harvard, Howells maintained always that the gentleman must be cultivated in letters and the world. He agreed with William James that the illiberally educated man, narrowed into one intellectual sphere, "literal, unable to suppose anything different from what he had seen, without imagination, atmosphere, or mental perspective," must "remain a cad, and not a gentleman." [49] The most painful of all the vulgarities was intellectual. Hence Basil March felt that one of the principal aims of the gentleman was toward "cultivated tastes"; and Lemuel Barker learned to feel that the things he had been taught by association with Bromfield Corey might well take the whole of his life-time to develop and enjoy. Yet Corey himself, "society veteran of that period when even the swell in Boston must be an intellectual man," knew that cultivation was the last and least of the gentlemanly attributes. It might baffle and bewilder people like the Laphams; but in the end it was only the "airy, graceful, winning superstructure" upon the basic requirements.[50]

Though Howells completely repudiated the squirearchical tradition in *The Son of Royal Langbrith,* he admired individual gentlemen who gave their talents to the good of society. If mankind were to be saved from itself at all, it must be saved by those of its members who were superior in morality, intellect, and esthetic power. He never tired of praising a man who, like the Brook Farmer, abolitionist, and educator G. W. Curtis, came forward to serve as a "Radical Gentleman" instead of remaining comfortably the "literary fine gentleman" with whom his magazine readers would have been satisfied.[51]

In *A Modern Instance* appears Howell's most intensive grapple with the problem of the function of the gentleman in his novels. When Ben Halleck is fatally and immorally (since she is still Bartley Hubbard's wife) attracted to Marcia, he is restrained by his friend Atherton in the name of the gentleman's responsibility for the welfare of society. Atherton's remonstrance takes on greater weight when we remember that every character in the book except poor, amoral Bartley regards divorce (in the mode of the day) as a crime against personality and society, if not against heaven. He says:

> It doesn't matter much, socially, what undisciplined people like Bartley and Marcia Hubbard do; but if a man like Ben Halleck goes astray, it's calamitous; it 'confounds the human conscience,' as Victor Hugo says. All that careful nurture in

the right since he could speak, all that lifelong decency of thought and act, that noble ideal of unselfishness and responbility to others, trampled underfoot and spit upon,—it's horrible! . . . the natural man is a wild beast, and his natural goodness is the amiability of a beast basking in the sun when his stomach is full . . . No, it's the implanted goodness that saves,—the seed of righteousness treasured from generation to generation, and carefully watched and attended by disciplined fathers and mothers in the hearts where they have dropped it. The flower of this implanted goodness is what we call civilization . . .[52]

With that as background it may be well to glance for a moment at the attitude towards sex in literature for which Howells was so thoroughly lambasted during the 'twenties. About the comparative sexual freedom which followed upon the cultural revolution after World War I much can be said. It has accomplished social good and evil both. And the freedom to write about sex artistically as well as technically was a necessary part of that revolution. Because Howells, the ancient Dean of American letters, was taken to be the champion of repression, he was bitterly attacked.

He was squeamish about sex. Partly that was because he was psychologically incapable of facing, even vicariously, brutal and sordid reality: and most of the treatments of sex in American literature have been sordid. Further, he believed that realistic literature which dealt with the *average* chaste and candid experience of American life (which to him was either upper middle-class Boston and New York or small-town Ohio seen through his father's eyes) was better than literature which lugged in lurid commercial eroticism.[53] With our current development of the historical romance into the type of which *Forever Amber* is the classic standard, many a reader and critic finds himself coming closer to Howells.

But there was a correlation between his ideal of the Christian gentleman and sex. From the mid-eighteenth century came the insistence that the true gentleman was chaste in thought, word, and deed. He was expected to marry and have children,— and beyond the bounds of marriage say nothing. Only the fine, false gentleman was promiscuous or ribald. Not everyone, as we have seen, accepted segregation into the ranks of the Richardsonians and their jittery prudishness. Emerson was capable of handling sex intelligently and healthily in "Initial, Demonic, and Celestial Love." In Allen Tate's *The Fathers* there is a fascinating confrontation of the balanced old gentleman, Louis Buchan, and the confused Victorian George Posey. Seeing a bull try to mount a cow, Posey blushes to the roots of his hair—and is met by the almost concealed contempt of Major Buchan for his inability to take the facts of life for granted. Acceptance of the old ideal of Sir Charles Grandison, reinforced in Howells by his neuroticism, made him label all sex as bad and try to harry it, an expression of "the beast-man," out of literature.

Like almost everyone else's mind, Howells's was not static throughout his long productive years. It changed in ways that became richly meaningful in his writings. Intensive study of his life would show four significant periods through which his mind passed: an early one of romantic melancholy and sensibility; a second one of maturing talent and command of the resources of the novelist which culminated with his first devotion to realism; the soul-stirring conversion to Tolstoian attitudes toward religion, society, and art; the final slackening of idealism and withdrawal toward comfort and convention which comes to most men in old age. To his ideal of the gentleman only the major, central turn to Tolstoi is really important, however.

## II

The advent of Tolstoi into Howells's life can be dated fairly readily. Having picked up *The Cossacks* by chance one day, he read *Anna Karenina* soon after, plunging on into Tolstoi with mounting excitement. Since he wrote Thomas Sargeant Perry on October 30, 1885, that he was then reading *Anna Karenina,* his "conversion," allowing for time to read further and digest it all, can reasonably be fixed as coming at the end of 1885.[54] The whole experience was much like that, he said, of "people converted at revivals." But he modified the traditional connotations of a radical overturn by adding at once: "What I had instinctively known before, I now knew rationally." [55] Though only a search beyond our present scope could really tell, presumably what he means is that his father's dormant religiosity has flamed up with the spark from Tolstoi. At any rate, he thought he had come "to the only true ideal, away from that false standard of the gentleman, to the Man who sought not to be distinguished from other men, but identified with them, to that Presence in which the finest gentleman shows his alloy of vanity." Christ, not the gentleman, was to be his model. And Tolstoi showed him how the world might be made over in Christ's image, "each one master of himself and servant to every other. He taught me to see life not as a chase of a forever impossible personal happiness, but as a field for endeavor towards the happiness of the whole human family." [56]

Typically of converts, Howells said something more than he meant when he talked of deserting the "false standard of the gentleman." For he deserted only the false, Holmesian standard. He set to work to revamp the high tradition and produced a new gentleman who was the normal, natural citizen of his utopian Altruria. Coming to Tolstoi, he said, he came to know rationally what he had before only felt emotionally. He had felt emotionally that courtesy was blended of emphatic kindliness and conscience. Now he "knew rationally" that in place of a competitive idea of social exclusion we must, for our salvation, substitute an ideal of social democracy. When Aristides Homos, the *Traveller from Altruria,* came to study conditions in benighted America, he shamed our half-gentlemen. And this was because inclusive society on the Altrurian plan had made "every man . . . a gentleman, and every woman a lady." [57]

The ideal of the inclusive society, developed furthest in the Altrurian books, Howells did not leave buried in them. It recurs all through the works of this period, especially in the Reverend Mr. Peck, the fascinatingly frustrated little idealist of *Annie Kilburn.* The most philosophic appeal is in the essay "Equality as the Basis of a Good Society." Its fundamental argument combines theoretical sociology and Howells's regular notion of courtesy. Groups, whether patrician or plebeian, are formed because within them men have the peace and ease of equality, he says. This goes to show that equality is the best natural condition of man. The truly best society, in fact, meets "in a region of absolute altruism" in which it is vulgar even to suppose that everyone is not equal. "In its finest and gentlest moments society will get rid of the inferiors altogether, and the equals will serve one another." The normal evolutionary tendency of true gentlemen will thus be in the direction of the inclusive society.[58] And the ultimate validation of this end to which Howells sees all good things pointing is that the gospel of Christ teaches "the spiritual unity of man." [59]

In this prophetic role he coupled with the new affirmation a biting denunciation of exclusive society. Able to instance the facts of Gilded-Age corruption of which he was aware years before such young friends as William Allen White, Frank Norris, Ray Stannard Baker, and Hamlin Garland, he had little trouble making a case. Exclusive society as the extension of capitalistic competitiveness was to him frivolous pretense supported by injustice and horrible exploitation. The best and most poignant of his usually melancholy poems expressed the point graphically:

### SOCIETY

I looked and saw a splendid pageantry
   Of beautiful women and of lordly men,
   Taking their pleasure in a flowery plain,
Where poppies and the red anemone,
And many another leaf of cramoisy,
   Flickered about their feet, and gave their stain
   To heels of iron or satin, and the grain
Of silken garments floating far and free,
As in the dance they wove themselves, or strayed
   By twos together, or lightly smiled and bowed,
Of curtseyed to each other, or else played
At games of mirth and pastime, unafraid
In their delight; and all so high and proud
They scarce seemed of the earth whereon they trod.

## II

> I looked again and saw that flowery space
>   Stirring, as if alive, beneath the tread
>   That rested now upon an old man's head
> And now upon a baby's gasping face,
> Or mother's bosom, or the rounded grace
>   Of a girl's throat; and what had seemed the red
>   Of flowers was blood, in gouts and gushes shed
> From hearts that broke under that frolic pace.
> And now and then from out the dreadful floor
>   An arm or brow was lifted from the rest,
> As if to strike in madness, or implore
>   For mercy; and anon some suffering breast
> Heaved from the mass and sank; and as before
> The revelers above them thronged and prest.[60]
>
> from *Stops of Various Quills*, 1895

And in the wide sense of the word, society fared no better from the competitive system which made life a matter for all men of "pushing and pulling, climbing and crawling, thrusting aside and trampling underfoot, lying, cheating, stealing . . . covered with blood and dirt and sin and shame . . . to a palace of our own, or the poor-house, which is about the only possession we can claim in common with our brother-man." [61]

America, he charged, had lost its democracy and become from mine to mansion a plutocracy.[62] And plutocracy was the bane of true gentlemanliness. There was as much competition in the world of 'Best Society' as in the business world; Holmes's gay gatherings seemed "a Stone-Age of social brutalities." [63] A man of gentlemanly character must think twice before he attends its gatherings. Perhaps his host would be some plutocrat like Dryfoos whose hospitality is "the profusion of a thief with his booty." [64] The conscience and cultivation of the gentleman simply cannot survive in a struggle so ruthless. Conditions under which a man "cannot be nobly unselfish without the fear of being a fool" choke off the production of gentlemen altogether.[65] Organized, competitive selfishness produces snobs,— "men who bully and truckle, and women who snub and crawl," [66]—and leaves the world at the mercy of the "moneyed vulgar" who make life unpleasant by their irrational exclusiveness because they do not know what else to do with themselves. Literary portraiture of such people, he said, carrying the new social theory into criticism, gives us instead of the gentleman the stock hero: "a painted barbarian, the prey of his passions and his delusions, full of obsolete ideals, and the motives and ethics of a savage" which "the guilty author" tries "to foist upon the reader as something generous and noble." It makes for bad art and worse morals.[67]

Howells hoped to elevate the worker to the refinement of the gentleman by giving him an ideal society in which to grow. But he called on the gentleman to rise first, to mend his ways first, to cease to hide behind his cultivation, and to drop his notions of special privilege. The reformation of the worker could come in God's time, but the time of the gentleman had almost run out. Howells came to wonder that the lightning of revolution had not struck already. To forestall it, he offered the gentleman the chance to rid himself of clinging savagery and perfect himself and society with him in Altruria. By adopting the ideal of inclusive society, Aristides Homos said, his country had not only made everyone a gentleman or lady, "we have already . . . given a whole continent perpetual peace; . . . founded an economy in which there is no possibility of want; . . . killed out political and social ambition; . . . realized the brotherhood of the race, and . . . have outlived the fear of death." [68]

It all hinged on the new validity Howells discovered in the tradition of the function of God's gentleman, as he thought both Emerson and Lowell had.[69] His old insistence that occupation barred no one from gentlemanliness was now positive. He became increasingly tender in his concern for the welfare of personal and household servants.[70] Chided by American associates for contravening good form in doing menial tasks and fraternizing with menials. Aristides Homos made it clear that in Altruria chances to perform services to meet another's need were rare and beautiful opportunities. As the philosophic young natural gentleman Emerance, of *The Vacation of the Kelwyns,* explains, there is personal dignity and impersonal dignity—and only the first matters. Impersonal dignity is a "superstition" that a man can be defiled by the things "which happen *to* him rather than those which happen *from* him." [71] When Homos was told that to black his own boots would offend the feelings of an American gentleman, he parried with a Socratic question:

> 'Then in America it is not offensive to the feelings of a gentleman to let another do for him what he would not do for himself?'
> 'Certainly not.'
> 'Ah, then we understand something altogether different by the word gentleman in Altruria.' [72]

The foreboding condition of an American culture which at the beginning of the twentieth century had hardly begun to recover from the shock of industrialization turned Howells and many other tender-minded men toward Christian socialism. And his Utopia was to be founded on the Christian socialist gentleman whose motto was the command: "If any is first among you, let him be your servant," as Howells rephrased it.[73] Nor was he alone in such feelings.[74] Halfway through our century, much of the hope has faded from the Christian socialist dream. But it has contributed importantly, and should continue to do so, in wakening awareness of the continuing problems and in helping to shape some of the more relevant solutions. That Howells, a pioneer in social criticism as in literary development, could so adapt the gentlemanly configuration testifies to its abiding versatility and vitality in American culture.

## CHAPTER ELEVEN

## *ARE THERE ANY GENTLEMEN NOW?*

SINCE Howells, the vitality of the gentlemanly ideal has been evident in a hundred ways. But the writers have reflected their bewilderment by fastening upon fragments of the configuration and refusing to try to deal with the whole. Some have walked alone, among them Sinclair Lewis, Dos Passos, Hemingway, Vachel Lindsay, Robert Frost and E. A. Robinson. Individually, they have had much to say about the gentleman in the twentieth century America. A number of other writers in treating of the gentleman have linked themselves, more or less loosely, within three groups. These are the Neo-Humanists, the Neo-Agrarians, and what may be called the Genteel Traditionists.

The Neo-Humanists show signs of being far from so moribund as some critics of the late thirties supposed. The two great prophets, Paul Elmer More and Irving Babbitt, are dead. Their disciples are split among far-fetched feuds. Yet their main ideas keep recurring and, in one form, command the most influential literary spokesman of the day, T. S. Eliot. The Neo-Humanists saw the approaching trial by fire of modern society. Some of them thought it a Last Judgement, as it may well be. They also resented the isolation of the intellectual in industrial society,

# ARE THERE ANY GENTLEMEN NOW?

and in criticism of these things they were often magnificent. Where they called up the best of the humane, gentlemanly tradition and strove to kindle contemporary minds with the old flame, they have spoken and still speak powerfully to the condition of the age. Where they gave way to conservative despair and bitterly espoused doctrines of "the elite," they turned away from the main American development of the tradition. In so doing they incur the danger of being shunted aside with Fisher Ames and Joseph Dennie.

The Genteel Traditionists divide raggedly into two groups. There are those who seek to cling to genteel traditions, to perpetuate outworn cultural forms of gentlemanliness. And there are the often bitter critics of both the futility of given genteel tradtions and the failure of our times to find new forms for the old values. The coiner of the phrase *"the* genteel tradition" was, of course, George Santayana. To the confusion of cultural critics who found the phrase useful, Santayana failed in "The Genteel Tradition in American Philosophy" and later in *The Genteel Tradition at Bay* to adopt clear referents for it. Then in *The Last Puritan* it turned out that he meant the genteel tradition left behind Unitarian Boston. But the damage had been done.

The main difference in kind between the Neo-Agrarians and the Genteel Traditionists lies in the former's being positive and much more deliberate. Though the old Vanderbilt group has been most articulate, Neo-Agrarians are not necessarily Southern. Louis Bromfield, among others, has gone that way strongly. Still, the agrarians have simply and deliberately turned to a genteel tradition. They have insisted on the oneness of soul and soil in a way which Otsego-loving Cooper might have liked had he known about it. And their program is essentially the same as his. A new agrarian way of life in America is possible enough. Yet when it does come, there seems little probability that it will be the Cooper-Vanderbilt ideal of the good gentleman guiding his flock of dependents from the pillared mansion. It is much more likely to be either the way of the independent middle-class farmer pooling machinery and work with his neighbors, or the industrialized factory in the field which is as yet hard to visualize as a way of life.

The attackers of genteel traditions have been among the most effective contemporary American writers. William Faulkner's lurid Mississippi, Ellen Glasgow's mildewed Virginia, Edith Wharton's and Robert Frost's rotting New England all cry protest at the inhumanity of trying to live within meaningless, obsolete forms. Much of the outcry against the small town made the same protest. J. P. Marquand's satire of the genteel tradition left over from Dr. Holmes's Boston has been less fervid, but culturally penetrating. In *B. F.'s Daughter* he seems to be starting a very interesting attempt to create new and useful expressions of the sorely frustrated ideals of the late George Apley and of H. M. Pulham, Esq.

Many of our historical novelists have been using the gentleman of the past for his effectiveness in the new romanticism of glamor. Joseph Hergesheimer is still probably the best of that crowd. James Branch Cabell has had a wonderful sort of field-day of fantasy during which he has been able to use the glamor-technique to satirize itself, the Virginia genteel tradition, and modern confusion. Yet he has been able to communicate his sense of the free magnanimity of the gentlemanly soul above all that as well. Beginning with *My Antonia* and *The Lost Lady*, Willa Cather was elegiac. The grand gentlemanly virtues were lost and gone. Then she turned and began to search for a tradition to revive, for forms which might be restored to cultural vitality now. W. A. Percy's *Lanterns on the Levee* is a rich elegy for the genteel tradition of his South. An inverted use of genteel traditions has been for the hard-boiled writer to project one in order to flout and deny it at every point.

The independents have on the whole been better writers and have made much more significant contributions than these others. They have cut loose from the past as much as they could (even from revolt against the past). And they have explored the human mind in our times; they have explored our times— often to find the trail ending in some limited affirmation of the ancient ideal of the gentleman. Sinclair Lewis stripped bare the shams of our culture one by one. Yet when that is done there is always the hand pointing to honesty—the final honesty of spirit which is honor. Dos Passos ranged all through industrial civilization to find at the last that decency, devotion to real duty, and readiness to sacrifice for larger goods than self are final values. Hemingway, for all he says about hating life, returns regularly to courage and magnanimity, the security of the spirit in facing down violence and tragedy. Steinbeck, to whom humanity as such means more than to these others, ends in decency, courage, and devotion, too. And Ma Joad and the Mayor of *The Moon is Down* show his sense of the need for self-denying responsibility.

The poets also have worked with gentlemanly values. Vachel Lindsay and Carl Sandburg have tried to reshape the Jeffersonian ideal to industrial times—as Whitman had begun to do in his latter years. A careful reader of Robert Frost could pry out from his poems a fairly complete picture of what he thinks the posture of the gentleman should be now. And Frost, on the Emersonian principle that "I am always inconsistent as always knowing there are other moods," would probably deny it! E. A. Robinson came close to the Neo-Humanists sometimes. But he went beyond them, too. A modern revaluation of the gentlemanly ideal could do much worse than start with "Flammonde" and "The Man Against the Sky."

In the end, our lack of a strong cultural direction toward which a new gentlemanly code could be turned seems clear. There are also cultural and ideological forces which oppose the traditions from which we would probably reshape our code. (Though a study of the Soviet gentleman would be a fascinating thing.) Yet our writers, like all the rest of us, keep reaching toward the values of the old ideal. It is still susceptible of vital expression. But until that new expression comes we must live in a welter of fragmented understandings and crumbling genteel traditions.

The vitality of the tradition is also evidenced by its secure place in the tremendous mass of popular, sub-literary art in our time. One of the surest appeals to the American mass-mind is that of the natural-gentleman "clean-cut young man." Such figures of myth as Ham Fisher's Joe Palooka, Milt Caniff's heroes, and the chivalric stereotypes imposed upon the athletic demi-gods of each recurrent season show the power over the national imagination of the popular gentleman. The muted idealism, also vastly popular, of Ernie Pyle's apotheosis of G.I. Joe was another facet of the same myth. Still another was the cult of Franklin Roosevelt's reputation for cheerful magnanimity. Yet others are the idealisms of the college fraternities, of the religious "youth movements," or of the Service Clubs.

The energy in the gentlemanly ideal, despite all the confusion of cultural forms about it, is clear enough evidence that there are still Americans trying to be gentlemen. But the years of the modern in America and now in England have made *code* and *class* considerations irrelevant. That is why the senile world of Marquand's George Apley and H. M. Pulham offers them no sustenance. Robbed of the old cultural firmness, the ideal is compensated by a new fluidity which matches the atomistic and bewildering conditions to date of industrial society. The modern gentleman cannot think of class. He needs self-respect, but narcissism is fatal to him. He is deprived of aristocratic glamor and is delivered over to the middle classes which still seem likely to dominate the coming century. But the return for lost glamor is the possibility that the gentlemanly ideal may save the bourgeoisie from themselves by securing the triumph of the Citizen Ideal within the middle-class configuration over the Success Formula part of it. Man for man, the "suburban gentleman" of our times is decenter, cleaner, more intelligent, and closer to the life of the mind than the gentry of any age.[1] And if his world survives, he has a reasonable expectation of future gains in the direction of the good life.

Like the question of aristocracy, the popular question of Victorian "chivalry" toward women has been made irrelevant by the healthy modern shift toward feminism. The relevant and important question for the gentleman now is of a self-validating way of life and thought. The tradition is valuable for its sense of the beauty, balance, and self-realization possible to individuals, and for the intelligent freedom and smoothness it lends to human relationships—a worth enhanced in an era of jumpy nerves. Its essence is the self-discipline of tender-minded persons for the furthering of social and cultural "values." Once that is established, the new cultural forms of gentlemanliness will be possible. As Emerson pointed out, codes and forms will rise from descriptions and imitations of the way the best gentlemen have met their responsibilities.

How can one be a gentleman nowadays? Doesn't it presume a personal heritage of generations of unconscious training? No, not necessarily. The discipline of gentlemanliness is like the discipline of an art. By thought, by awareness, and especially by self-discipline to constant performance of the right action, however small, some people can cultivate unpretending, organic courtesy. Anyone can do it in some degree. Like an art or an athletic skill, however, it is finally ruled by individual capacity. Natural gentlemen, like genuine talents or natural athletes, start with immense advantages. Some people, born duffers, might never see what courtesy is all about; but that offers no validation for the mucker pose.

What is a gentleman? A gentleman is a man whose inner balance of sensibility, good-will, and integrity issues in moral dependability (the instinct to act rightly in a crisis); in courtesy (the instinct to serve other people's physical and psychological needs); and in the excellent performance of some good social function. Or it is anyone who is sincerely trying to be a gentleman.

# NOTES

## CHAPTER ONE

[1] George Sitwell, "The English Gentleman," *The Ancestor*, I (April, 1902). There are such a number of excellent works on all of this background material that one can hardly do more than pay his respects and acknowledge his gratitude for the clarity and suggestiveness of their analyses. The most readable of the scholarly works is Esmé Wingfield-Stratford, *The Making of a Gentleman*, London, 1938; other scholarly and highly useful works are: Ruth Kelso, *The Doctrine of the English Gentleman*, University of Illinois Studies in Language and Literature, XIV (February-May), 1929; John Mason, *Gentlefolk in the Making*, Philadelphia, 1935; A. Smythe-Palmer, *The Ideal of a Gentleman*, London, n.d.; Virgil Heltzel, *Chesterfield and the Tradition of the Ideal Gentleman*, University of Chicago dissertation, unpublished, 1928; W. Lee Ustick, "Changing Ideals of Aristocratic Character and Conduct in the Seventeenth Century," *Modern Philology*, XXX (November, 1932). There are also various works more personal than scholarly, of which Henry Dwight Sedgwick's rather bitter *In Praise of Gentlemen*, Boston, 1935, struck me as best.

[2] See the introduction to Charles Moore, *George Washington's Rules of Civility and Decent Behavior in Company and Conversation*, Boston, 1926.

[3] "The Parallel of Deism and Classicism," *Modern Philology*, XXIX (February, 1932), 281-299.

[4] The compelling clarity of terms and method in Ralph Linton's *The Cultural Basis of Personality*, New York, 1945, has been particularly helpful here.

[5] "The Genteel Tradition in American Philosophy," *Winds of Doctrine*, New York, 1913, and *The Genteel Tradition at Bay*, New York, 1931.

[6] *The Beginnings of Critical Realism in America*, New York, 1930, 52, 53, 54.

[7] *Ibid.*, 52.

## CHAPTER TWO

[1] This successful struggle has been so well sketched by Professor Morison in *Builders of the Bay Colony,* New York, 1930, (especially Chapters III, VII, and VIII) that it seems superfluous to summarize him.

[2] Daniel Neal, *A History of New England,* London, 1747, II, 322. Excellent handlings of such questions as they relate in particular to affairs at Harvard are given in S. E. Morison, "Procedence at Harvard College in the Seventeenth Century," *Proceedings of the American Antiquarian Society,* n.s. XLII, 377-78; and in the same historian's *The Founding of Harvard College,* Cambridge, 1935, *passim.*

[3] *The Founding of Harvard College,* p. 250.

[4] S. E. Morison, *Harvard in the Seventeenth Century,* Cambridge, 1935, 165.

[5] For assurance on this point as well as for any number of insights into Puritanism, I am indebted, as any student of the subject must be, to Perry Miller's *The New England Mind,* New York, 1939. Especially valuable, because of the excellence of its anthologized materials, is Perry Miller and Thomas Johnson, *The Puritans,* New York, 1938.

[6] On September 27, 1631, Josias Plastowe, caught stealing corn, was sentenced "hereafter to be called by the name Josias, & not Mr., as formerly hee used to be." Morison, "Precedence . . .," 378.

[7] In Morison, *Builders of the Bay Colony,* the account of Winthrop is swift-paced and generally excellent. The place to find the man himself, however, is in his own journal, the best edition of which is John Winthrop, *The History of New England from 1630 to 1649,* J. K. Hosmer, ed., Boston, 1908.

[8] The correspondence between father and son may be followed through the first volume of *The Life and Letters of John Winthrop,* ed. by R. C. Winthrop, Boston, 1864.

[9] *The Colonial Mind, 1620-1800,* 88 ff.

[10] Though it is not necessarily conclusive evidence, Sewall echoed the Puritan main tradition in roundly condemning avarice as a motive for slave-keeping in his pioneer anti-slavery pamphlet, *The Selling of Joseph,* 1700. He was the "only writer" of the age "who examined economic considerations in slavery and servitude," says E. A. J. Johnson, *American Economic Thought in the Seventeenth Century,* London, 1932, 109.

[11] William Mathews, *American Diaries . . .,* Berkeley, 1945, calls Sewall's "probably the best American diary." Quotations here are from *Samuel Sewall's Diary,* ed. Mark Van Doren, New York, 1927. Interesting if sometimes untrustworthy accounts of Sewall may be found in N. H. Chamberlain, *Samuel Sewall and the World He Lived In,* Boston 1898, and Henry Cabot Lodge, "A Puritan Pepys," *Studies in History,* New York, 1892.

## CHAPTER THREE

1 *The Massachusetts Magazine,* II (1790), 36.
2 II (1791), 566-567.
3 There is some conservative malice in Tyler's treatment of Jonathan. Jonathan is intended to be a comic character and therefore be a bumpkin. But he is a leveller, too, saying, "we don't make any great matter of distinction in our state, between quality and other folks," and only Manly has saved him from participation in that carnival of iniquity, Shays' Rebellion.
4 Careful reading of the defence of duelling made by Dr. Johnson will show its lack of seriousness. Boswell, indeed, in a note (Everyman ed. II, 264n.) is at some pains to point out that Johnson was rowing against the stream, as he loved to do. Johnson's argument boils down to the assertion that a man sometimes is forced to do that which he knows is wrong. His analogy, in fact, is that duelling is private war and that private war is no more contrary to Christianity than public war,—we go to ingenious lengths to justify the latter by the gospels, why not the former? It is a clever conversational rationalization, and Boswell indicates that Johnson knew that it was.
5 See William Oliver Stevens, *Pistols at Ten Paces, The Story of the Code of Honor in America,* Boston, 1940, 12-13.
6 See the Burr-Hamilton correspondence in the New York State Historical Museum, Coopertown, and Wandell and Minnegerode, *Aaron Burr,* New York, 1928, Part V, Chapter V.
7 George Ripley and Bayard Taylor, *Cyclopedia of Literature and the Fine Arts,* New York, 1853, 263.
8 Chas. Warren, *Jacobin and Junto, Cambridge,* 1931, 95.
9 *Ibid.,* 50.
10 See especially Alice M. Baldwin, *The New England Clergy and the American Revolution,* Durham, 1928.
11 For *The Nature of True Virtue* see the excellent discussion in C. H. Faust and T. H. Johnson, *Jonathan Edwards,* New York, 1935, lxxvciii. For *Charity and Its Fruits* see the review in *New Englander,* X (May, 1852), 229-244.
12 *Port Folio,* IV (Nov., 1810), 482.
13 *Port Folio,* IV )Nov., 1807(, 308.
14 Quoted by Milton Ellis, *Joseph Dennie and His Circle,* Austin, 1915, 118.
15 Porter G. Perrin, *Life and Works of Thomas Green Fessenden,* Orono, 1925, 73, 102-103.
16 *Works of Fisher Ames,* Boston, 1809, 432. The Adamses regarded Ames and his exaggerated pessimism as being insane. John Adams spoke of "poor Ames's distempered imagination," *Works,* IX, 631. And when a group of Ames's "friends" issued his works after his death, John Quincy Adams wrote a long review of them which was printed as a pamphlet, *American Principles,* Boston, 1809. He admitted that Ames

had "genius and virtue," but charged that association with Hamilton
had "warped his judgement and trammelled the freedom of his mind."
Unreasoning fear of France had combined with physical weakness to
make Ames hysterical. His platform was "Suberviency to Britain—
Abhorrence to France—and contempt for the American people." He
had come to the point where all his writing inspired "not *exertion*
but *despair*" and " I know that in penning those billingsgate invectives against his country, he could not be in possession of a sound
mind." The younger Adams's whole point is that the publication of
Ames's works at that particular moment by the group which brought
them out was not a legitimate act of political piety but an attempt by
the mercantile, Hamiltonian Federalists to return to power by reviving
the outworn scare campaign in an effort to frighten the American
people into submitting to their "select and exclusive church."
17 See his long poem *Greenfield Hill*, especially part II, and *Travels in
New England and New York*, New Haven, 1821-22, III, 473; IV, 421.
18 See *Virtuous Rulers a National Blessing*, Hartford, 1791, 20.
19 *Travels*, I, 514. Dwight used "accomplishments" as the third of the
definitions in Johnson's *Dictionary:* "Embellishment; elegance; ornament of mind or body."
20 *Travels*, I, 335-6; IV, 355.
21 *A Sermon on Duelling.* . . . New York, 1805.

## CHAPTER FOUR

1 He had read, for instance, in the following authors, most of whom
have previously been mentioned in this study: Addison, Bolingbroke.
Burke, Chesterfield, Cicero (whose essays he knew almost by heart.
*Works*, X, 388), Dr. Johnson, La Bruyere, Locke, Montaigne, Plato,
Pope, Richardson, Scott, Shakespeare, Steele and Swift.
2 *The Works of John Adams*, Charles Francis Adams, ed., Boston, 1856,
hereafter indicated by the capital Roman numeral of the volume, 1, 58.
3 I, 30.
4 III, 452.
5 II, 10.
6 *Journal of William Maclay*, ed. by Edgar S. Maclay, New York, 1890,
5. See also 49, 127, 137, and 140.
7 VI, 457, 495, 504. While editor at once of two Federalist papers in
New York, the *American Minerva* and the *Herald*, Noah Webster put
out a booklet entitled *The Revolution in France considered in respect
to its Progress and Effects* (1794). There, in his best lexicographical
form, Webster defended Adams's definition of aristocracy. In America
"aristocracy" must always denote "that *personal influence* which men
derive from offices, the merit of eminent services, age, talents, wealth,
education, virtue, or whatever other circumstance attracts the attention
of the people . . . the circumstances which do actually give this *personal
influence,* which forms a kind of natural or customary aristocracy, exist
universally among men."

8 VI, 451-452.
9 VI, 458; 477-478.
10 VIII, 507. Yet Jefferson's earlier fear that Hamilton and Adams meant to create an American monarchy must have had some basis in Adams's behavior in the late '80's. See I, 356, 417; XVI, 93. And cf. Mercy Warren to Adams in Stedman and Hutchinson, *Library of American Literature*, III, 124-126.
11 VI, 457-458.
12 V, 372.
13 VI, 210.
14 VIII, 370. See also X, 64; VI, 236 and 249.
15 VI, 241-2.
16 VI, 506. Cf. VII, 79. It is interesting in this connection to notice that Adams was, in distinction from the financier Hamilton, an agrarian Federalist. In his "vocabulary, the word *property* meant land" (I, 639). And there is strong evidence that his adherence to an agrarianism not too unlike Jefferson's own was the cause of the downfall of the Federalist party. The Hamiltonians, eager to seize control of the party to further their commercial interests, forced Adams and his close adherents out of the party, thus weakening themselves and strengthening Jefferson at one stroke, with the result that Federalism's power was permanently broken. See M. J. Dauer, *The Basis for the Support for John Adams in the Federalist Party*, abstract of University of Illinois dissertation, Urbana, 1933.
17 VI, 452.
18 VI, 421-422.
19 VI, 460; cp. 453-454.
20 VI, 232-234.
21 VI, 245.
22 VI, 235-238.
23 III, 448-449.
24 VI, 248.
25 VI, 97.
26 See variously VI, 458; 263; 97; 276-277.
27 X, 24.
28 IV, 290-291.
29 VI, 184.
30 IV, 289, 290.
31 IX, 524.
32 VIII, 192.

## CHAPTER FIVE

1 Dixon Wecter, *The Saga of American Society*, New York, 1937, 23.
2 Quoted in Sarah N. Randolph, *The Domestic Life of Thomas Jefferson*, Cambridge, 1939, 13-14.
3 *The Writings of Thomas Jefferson*, Monticello Edition, Washington, 1903-4, hereafter indicated by the capital Roman numeral of the volume, V, 83.

[4] Randolph, 288.
[5] *Ibid.*, 240-241.
[6] *Ibid.*, 273. See also XII, 198-200.
[7] XI, 413.
[8] XII, 199.
[9] I, 222-3. See also XVIII, 248.
[10] IX, 376; XVI, 59-60.
[11] Randolph, 310.
[12] V, 188.
[13] VI, 262.
[14] XIX, 217.
[15] XV, 167.
[16] Randolph, 314-315.
[17] XIV, 7-8.
[18] XIV, 140-1, 143.
[19] *Writings of Thomas Jefferson*, ed. P. L. Ford, 1899, X, 23-24.
[20] XIII, 396-7. This faith in a natural aristocracy was an argument generally used by ardent democrats against hereditary nobility. Even the fiery Thomas Paine wrote that "Nature is often giving to the world some extraordinary men who arrive at fame by merit and universal consent, such as Aristotle, Socrates, Plato, &c. They were truly great or noble. But when government sets up a manufactory of nobles, it is . . . absurd." (Conway ed., III, 269-70). And a transplanted Italian democrat named James Ph. de Puglia wrote that "titles were given to distinguish the mental qualities of men and not their personal . . . A man who buys nobility with ambition and money, . . . may find distinction among the idiots and ignorant, but not in the eyes of an enlightened people . . . Juvenal therefore was of my sentiment saying, that it is better to be Thersites' son but be wise and useful to mankind, than to have Achilles for a father and to be Thersites himself." *Man Undeceived*, Philadelphia, 1793, 10-11.
[21] VIII, 405.
[22] XIII, 396.
[23] V, 396-397.
[24] VI, 3-4.
[25] V, 153.
[26] XIII, 398-399.
[27] XIV, 76.
[28] I, 73-4.
[29] XV, 35-36.
[30] XIX, 213.
[31] XIX, 213-217.
[32] XV, 156; II, 203.
[33] XIII, 400.
[34] In Stedman and Hutchinson, *A Library of American Literature*, New York, 1889, IX, 184-186. This is also one of the leading ideas in W. C. Brownell, *Democratic Distinction in America*, New York, 1927.
[35] See Arthur M. Schlesinger, Jr., *The Age of Jackson*, Boston, 1945, esp. 10-17, and 267.

36 See Henry Christman, *Tin Horns and Calico*, New York, 1945, the excellent account of New York State's Anti-Rent War which eventuated in the liquidation of the remnants of the patroon system.

## CHAPTER SIX

1 See Schlesinger's brilliant analysis of "The Southern Dilemma," especially pp. 248-249. With such a situation as that he portrays, Southern adherence to the agrarian dream could be little more than wishfulness.

2 Dixon Ryan Fox, *The Decline of Aristocracy in the Politics of New York*, New York, 1919, 136.

3 See, for instance, the letter he wrote to William Dunlap explaining that he could not forget his obligations as an American gentleman (*Diary of William Dunlap*, New York, 1931, III, 644). After his death, he was described by the sculptor Horatio Greenough as "my ideal of an American gentleman"; and H. T. Tuckerman lost his prejudices against Cooper instilled by the adverse press simply through meeting the man and finding him "a most interesting companion and a noblehearted gentleman." (In Dorothy Waples, *The Whig Myth of James Fenimore Cooper*, New Haven, 1938, 126; 137.) From Paris Susan Cooper, always a candid lady, wrote that "had we been so disposed, we might have been in a constant round of Dissapation (sic), Mr. Cooper had almost affronted the Lords, the Dukes and Princes, by declining their invitations—but after satisfying Curiosity, we thought it would be quite as wise, to stay Home, and save our Purse, for other purposes." (*Correspondence of James Fenimore Cooper*, J. F. Cooper ed., New Haven, 1922, hereafter called *Correspondence*, I, 127-128). This Samuel F. B. Morse confirmed, saying that Cooper was "courted by the greatest and most aristocratic, yet he never compromises the dignity of an American citizen . . ." (in H. W. Boynton, *James Fenimore Cooper*, New York, 1931, 221).

4 The most detailed treatment of this is Ethel R. Outland, *The "Effingham" Libels on Cooper*, University of Wisconsin Studies in Language and Literature, No. 28, Madison, 1929. It should be checked by reference to Waples and Schlesinger but most especially by Robert E. Spiller, *Fenimore Cooper, Critic of His Times*, New York, 1931.

5 Spiller, 211. For his distrust of mercantile Federalism cp. *Homeward Bound*, 502-503. All references to novels, unless otherwise indicated, are to the *Works of J. Fenimore Cooper*, New York, 1892.

6 See Gregory Paine, *James Fenimore Cooper as an Interpreter and Critic of America*, University of Chicago dissertation, 1924, 156.

7 *Notions of the Americans: Picked Up by a Traveling Bachelor*, Philadelphia, 1828, hereafter called *Notions*, II, 172, 175, 183-4. Schlesinger shows that, contrary to much Whig propaganda Jacksonians as a group were led by rather distinguished gentlemen, and Old Hickory himself was, as "direct testimony agrees, . . . a man of great urbanity and distinction of manner" (37-38 *et passim*).

8 *Notions*, II, 314-315; cf. I, 144-145.

9 *Ibid.*, I, 95-96.

10 *Ibid.*, I, 153-154.
11 *Ibid.*, II, 194-197.
12 *Ibid.*, II, 295.
13 *The American Democrat,* Cooperstown, New York, 1938, 91-92.
14 *Ibid.*, 97.
15 P. 248.
16 *Home As Found,* 84.
17 In Outland, 79.
18 I am not thoroughly convinced by Mr. Schlesinger's conclusion that Cooper came at the very end to look to "the commercial oligarchy . . . as the only bulwark of property" (p. 380). As *The Monikins* shows in purest form, Cooper always had believed that property, badly threatened, would take steps to protect itself. And it is always extremely difficult to show much from any one statement by Cooper, who loved to be bluff, who gloried in facing tough facts and then arguing around them, and who had come to specialize in Jeremiad epigrams on American social and political topics. There can be no doubt, however, that in his last years Cooper was progressively more deeply exasperated; and he might very possibly have been turning to mercantile obligarchy as better than *sans-culottism*. But it would represent an entire failure of nerve in him.
19 *The Sea Lions,* 5.
20 *Home as Found,* 21.
21 *The Prairie,* 248.
22 *The American Democrat,* 135. Cp. *Notions* and the Anti-Rent Trilogy *passim.*
23 *The Crater,* 207.
24 *The Monikins,* Ch. XXVII. Cf. *Home as Found,* 55.
25 *Afloat and Ashore,* 422.
26 *Notions,* II, 315.
27 *Ways of the Hour,* 43-44.
28 *Notions,* I, 108.
29 *Chainbearer,* 268-269.
30 All Cooper's pedantic Yankee Schoolmasters, especially Jason Newcomb of the Littlepage Manuscripts, embody this dislike.
31 *Redskins,* 487.
32 *Homeward Bound,* 502.
33 *Lionel Lincoln,* 323; *Notions,* II, 294.
34 *The Pilot,* 127. See also *Lionel Lincoln,* 395; *The Spy,* 602; *Chainbearer,* 460; *The Sea Lions,* 11; and *Ways of the Hour,* 117.
35 *Notions,* II, 295. See also I, 194.
36 *Chainbearer,* 171.
37 *Ways of the Hour,* 40; cf. *Oak Openings,* 109.
38 A good analysis of the evolution of Cooper's religion may be found in *The Clergyman in Representative American Novels,* University of Wisconsin, unpublished dissertation, 1943, by Emerson Clayton Shuck.
39 *Gleamings in Europe: England,* ed. Spiller, New York, 1930, 305.
40 *Gleamings in Europe: France,* ed. Spiller, New York, 1928, 190. Cf. *Redskins,* 541; *Notions* I, 171; II, 60.

41 *Notions* I, 174.
42 *Ibid.*, I, 88. Cf. *The Spy*, 626; *The Pilot*, 177; *Last of the Mohicans*, 150; *Satanstoe*, 481; *Chainbearer*, 374; *Ways of the Hour*, 51.
43 *Ways of the Hour*, 125. This is a motif running all the way through Cooper; see *Precaution*, 585; *The Spy*, 448; *Home as Found*, 131; *Homeward Bound*, 484.
44 *The American Democrat*, 123-124.
45 *Homeward Bound*, 677.
46 *Gleanings . . . England*, 118; cf. *Redskins*, 503.
47 *Homeward Bound*, 521.
48 *Notions*, I, 2-3.
49 *Gleanings . . . France*, p. xx. Cp. Bryant's description of Cooper's personality in his *Discourse of the Life and Genius of Cooper*, in *William Cullen Bryant*, Tremaine McDowell ed., New York, 1935, 281.
50 *Miles Wallingford*, 348. Cf. *The Crater*, 162-3, 148; *Gleanings . . . England*, 22, 111; *Redskins*, 504.
51 *Deerslayer*, 4.
52 *Pathfinder*, 542; *Deerslayer*, 215.
53 *Pathfinder*, 508.
54 *Deerslayer*, 234. The meaning is sometimes obscured by such usages as that of Natty in observing that Jasper Western had "a nat'ral gift" for sailing *(Pathfinder,* 512), but in the main it is clear as in *ibid.*, 506. Cp. *Wyandotté*, 3.
55 *The American Democrat*, 47.
56 *Redskins*, 632.
57 *Home as Found*, 86.
58 *Miles Wallingford*, 328.
59 *Satanstoe*, 488.
60 *Satanstoe*, 229.
61 *Home as Found*, 113.
62 *Prairie*, 377.
63 *Deerslayer*, 44.
64 *Deerslayer*, 42.
65 *Home as Found*, 86. Cf. *Monikins*, 395-396; *Gleanings . . . England, passim.*

## CHAPTER SEVEN

1 *Notions of the Americans*, I, 88.
2 G. L. Paine, *op. cit.*, 98; and Spiller, 11.
3 *Deerslayer*, 4-5.
4 *Pathfinder*, 500.
5 *Deerslayer*, 114.
6 See Boynton, 113.
7 *Pathfinder*, 364.
8 *Deerslayer*, 157.
9 *Ibid.*, 49.
10 *Pathfinder*, 454.
11 *Ibid.*, 537.

12 *Deerslayer*, 42.
13 *Pathfinder*, 533.
14 *Ibid.*, 365.
15 With each successive novel Natty became more glamorous and more gentlemanly. The novels were actually written: *Pioneers*, 1823; *Last of the Mohicans*, 1826; *Prairie*, 1827; *Pathfinder*, 1840; *Deerslayer*, 1841. By the last book Cooper was prepared to apologize for Natty's earlier gaucheries by explaining that it had seemed necessary to endow him with crudities in order to preserve the fictional *"vraisembable"* of the woodsman and to keep Natty from seeming "a 'monster' of goodness." *(Deerslayer, 5).*
16 *Prairie*, 248.
17 *Pioneers*, 784.
18 *Prairie*, 278.
19 *Homeward Bound*, 584.
20 *Gleanings . . . England*, 123.
21 *Satanstoe*, 480.
22 This was, of course, a central concern of novels ranging in time of composition from *The Pioneers* through *Homeward Bound, Home as Found*, to the group just preceding *The Crater*, including *Afloat and Ashore, Miles Wallingford*, and the Anti-Rent trilogy.
23 *Homeward Bound*, 478 and 484.
24 *Ibid.*, 478, 480, and 677.

## CHAPTER EIGHT

1 "Dr. Holmes: A Re-Interpretation," *New England Quarterly*, XII, (March, 1939), 20.
2 *Writings of Oliver Wendell Holmes*, Boston and New York, 1892, hereafter indicated by Roman numeral, II, 204.
3 II, 139-140. The italics here, as in all the quotations from Holmes, are his.
4 See the illuminating account by Mrs. James T. Fields of the way Holmes came to dinner, ate little, and talked sparklingly all through an evening on all his favorite topics. *Memories of a Hostess*, M. A. DeWolfe Howe ed., Boston, 1922, 46-48.
5 William Dean Howells, *Literary Friends and Acquaintance*, New York, 1900, 147.
6 VIII, 9.
7 V, 3-6.
8 XI, 2.
9 VIII, 410-411.
10 I, 195.
11 V, 4; III, 276.
12 V, 5.
13 I, 20-23.
14 I, 260; Cf. II, 151; V, 1-2.
15 III, 294-295.

16 See I, 178; V, 59; VII, 54-5, 76; X, 193.
17 In John T. Morse, *Life and Letters of Oliver Wendell Holmes*, Boston, and New York, 1896, hereafter called, Morse, I, 123.
18 V, 482-483.
19 V, 20.
20 I, 260.
21 Morse, II, 168-169.
22 II, 121.
23 VII, 32.
24 V, 2.
25 V, 11-12.
26 I, 23.
27 I, 89.
28 I, 23; IV, 74.
29 Morse, II, 311. For comment on Holmes and the classics, Clark, *op. cit.*, is interesting. Cf. the abortive Autocrat paper in *The New England Magazine*, II (Feb., 1832), 134; and in Morse, II, 222; in Holmes, IV, 96; V, 172-3. Though Mrs. Fields noticed that Holmes in familiar discouse habitually said "ain't," he was inclined like Cooper to make of speech a particular criterion of gentility. He admitted that even "gentlemen in fine linen, and scholars in large libraries" might occasionally make a mistake *(ibid.,* II, 44) but he held speech, and especially diction, a valid criterion nevertheless. " 'Fust-rate,' 'Prime,' 'a prime article,' 'a superior piece of goods,' 'a handsome garment,' 'a gent in a flowered vest,'—all such expressions are final," he said. "They blast the lineage of him or her who utters them, for generations up and down." They are "decisive of a man's social *status.*" *(ibid.,* I, 28). Indeed, "the touchstone of New England Brahminism" is the ability to pronounce "view" properly! Pure vulgarisms aside, Holmes had no patience with the argot of the upper classes either. "I have known several very genteel idiots whose whole vocabulary had deliquesced into some half dozen expressions," the Autocrat commented, listing several. ". . . These expressions come to be the algebraic symbols of minds which have grown too weak or indolent to discriminate. They are the blank checks of intellectual bankruptcy." *(ibid.,* I, 256-7). Holmes, himself, says his nephew and late contemporary, Morse, "wrote a simple, what may be called a gentlemanlike style, and of great purity, but crowded with allusions . . . for educated and well-read audiences." (Morse, II, 16). He read his own poetry too, "like a gentleman; that is to say, with much simplicity, yet with a sympathy of expression in voice and feature which was very charming." (Morse, I, 240-1). While such comments do not have the authority of statements by Holmes himself, I think they may be taken to represent his own goals.
30 I, 51.
31 I, 115.
32 II, 95.
33 II, 133.
34 III, 103.

35 V, 94.
36 II, 150-1. Cf. I, 258-9; II, 45; V, 103.
37 Murray Bradshaw in *The Guardian Angel*, VI, 255-256.
38 I, 312; V, 412; XI, 26-27.
39 Morse, II, 144, 146, 150-151.
40 Report of a lecture on Byron and Moore, *Boston Daily Evening Transcript*, March 26, 1853.
41 I, 116.
42 See I, 193; II, 150-1; III, 270; and V, 9-10.
43 I, 10 and 258-259.
44 See Howells *op. cit.*, 165-6; I, 23, and Morse II, 33.
45 I, 271. His reaction to the coldness of British aristocracy throughout his *One Hundred Days in Europe* is much the same.
46 III, 334-335.
47 I, 260-261 *n*.
48 *Ibid*. Cf. IV, 151, and Morse I, 105.
49 I, 171.
50 V, 39-40.
51 II, 279.
52 II, 133.
53 H. H. Clark, *op. cit.*, 19, 34.
54 II, 133-4. See the crude, original Autocrat, *New England Magazine*, I (Nov., 1831), 428; and *Elsie Venner*, V, 31, 83-4; also IV, 222-3, 236; X, 121.
55 II, 283.
56 *Studies of a Biographer*, London, 1907, II, 174-175.

## CHAPTER NINE

1 *The Casket*, Jefferson, Ohio, II (August, 1853), 126-127.
2 *The Complete Works of Ralph Waldo Emerson*, Centenary Edition, hereafter indicated by the capital Roman numeral of the volume, III, 120-2; see also IV, 3; X, 312.
3 X, 36.
4 I, 261.
5 III, 122-123.
6 *Journals of Ralph Waldo Emerson*, E. W. Emerson and W. E. Forbes eds., New York, 1912, hereafter called *Journals*, X, 312. Quoted by permission of the publisher, Houghton Mifflin Co.
7 I, 386.
8 I, 387.
9 XI, 537.
10 *Journals*, I, 389.
11 III, 123.
12 *Sir Walter Raleigh*, New York, 1905, 18. Cf. 58, 68, 80-82.
13 IV, 247.
14 *Journals*, II, 120.
15 III, 125-126. See essay on *Wealth* and *Works* I, 240; *Journals*, V, 260; VI, 34; *Uncollected Writings*, 120.

[16] IV, 26, 61.
[17] X, 38-39; 52.
[18] III, 130, 148.
[19] III, 132; and VI, 170.
[20] In O. W. Holmes, *Ralph Waldo Emerson,* Boston, 1885, 164-165.
[21] *Journals,* IX, 556.
[22] *Ibid.,* X, 96-97.
[23] III, 155.
[24] III, 127-128.
[25] V, 192.
[26] *Journals,* VII, 519.
[27] *Ibid.,* VIII, 190-192.
[28] IV, 223-258.
[29] III, 142-147.
[30] IV, 170-171.
[31] *Journals,* VIII, 192.
[32] *Ibid.,* IX, 187.
[33] *Ibid.,* IX, 148.
[34] V, 187.
[35] *Journals,* IX, 556.
[36] III, 140-141.
[37] *Journals,* X, 50.
[38] VIII, 102-103.
[39] III, 143.
[40] Alexis De Tocqueville, *Democracy in America,* Philip Bradley ed., New York, 1945, I, 52.
[41] *Journals,* VIII, 471; *Writings,* IV, 264.
[42] *Journals,* VIII, 481.
[43] IV, 268.
[44] *Journals,* VIII, 417.
[45] *Ibid.,* IX, 63.
[46] VI, 164.
[47] *Journals,* VII, 516.
[48] IV, 289-290.
[49] IV, 57.
[50] VI, 216; Cf. X, 55.
[51] *Journals,* III, 494.
[52] X, 65-66.
[53] I, 391.
[54] III, 145.
[55] See "Natural Aristocracy," *Journals,* VIII, 75-6.
[56] III, 95.
[57] *Journals,* IX, 187-188. Cf. *Journals,* X, 432 ff.
[58] *Ibid.,* VII, 321.
[59] I, 390.
[60] XI, 280-281.
[61] III, 284-285.
[62] VI, 164.

63 III, 153-154.
64 XI, 230.
65 *Journals,* VII, 10.
66 VI, 196.
67 VI, 197.
68 *Journals,* VII, 384.

## CHAPTER TEN

1 *Years of My Youth,* New York, 1917, 13. See William Cooper Howells, *Recollections of Life in Ohio, 1813-40,* Cincinnati, 1895, 144.
2 *Years of My Youth,* 124.
3 *Ibid.,* 81. Cf. *My Literary Passions,* New York, 1910, 95.
4 *The Kentons,* New York, 1902, 144.
5 *Life in Letters of William Dean Howells,* Mildred Howells, ed., New York, 1928, hereafter called *Letters,* I, 14.
6 *Ibid.,* I, 19.
7 *Years of My Youth* has a glowing account of his Columbus experience which is substantiated by the thirty-odd letters written to General Comley, the friend of his youth who took over his old paper, *The Ohio State Journal,* after the Civil War. The letters are preserved in the Ohio State Historical and Archaeological Museum.
8 *Letters,* II, 221; Cf. I, 141-142.
9 See James Russell Lowell's praise of just these qualities when Howells was still a rising young man: *The Function of the Poet and Other Essays,* Newton Arvin ed., New York, 1920, 146-148.
10 *Literary Friends and Acquaintance,* 251.
11 *Venetian Life,* London, 1866, 344.
12 Morse, II, 44.
13 In Cambridge itself Howells dined with Longfellow regularly "about once in three weeks," formed part of the distinguished group about the James family, and did the honors for all Cambridge and Boston when Bret Harte was his guest in 1871 *(Letters,* I, 161, 176, 182). Thus and as steady members of the group around the publisher Fields, the Howellses were "good society" in Boston. At Henry Adams's he dined successively with Lord Houghton and William Waldorf Astor, entertaining the latter in his own home. In New York he met assorted Vanderbilts, John Jacob Astor, Tilden and Bryant, and his Columbus friend, Whitelaw Reid *(Ibid.,* I, 168-9, 213-214, 240, 253). In England, later, Lowell and Henry James brought him into the international game. As earlier in Columbus, however, Howells quickly found such sport wearing thin; it "demoralized" him; and, though he was always available to friends or to young writers, he found himself gradually withdrawing from Society *(Ibid.,* II, 30).
14 *Literary Friends and Acquaintance,* 141. See also the discussion below of the "conventional-unconventional conflict" as a Howells theme.
15 *Ibid.,* 146-147.
16 See *Letters,* I, 152-153.

[17] *Literary Friends* . . ., 273. William M. Sloan reported that Howells, unable to attend a Lowell centenary dinner, had telegraphed him that "on almost every page written by him he has felt his indebtedness to Mr. Lowell." *Commemorations of the Centenary of the Birth of James Russell Lowell* . . . *American Academy of Arts and Letters*, New York, 1917, 33.

[18] Harry Hayden Clark in the introduction to *James Russell Lowell* in the American Writers Series, shows there that Lowell, dismayed by the Gilded Age, turned from the optimistic nationalism of his Civil War period toward hope from the cultivation of ideal American gentlemanliness (see esp. pp. lxix-lxxvi). He dates the beginning of this shift in Lowell's thinking at about 1867.

[19] *The Complete Writings of James Russell Lowell*, Elmwood Edition, Cambridge, 1904, II, 138, 248.

[20] *Ibid.*, VII, 212.

[21] Cp. *Venetian Life*, 338, with "Equality as the Basis of Good Society," *Century Magazine*, n. s. XXIX (Nov., 1895), 64; and with *The Vacation of the Kelwyns*, New York, 1920, 3. Howells's plutocrats are always vulgar and usually damned by their wealth, like Northwick in *The Quality of Mercy* and Dryfoos in *A Hazard of New Fortunes*.

[22] *Letters*, I, 174.

[23] *Out of the Question*, Boston, 1877, 147-148.

[24] *Ibid.*, 143-144.

[25] *Ibid.*, 175.

[26] *Ibid.*, 179.

[27] *Ibid.*, 82-83.

[28] *The Minister's Charge*, New York, 1887, 368; 446-447.

[29] *Ibid.*, 387.

[30] *The Landlord at Lion's Head*, New York, 1910, 300-301.

[31] *Ibid.*, 100-101.

[32] *Ibid.*, 399.

[33] *Imaginary Interviews*, New York, 1910, 85.

[34] *Their Wedding Journey*, Boston, 1885, 94.

[35] Preface to *English Society* by George Du Maurier, New York, 1897, 7.

[36] *A Chance Acquaintance*, 66-67.

[37] *Ibid.*, 144.

[38] *Ibid.*

[39] *Ibid.*, 137-138.

[40] *Ibid.*, 150.

[41] *Ibid.*, 151.

[42] *Ibid.*, 260.

[43] *The Son of Royal Langbrith*, New York, 1905, 78.

[44] *Ibid.*, 316-317.

[45] *The Landlord at Lion's Head*, 207.

[46] *A Hazard of New Fortunes*, New York, 1911, 412-418, 408, 438. See also *The Minister's Charge*, 408; *The Quality of Mercy*, 182-183.

[47] *The Rise of Silas Lapham*, Boston, 1885, 423. Cf. *A Woman's Reason*, Boston, 1884, 137.

48 *Literary Friends* . . ., 144-145. Cp. Longfellow, 200; and Dr. Palfrey, 285.
49 William James, *Some Problems of Philosophy,* New York, 1919, 7.
50 *The Rise of Silas Lapham,* 194.
51 "George William Curtis," *North American Review,* CVII (July, 1868), 114-115. Cf. *Literary Friends* . . ., 109, 129-130, 288.
52 *A Modern Instance,* 471-472.
53 *Criticism and Fiction,* New York, 1910, 262-263. Howells always identified Europe with sexual license, America with chastity and innocence: see *Letters,* I, 58-59; *Venetian Life, passim; The Lady of the Aroostook,* 280; "An Obsolete Fine Gentleman," *Atlantic Monthly,* XXXVI (July, 1875), 90-106.
54 *My Literary Passions,* 185; *Letters,* I, 372.
55 "Lyof N. Tolstoy," *North American Review,* CLXXXVIII (1908) 852.
56 *Literary Passions,* 183-184.
57 *A Traveller from Altruria,* New York, 1894, 120, 296.
58 *Century Magazine,* loc. cit., 63-67.
59 *Minister's Charge,* 458. Cf. *Literature and Life,* New York, 1902, 34; *Criticism and Fiction,* 232.
60 *Stops of Various Quills,* New York, 1895, XXVI.
61 *A Hazard of New Fortunes,* 507.
62 "Are We a Plutocracy?" *North American Review,* CLVIII (Feb., 1894), 185-196. Cf. *Impressions and Experiences,* 42.
63 *Annie Kilburn,* 130.
64 *A Hazard of New Fortunes,* 379.
65 *Through the Eye of the Needle,* New York, 1907, 4. Cf. *Traveler From Altruria,* 201-2, 213; *Quality of Mercy,* 368; *Impressions and Experiences,* 234-235.
66 *Literary Passions,* 98.
67 *Criticism and Fiction,* 240.
68 *A Traveller from Altruria,* 310.
69 *The Vacation of the Kelwyns,* 92-93.
70 "The Superiority of Our Inferiors" in *Imaginary Interviews; Through the Eye of the Needle,* 34-35.
71 *The Vacation of the Kelwyns,* 87.
72 *A Traveler From Altruria,* 127-128.
73 *Ibid.,* 20-21.
74 See Crothers, *The Gentle Reader,* 225-6; C. F. Dole, *The Religion of a Gentleman,* New York, 1900, 8. Also Ephraim Emerton, "The Gentleman and Scholar," *Atlantic,* LXXXVI (June, 1900), who cites Howells; and H. C. Morton, "The American Notion of Equality," *Atlantic,* LXXX (September, 1891).

## CHAPTER ELEVEN

1 Esmé Wingfield-Stratford, *The Making of a Gentleman,* 308-309.

# INDEX

## A

Adams, Henry, 150
Adams, Jas. T., 25
Adams, John, 18, 20, 30, 59, 61, 63, 67, 68-83, 89-90, 92-97, 99, 103, 110
Adams, John Quincy, 214-215
Addison, Joseph, 9
Agrarianism, 103-105, 109-111
Alger, Horatio, 152, 160-162
Allstree, Richard, 8
American gentleman, 100-101, 105-111, 115, 125-126, 128, 155, 163-164, 168, 174-175, 188
Ames, Fisher, 66, 67, 207
Amory, Cleveland, 23. See Brahmin caste
Anthropology, See Culture
Aristocracy, See Gentry, class of
Aristotle, 2
Arnold, Matthew, 15
Atherton, Gertrude, 60

## B

Babbitt, Irving, 206
Beauty, 79, 91, 172, 173, 179, 182
Birth, 7, 9-10, 18, 20, 73, 78-79, 100-101, 106, 115, 116, 148, 150 156. See Natual Gentleman.
Brackenridge, H. H., 61.
Brahmin caste of New England, 17, 42, 149-150, 150-151, 167, 176-178, 184. Vs. "Proper Bostonian," 23

Brathwaite, Richard, 6
Bromfield, Louis, 207
Brown, John, 181
Brownell, W. C., 217
Bryant, W. C., 101, 220
Bumppo, Natty, 17, 20, 111, 123, 127, 134-138
Burr, Aaron, 38-60
Byrd, William, 17, 53

## C

Cabell, J. B., 208
Cable, G. W., 27
Calling, doctrine of, 8, 42-43, 49-50, 166
Calvert, George, 55
Caniff, Milt, 210
Carlyle, 15
Castiglione, 9, 11, 43
Cather, Willa, 31, 208
Cervantes, 3, 185
Character, 5-6, 43, 70, 86-87, 101, 118,119, 134, 152, 156, 165, 179, 181-82, 193, 197
Chaucer, 3
Chesterfield, 9, 12-13, 45, 53, 56-57, 64, 81, 86, 154
Chivalry, 4
Christian gentleman, 11, 12, 13-15, 52-67, 62, 86, 118-120, 155-156, 161, 184, 199-200, 201, 204-205
Cicero, 2
Clark, Harry Hayden, viii, 147, 222, 223, 226
Clemens, S. L., 31, 60-61, 115

Cobbett, Wm., 62
Cogdell, John L., 32
Cooper, J. F., 17, 20, 21, 27, 31, 103-126, 127-145, 156, 157, 160, 194 207
Cotton, John, 35, 166
Courtesy, 6, 12, 15, 21, 61, 87-89, 107, 120-121, 134, 154, 171, 182-183, 193-196
Courtesy books, 5, 9, 13, 34
Cowper, Wm., 13
Criticism, 29-30, 127, 204
Crothers, S. M., 55
Culture (anthropological sense), 2-3, 22, 23, 24, 27-28, 30
Curti, Merle, vii
Curtis, G. W., 198

D

Defoe, 9
Democracy and the gentleman, 92, 93-95, 97-99, 100, 100-101, ,105-107, 110, 122, 126, 157, 158, 160-162, 163-164, 186, 189, 201-205
Dennie, Joseph, 64-65, 67, 104, 207
De Tocqueville, 175-176
de Puglia, J. P., 217
Dickens, 13, 15, 24
Dos Passos, 31- 206, 209
Duelling, 58-61, 67, 88-89, 118, 157-158, 179
Du Maurier, 15
Dunlap, Wm., 218
Dwight, Timothy, 61, 63, 66-67

E

Education, 12, 17, 40, 41-42, 61, 67, 73, 90-91, 97-99, 101, 117, 125, 153, 189, 197-198. See Courtesy book
Edwards, Jonathan, 63

Eliot, Chas. W., 100-101
Eliot, T. S., 206
Ellis, Milton, 214
Elyot, Thos., 6
Emerson, 19, 31, 44, 100, 108, 147, 155, 156, 158, 160-183, 189, 200, 211
Etiquette, 70-72, 89-90, 120-123, 195-196

F

Fashion, See Etiquette, Manners
Faulkner, Wm., 31, 208
Federalist party, 59, 61-67, 97, 101, 103, 104-105
Feminism, 211
Fessenden, Thos., 65, 104
Fielding, 9
"Fine" gentleman, 11, 12, 52-67, 69, 147, 154-155, 158-159
Fitzgerald, Scott, 31
Forbes, John M, 174-175
Freneau, Philip, 61
Frontier, the, 16-17, 52, 85, 112-113
Frost, Robert, 206, 208, 209
Function of gentleman, theory of, 7-8, 17, 21, 25, 38, 99, 104, 110, 137-138, 141-142, 144-145, 152-153, 158, 166, 173, 198-199

G

Gainsford, Thos., 6
Genteel traditions, some, 17, 23-27, 51, 63, 67, 92, 104, 126, 168-170, 177-178, 188, 207-208
Gentleman, the, See American, Christian, "Fine," Natural, and Southern; see Democracy and, Function of, Literature and, Sex and
Gentleman, ideal of, 3, 9-10, 16-

19, 92, 100, 101-102, 162, 183
Gentry, class of, 2-3, 9-10, 16-19, 34, 38, 53, 61, 63, 65, 74, 78, 92, 95-96, 99, 100, 101, 103, 105-106, 110, 122, 125, 126, 160-161
George III, 20
Gerry, Elbridge, 62
Glasgow, Ellen, 27, 3, 208
Greenough, Horatio, 218
Goethe, 165, 177-178

H
Hakluyt, R., 6
Hamilton, Alexander, 58-60, 64, 109, 216
Hawkins, Frances, 8
Hawthorne, Nathaniel, 31, 56
Heltzel, Virgil, 212
Hemingway, Ernest, 31, 206, 209
Hergesheimer, Joseph, 31, 208
Heywood, John, 4
Hicks, Granville, 25
Hobbes, 9
Holmes, Dr. O. W., 19, 20, 21, 31, 101, 146-159, 160, 167, 184, 187, 191, 203
Homer, 29
Honor, See Character, Christian gentleman, Duelling
Horace, 2, 64, 154
Howells, Wm. Cooper, 185, 186, 199, 201
Howells, W. D., 19, 20, 21, 31, 100, 148, 156, 174, 184-205
Hubbard, Wm., 36
Hutchinson, Anne, 36

I
Indians, Cooper's, 129-134
Irving, Washington, 27, 31, 90, 101
Isocrates, 2

J
Jackson, Andrew, 105, 108, 218
Jacksonians, 101, 105, 126
James, Henry, 28, 31, 174, 190
James, William, 197-198
Jay, John, 128
Jefferson, 15, 18, 19, 20, 26, 30, 60, 64, 67, 72, 75, 78, 85-102, 103, 105, 157, 158
Jeffersonians, 61-62, 63, 77, 100-102, 185-186, 194, 209
Jewett, S. O., 27
Johnson, Samuel, 9, 13, 214
Johnson, Thomas, 213
Joyce, James, 28

K
Kelso, Ruth, 212
Kennedy, J. P., 31
Knight, Sarah K., 17

L
Lanier, Sidney, 4
Lee, Robert E., 60
Lewis, Sinclair, 31, 206, 209
Lewisohn, Ludwig, 25
Lincoln, 20, 167-168
Lindsay, Vachel, 31, 206, 209
Linton, Ralph, 212
Literature and culture, 27-29
Literature and the gentleman, 29, 127-145
Locke, 9, 15, 62
Longfellow, 31, 187, 193
Lovejoy, A. O., 10
Lowell, Frances C., 180
Lowell, J. R., 31, 101, 153, 188-189, 193

M
Maclay, Wm., 70-71
Manners, 2-3, 12, 69, 87-90, 107, 120-122, 154, 166-167, 171, 173-174, 176, 186-187

Marquand, J. P., 31, 159, 208, 210
Marxianism, 25-26
Mason, John, 212
Mather, Cotton, 21, 34, 37, 40-41, 43, 44
Melville, Herman, 28, 31, 56
Metaphoric animism, 23, 26
Miller, Perry, 213
Milton, John, 6, 172, 179
Mitchell, Jonathan, 37
Moore, Charles, 212
More, P. E., 206
Morison, S. E., 40, 44
Morse, S. F. B., 218
Mucker pose, the, 25

N
Napoleon, 108, 164, 165, 169, 171
Nationalism, See American gentleman
Natural gentleman, 7, 10, 18, 20, 61-62, 72-75, 77-78, 82, 92, 94, 100-101, 105, 106, 113, 123, 140, 150, 161, 164-168, 189-196. See Birth; Bumppo, Natty
Neo-Humanism, 206-207, 209
Newman, 15, 21
*Noblesse oblige,* See Character, Function of gentleman
Norris, Frank, 31
Norton, C. E., 194

O
Ovid, 2

P
Page, T. N., 27
Paine, R. T., 66
Paine, Thos., 61, 66, 75, 217
Palooka, Joe, 20, 210

Parrington, V. L., 26-27, 44, 48
Peacham, Henry, 6, 8
Percy, W. A., 31, 208
Perrin, Porter, 214
Plato, 2, 79, 164, 177-178
Plutarch, 2
Poe, E. A., 31
Politeness, See Etiquette, Manners
Pope, Alexander, 82-83
Ptah-Hotep, 1
Pufendorf, 9, 62
Puritanism, 8, 16, 33-51, 63, 81, 169
Pyle, Ernie, 210

Q
Quintilian, 2

R
Raleigh, Sir Walter, 164-165
Revolution, American, 18, 61
Richardson, Samuel, 11, 13-14, 53, 56-58, 200
Robinson, E. A., 31, 64, 206, 209
Roosevelt, Franklin, 210
Roosevelt, Theodore, 31

S
Sand, George, 169
Sandburg, Carl, 209
Santayana, 24-25, 159, 169, 207
Schlesinger, A. M., Jr., 217-219
Scott, Sir Walter, 4, 31, 60, 115, 162, 169
Sedgwick, H. D., 212
Sensibiilty, 14
Sewall, Jonathan, 69
Sewall, Samuel, 48-51
Sex and the gentleman, 199-200
Shakespeare, 5, 168, 185
Sheridan, Richard, 57

Sidney, Sir Philip, 162, 172, 181
Simms, W. G., 31
Sitwell, Sir George, 2, 212
Smith, Bernard, 25
Smith, Sir Thomas, 4
Smythe-Palmer, A, 212
Snobbery, See Courtesy, Etiquette, Manners
Southern gentleman, 16, 32, 60, 85-86, 91-92
Spiller, Robert, 218-220
Steele, 9, 11, 64
Steinbeck, John, 31, 209
Stephen, Leslie, 158
Sterne, 56-57
Stevens, W. O., 214
Stowe, H. B., 53
Swift, Jonathan, 29

T

Tate, Allan, 27, 200
Tennyson, 4
Thackeray, 15, 185
Theocracy, 33-51, 178. See Puritanism
Theophrastus, 2
Thoreau, 164-165
Tolstoi, Lyof, 100, 184, 188, 200-201
Travel, 57, 90-91, 117
Trumbull, John, 55-56

Tyler, Royall, 56-58

U

Ustick, W. L., 212

V

Veblen, Thorstein, 21, 80

W

Walpole, Horace, 11
Warren, James, 71
Warren, Mercy, 53, 216
Washington, George, 8, 18, 56-58, 60, 87, 108, 129, 165
Wealth, 6, 20, 42, 48, 78, 80-81, 106-107, 116-117, 151-153, 170-171, 182, 203
Webster, Noah, 63, 215
Wecter, Dion, vii, 35-36
Wharton, Edith, 31, 208
Whig party, 109
Whitman, Walt, 209
Whittier, J. G., 31
Wilde, Oscar, 15, 21
Williams, Roger, 37, 46
Wingfield-Stratford, Esme, 212
Winslow, Edward, 37
Winthrop, Governor John, 34-39, 44-46
Winthrop, John, Jr., 40, 45-47
Wise, John, 62

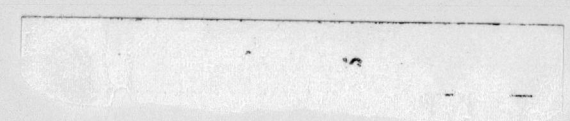